Life and Words

A

Philip E. Lilienthal

B O O K

The Philip E. Lilienthal imprint honors
special books in commemoration of a
man whose work at University of
California Press from 1954 to 1979 was
marked by dedication to young authors
and to high standards in the field of
Asian Studies. Friends, family, authors,
and foundations have together endowed
the Lilienthal Fund, which enables
UC Press to publish under this imprint
selected books in a way that reflects the
taste and judgment of a great and
beloved editor.

Life and Words

VIOLENCE AND THE DESCENT INTO THE ORDINARY

Veena Das

Foreword by Stanley Cavell

UNIVERSITY OF CALIFORNIA PRESS

BERKELEY   LOS ANGELES   LONDON

University of California Press, one of the most
distinguished university presses in the United States,
enriches lives around the world by advancing scholarship
in the humanities, social sciences, and natural sciences. Its
activities are supported by the UC Press Foundation and
by philanthropic contributions from individuals and
institutions. For more information, visit
www.ucpress.edu.

Several chapters are revised versions of earlier essays, which
are listed in the acknowledgments on pages 267–269.

University of California Press
Berkeley and Los Angeles, California

University of California Press, Ltd.
London, England

Library of Congress Cataloging-in-Publication Data

Das, Veena.
    Life and words : violence and the descent into the
ordinary / Veena Das ; foreword by Stanley Cavell.
        p.   cm.
    "Philip E. Lilienthal Asian studies imprint."
    Includes bibliographical references and index.
    ISBN-13, 978-0-520-24744-4 (cloth : alk. paper)
    ISBN-10, 0-520-24744-2 (cloth : alk. paper)
    ISBN-13, 978-0-520-24745-1 (pbk. : alk. paper)
    ISBN-10, 0-520-24745-0 (pbk. : alk. paper)
    1. Violence—India.   2. India—History—Partition,
1947.   3. Sikhs—Crimes against—India.   4. Riots—
India—History—20th century.   5. Suffering—India.
6. India—Politics and government.   7. India—Social
conditions.   8. India—Social life and customs.   I. Title.

    GN635.I4D2662   2007
    303.60954—dc22   2006003041

Manufactured in the United States of America

15   14   13   12   11   10   09   08
10   9   8   7   6   5   4   3   2

This book is printed on New Leaf EcoBook 50, a 100%
recycled fiber of which 50% is de-inked post-consumer
waste, processed chlorine-free. EcoBook 50 is acid-free
and meets the minimum requirements of ANSI/ASTM
D5634–01 (*Permanence of Paper*).

For
Saumya, Jishnu, and Sanmay—
for their gift of love
and
Ranen—
for the generosity of spirit with which he has
nourished our life together

CONTENTS

FOREWORD

VEENA DAS speaks of her "repeated (and even compulsive) reliance on Wittgenstein" as playing a role in the philosophical friendship that has developed between us. Beyond the clear evidence for this observation, the truth of it, from my side of things, is further confirmed, if perhaps less clearly, in an early and in a late thought of mine, each expressing my sense of an anthropological register in Wittgenstein's sensibility, thoughts not reflected in Wittgenstein's well-known recurrence, in his later (or as the French put it, his second) philosophy, to imaginary "tribes" different from "us." I would like to mark my pleasure in contributing prefatory words for Das's wonderful book *Life and Words* by putting those easily lost thoughts into words, into the world.

My early thought was directed to a passage in *Philosophical Investigations* that roughly sounds to me like a reflection on a primitive allegory of incipient anthropological work: "Suppose you came as an explorer into an unknown country with a language quite strange to you. In what circumstances would you say that the people there gave orders, understood them, obeyed them, rebelled against them, and so on? The common behaviour of mankind is the system of reference by means of which we interpret an unknown language" (§206).

This may, as other moments in Wittgenstein's text may, seem either too doubtful or too tame to be of much intellectual service. "Common behavior" seems quite unargumentative in referring to the behavior of salmon and mallards and anthropoid apes, not quite in referring to that of human beings. But let's turn the card over. Take it that the allegorical air comes rather from the fact that to ask a question of the form "In what circumstances would you say . . . ?" is precisely Wittgenstein's most obvious (ordinary language) procedure directed to and *about us,* about us as philosophers when we are, as we inevitably are, variously tempted to force our ordinary words to do what they, as they stand, will not do, disappointed by finitude. It is *our* language that is, or that we perpetually render, foreign to us. The point of the allegory would then be that the explorer coming into an unknown country with a strange language is a figure of the philosopher moved to philosophical wonder by the strangeness of the humans among whom he lives, their strangeness to themselves, therefore of himself to himself, at home perhaps nowhere, perhaps anywhere. (I have spoken of the *Investigations* as a portrait more specifically of the modern subject.)

Asking us either to find our behavior strange (*seltsam*), or not strange, is a familiar gesture in the *Investigations,* anticipated, for example, in Plato's image of the everyday as a cave, and in Rousseau's fantasm of the first word (the first naming of the human other) as a giant, and in Thoreau's perception in the opening pages of *Walden* of his fellow townsmen as self-tormenting "Bramins" (Thoreau's spelling). The intersection of the familiar and the strange is an experience of the uncanny, an intersection therefore shared by the anthropologist, the psychoanalyst, and the Wittgensteinian (Socratic, Rousseau-like, Thoreau-like, etc.) philosopher. (Here an anthropological perspective is the counter to what is sometimes called, and disapproved of as, a humanist perspective, satisfied in its knowledge of what humanity should be. What I call Wittgenstein's anthropological perspective is one puzzled in principle by anything human beings say and do, hence perhaps, at a moment, by nothing.)

This brings me to the second, later thought prompting the sense of Wittgenstein's seeking perspective on his unknown culture. I once shared a podium to discuss, perhaps debate, Wittgenstein's later views with a friend who is fully recognized as one of the most accomplished philosophers of our generation. In his introductory remarks he asked, in effect: Why is Wittgenstein content to accord the status of a culture or an imaginary tribe to virtually any group of strange creatures with apparently the sole exception of philosophers? When my turn to speak came I replied that for Wittgenstein philosophy is not a culture, not one among others. It is without (no matter how persistently it craves to have) a persistently accepted and evolving language of its own, retaining only some local terms that will be disputed and repudiated by other philosophers; "houses of cards" Wittgenstein will call its parade of discourses. The locale of its originating form of life is the singular human being dissatisfied with itself, a fate inherent, or say natural, within any civilized human society. We (moderns, philosophers) are likely often to accede to the idea that philosophy has become a profession like others, say, since its incorporation into the Western university curriculum over the past two and a half centuries. But that is something Wittgenstein fairly clearly finds as strange as it is familiar.

It seems clear to me that Das's sense of compulsive turning to a companionship with Wittgenstein's later work is her recognition that his address to the human other is, like her own, one that can be said to revolve characteristically around the study of pain. I have heard this tropism of Wittgenstein's criticized as in effect making things too easy for himself, since the criteria of pain are epistemologically so well defined, the feeling so well known. This strikes me merely as one of numberless ways of defending oneself against Wittgenstein's uncovering of philosophy's defenses, say, against the everyday, against finitude. But the question of the sense of pain's pressure in Wittgenstein's text is a good one. Since I have for a long time been following out my sense of Wittgenstein's work as directed to an understanding of skepticism, I am likely to regard pain as especially suited to be a philosophical example for him precisely because of its commonness and its recognizability, something knowable about the other if anything is. And I would emphasize two other facts of the phenomenon, first that over a large range of its occurrences its manifestation is more or less repressible or disguisable (paradoxically more easily than the manifestation of joy or mild surprise or a prompting of laughter), so that one may be said in such cases to have to care whether to understand what is happening; second, that unlike joy or surprise or laughter, with pain there is a moral demand to respond to its expression. (A killjoy is obnoxious but not immoral.) I find that one appropriate use of Das's work is as a companion to Wittgenstein's preoccupation with the other.

What kind of task is it to study social suffering? To follow Das into events in which social convulsion lays bare the question of a society's will and its right to exist, to name and honor itself, is to arrive repeatedly at the feeling that to know a society is to know its capacity to inflict suffering upon itself. In her perception of the cases she principally studies, the extended total event of the Partition and the comparatively confined event of the aftermath of the assassination of Indira Gandhi, states of chaos are as if called upon to hold the mirror up to what society has called its order. Here the philosophical image or myth of pervasive but hidden chains or iron bars keeping us in place—yet variously perceptible in Plato (where in the Cave we are each chained) and in Rousseau (where we are free and everywhere in chains) and in Thoreau (where we are caged in the woods) and in Marx (where most of us have nothing to lose but our chains)—can seem to come to a terrible enactment in the moment at which these bonds bewilderingly are broken. In the instances Das places before us, a reality of pain is released for which she finds that there are no standing words.

She nevertheless discovers a path of articulation into this chaos by confronting the tradition of philosophy and transforming or reinhabiting— and, what is more, showing the resultant relation of—two of its familiar sites of perspective on our common lives, that of the social contract establishing consent to the political order, and that of our common language appearing as inherently unreliable. She takes on the perception that the social contract has been sexualized, that the roles of men and women are systematically contrasted in the events of partitioning, where consent is declared and forced (hence horribly parodied) by symbolizing it in the abduction of women, and where this violation simultaneously produces silence in women and, in men, a volubility that fails to express what they see and do. Das characterizes the men's speech as taking on the register of rumor, as if the events they describe were caused otherwise than by themselves, as if they have made themselves into creatures lacking both desire and responsibility. This psychic catastrophe is a kind of living parody of something philosophy has meant to capture in its portraits of skepticism, where one is invited to feel that it is language itself that causes the human being's ignorance of itself and of its role in the world, and not a self-distancing and self-blinding relation to one's words.

Something that has kept drawing me back to the topic of skepticism, from the time of completing my doctoral dissertation, so largely concerned with understanding Wittgenstein's *Philosophical Investigations* as an original response to the threat of skepticism, was my sense that skepticism with respect to other minds was, whenever I heard it discussed in classes and conferences, made derivative from, or made to imitate, skepticism's modern inception in Descartes and its continuation in Hume and its opposition in Kant, each of whom had treated skepticism essentially with respect to material objects, or, say, to the system of objects philosophers have called the external world. Hence the philosophical problem of others was shaped as one of assessing whether, or how, we know about others what we claim to know. A decisive turn in my own studies in skepticism came from the realization that a skeptical process toward other human beings (others like myself, Descartes says) results not in a realization of my ignorance of the existence of the other, but in my denial of that existence, my refusal to acknowledge it, my psychic annihilation of the other. That there is a violence that is not directed to the defense of the self's integrity or to a rightful demand for equality or for freedom, but expresses this wish for the other's nonexistence, strikes me as a further way to take up Das's insight of "healing [the consequences of violence] as a kind of relationship with death."

I was prompted to ask myself whether her cases of extreme manifestation of a society's internal, one could say, intimate and absolute violence are comprehensible as extreme states, or suddenly invited enactments, of a pervasive fact of the social fabric that may hide itself, or one might also say, may express itself, in everyday encounters. The background of my question is double, one part coming from a further perception of Das's, and one part coming from my having in recent years begun to register unacknowledged yet inevitable manifestations of what Wittgenstein pictures as the pervasive, irreducible recurrence of human nervousness or restlessness, as it were the human incapacity for and refusal of peace (which Wittgenstein specifically pictures as features of the modern subject, ones he portrays as torment, perverseness, disappointment, devastation, suffocation, and so on), a kind of perpetual preparation for violence that has led me to speak of our dealing among ourselves "the little deaths of everyday life," the slights, the grudges, the clumsiness, the impatience, the bitterness, the narcissism, the boredom, and so on (variously fed and magnified and inflamed by standing sources of social enmity, say, racism, sexism, elitism, and so on). No wonder a philosopher (I am thinking at the moment of Thoreau) will from time to time allow himself to be overcome with the feeling that human life, as it stands, stands in need of, and is without, justification, as when, adding up the amount he has spent on food in a year, that is, on supplies to keep himself alive, he announces, "I thus unblushingly publish my guilt."

The further insight of Das's that I refer to is her recognition that in the gender-determined division of the work of mourning the results of violence, the role of women is to attend, in a torn world, to the details of everyday life that allow a household to function, collecting supplies, cooking, washing and straightening up, seeing to children, and so on, that allow life to knit itself back into some viable rhythm, pair by pair. Part of her task is to make us ponder how it is that such evidently small things (whose bravery within tumultuous circumstances is, however, not small) are a match for the consequences of unspeakable horror, for which other necessaries are not substitutes. (Here the pity and terror that Aristotle finds in the catharsis provided for the witnesses of tragedy seem in everyday time to yield healing for the healers of catastrophe.)

In the background of my sense of these matters a remark from Wittgenstein's *Journals,* collected in a volume entitled *Culture and Value,* plays a role that I know I still imperfectly, or only intermittently, understand but that I feel sure is illuminated by this nearly inconceivable mismatch of harm and healing: "The whole planet can suffer no greater torment than a single soul." We are touching here on matters that will seem to take moral philosophy, with its assessment of goods and its exhortations to duty and to contracts, quite beyond its accustomed paths.

A parting word. I spoke just now of evidently small things in response to tumultuous things, and I spoke earlier of Das's work as reciprocating Wittgenstein's preoccupation with the everyday life of the other, where the modification "everyday" asks attention to the specificity (however perhaps normally missed) of a current locus of interest and desire and need. The bridge for me here between these representatives of philosophical and anthropological work is my perpetual harboring for philosophy an idea or image—I guess in unpropitious times—of the first virtue of philosophy as responsiveness. I have sometimes put this thought by saying that philosophy does not speak first. It is a recurrent cause of wonder to me that in philosophy's modern rebeginning, where philosophy finds the power to wipe clean the intellectual slate and ask for proof that we know anything exists—most poignantly expressed as wanting to know whether I am alone in the world—Descartes passes by, I have to say denies, the answer provided in the existence of the finite neighbor. My heartfelt gratitude to Veena Das for her *Life and Words.*

Stanley Cavell
Walter M. Cabot Professor Emeritus
of Aesthetics and the General Theory of Value
Harvard University

ONE

The Event and the Everyday

IT SO HAPPENS THAT FOR MANY YEARS NOW I have been engaged in thinking and writing about violence and asking what kind of work anthropology does in shaping the object we have come to call violence. I have a picture of this book as some kind of map (or a fragment of one) of the distance that I have traveled since I first realized how much of my intellectual biography was tied up with questions around violence: my journey is not about going forward, but rather about turning back, about collecting words and thoughts that I think of as having forged connections between me and my interlocutors in the field. Two major events have anchored my ethnographic and anthropological reflections, but the book is not *about* these events in the sense that a historian or a psychoanalyst might construe them.[1] Rather, it narrates the lives of particular persons and communities who were deeply embedded in these events, and it describes the way that the event attaches itself with its tentacles into everyday life and folds itself into the recesses of the ordinary. My attention is captured in this book by both the larger possibilities of phenomena and the singularity of lives.

I was educated into asking these kinds of questions by those who, in anthropological parlance, are my informants—except that the book is a response to them—and so if one has a picture of an informant as one who informs about some prethought questions, then this was not the relation I bore with them. The burden of the book is not to render their trauma visible or knowable in the way in which much fine work on war veterans or victims of major catastrophes has made familiar. I briefly visit those debates, but my concern is with the slippery relation between the collective and the individual, between genre and individual emplotment of stories. Thus, I asked such questions as: What it is to inhabit a world? How does one make the world one's own? How does one account for the appearance of the subject? What is it to lose one's world? What is the relation between possibility and actuality or between actuality and eventuality, as one tries to find a medium to portray the relation between the critical events that shaped large historical questions and everyday life? Since the two events I address—that of the Partition of India in 1947 and the assassination of the then prime minister Indira Gandhi in 1984—span a period in which the nation-state was established firmly in India as the frame of reference within which forms of community found expression, the story of lives enmeshed in violence is part of the story of the nation. The two concepts that are knotted together in various ways in the chapters of the book are the concepts of the voice and the everyday. I have learned to engage these concepts from the writings of two philosophers, Ludwig Wittgenstein and Stanley Cavell. On another register, the book, then, is about how these concepts may be received in anthropology for those who want to think of these matters.[2]

It would be obvious that the questions I ask did not simply come my way in the course of my work among urban Punjabi families (intensively in 1973 and 1974 and then intermittently until 1980) who had migrated to India as refugees from various parts of the Punjab during the traumatic riots of the Partition in 1947. Nor were the questions posed quite in this way by the survivors of the riots against the Sikhs in Delhi in 1984, among whom I worked for more than a year. I had to learn to recognize these questions as somehow mine, animating my life and work: they were not there because of some textbook formulations on these issues.

In repeated attempts to write a book on the subject of violence, I felt that every time I succeeded in saying something, I was left with a sense of malaise, a disappointment with what I had said. Given that there is a certain air of obviousness with which notions of the everyday and of voice are often spoken of in anthropological writing, I have been amazed at how difficult I found it to speak of these matters. Thus, what I present here is not a piecemeal improvement on what I have written earlier or a filling up of some details that were missing. Rather, having presented a large part of my ethnography in the form of papers, I feel that I want to see my ethnographic practices, my models of reading and writing if you will, as responding to the pressure of questions on voice and the ordinary, or better, the voice in the everyday. As the disastrous violence against Muslims in Gujarat in March 2002 makes clear, the events of collective violence continue to shape the intertwining of experiences of community and state and continue to become more lethal, especially for minorities in India, though the development of increasingly critical practices to counter this is also important to note. I need to find the right distance or the right scale at which this picture might be sketched.

RELATIONS

Marilyn Strathern has eloquently addressed questions of scale and complexity within the discipline of social anthropology. As she says, "Social anthropologists route connections through persons. They attend to the relations of logic, of cause and effect, of class and category that people make between things; it also means that they attend to the relations of social life, to the roles and behavior through which people connect themselves to one another. And habitually they bring these two domains of knowledge together, as when they talk about the relation between culture and society." Further, on the tradition of social anthropology in Britain, she adds, "And the enunciation of rules was understood as the moment at which people became articulate about relationships. . . . Social structure inhered in relationships relevant to people's acts and intentions. . . . This model could be *enacted* over and again in fieldwork. The tradition of fieldwork meant that anthropologists learnt about systems by entering into relationships with those whose social life they were studying. Like Saem, the apprentice gained knowledge in the course of interaction."[3]

Relationships appear crucial to Strathern because they are both the objects of study and the means through which anthropologists arrive at an understanding of both abstract and concrete patterns of sociality. Once we comprehend how concrete relations and abstract relations are connected, we begin to see questions of scale and complexity in a very different light. Thus, small-scale societies are not simply those in which face-to-face relations make it easier to grasp social relations in their totality, nor are complex societies those in which there is an absence of face-to-face relations. Indeed, Strathern gives many examples of the complexity of so-called simple societies and calls upon notions of tacit knowledge to show how concrete relations are implicated in the production of new forms of sociality corresponding to dramatic changes in technology.

I take two important formulations from Strathern's attention to relations. First, that concrete relations that we establish in living with others are like shadows of the more abstract questions—that is, we learn about the nature of the world in the process of such living. Second, that we cannot assign a scale to patterns of sociality independent of perspective. Indeed, to be able to establish a perspective is to enlarge the field of our vision. The question, then, is not that of part–whole relations but of establishing the horizon within which we may place the constituent objects of a description in their relation to each other and in relation to the eye with which they are seen.[4] One might also express this in terms of the relation between the subject and the world. (I would like to note here for later discussion that I see the problems of uncertainty, doubt, and skepticism as embedded in the concreteness of relations—if I come to doubt such things as my relations to my parents, the fidelity of our love, or the loyalty of my children, these are doubts that put my world in jeopardy. They are like shadows of the more abstract philosophical doubts about the reality of the world.) For the moment, I return to some initial formulations on the question of the subject and the world.

Let us take Wittgenstein's statement that "the subject does not belong to the world; rather it is the limit of the world."[5] In interpreting this statement several scholars have suggested that the relation of the subject to the world is like that of the eye to the visual field—the eye is not itself in the visual field that it defines. Without going into a sustained defense of my interpretation at this point, I suggest that in thinking of the subject as constituting the limit of the world, Wittgenstein is proposing that the experience of being a subject is the experience of a limit. The world is not invented by me (as the cliché goes), but then how do I make the world mine? How am I, as a subject, implicated in experience, for I take it that there is no pregiven subject to whom experience happens or on whom experience can be predicated? It is Wittgenstein's thought that the subject is the *condition* of experience.[6] Given that he considers the human form of life as one complicated enough to have language, the question might also be put as one of taking responsibility for language.[7] If the subject is also the boundary of the world, there is clearly no particular point in the course of my life that I can locate as the point at which my subjectivity emerges. Hence it is Wittgenstein's thought that the subject is never closed or done with. Being able to draw a boundary itself raises the issue of the experience of limit. Then how should we see the violence of the events that frame the ethnography—should we regard the violence as that which exceeded the boundaries of the world, as it was known? These are complicated pictures of what it is to make and remake a world, bringing into question the pictures of totalities, parts, fragments, and boundaries that we may have. These pictures are tied up with questions of what it is to write an ethnography of violence—one that is not seen as bearing an objective witness to the events as much as trying to locate the subject through the experience of such limits.

FRAGMENTS, BOUNDARIES, LIMITS

A body of critical theories has emerged in recent years marked by the "rhetoric of mourning." Eric Santner characterizes it thus:

> By the "rhetoric of mourning," I mean the recurrence, in so many post-modern theoretical discourses, of a metaphysics of loss and impoverishment. The appeal in these discourses to notions of shattering, rupture, mutilation, fragmentation, to images of fissures, wounds, rifts, gaps and abysses, is familiar enough. These discourses, primarily post-structuralist in inspiration, appear committed to the vigilant and radical critique of what are taken to be narcissisms and nostalgias central to the project of modernity—namely, Enlightenment faith in progress—and the Western tradition more generally. These discourses propose a kind of perpetual leave-taking from fantasies of plenitude, purity, centrality, unity and mastery. Such fantasies and their various narrative performances, whether cast in the rhetoric of totalization or of liberation, are in turn seen as the primary sources of violence in history.[8]

The idea I use of a fragment shares in Santner's sense of loss and impoverishment but is not directly related to a critique of the Western Enlightenment project. My sense is to think of the fragment here as different from a part or various parts that may be assembled together to make up a picture of totality. Unlike a sketch that may be executed on a different scale from the final picture one draws, or that may lack all the details of the picture but still contain the imagination of the whole, the *fragment* marks the impossibility of such an imagination. Instead, fragments allude to a particular way of inhabiting the world, say, in a gesture of mourning. I have in mind a picture of destruction, such as that sketched by Stanley Cavell in his writings on philosophy, literature, and film. Cavell takes up Wittgenstein's famous comment—of his investigations destroying everything that is great and important, "leaving behind only bits of stone and rubble"—and suggests that the color that is lent to this abstract conceptual moment is of a particular hue. In his words: "Could its color have been evoked as the destruction of a forest by logging equipment, or of a field of flowers by the gathering for a summer concert or by the march of an army? Not, I think if the idea is that we are going to have to pick up the pieces and find out how and whether to go on, that is go on living in this very place of devastation, as of something over."[9] What it is to pick up the pieces and to live in this very place of devastation? This is what animates the description of lives and texts in this book.

VOICE AND THE EVERYDAY

The repression of voice and hence of confession, of autobiography, in philosophy is an abiding theme of Cavell's work. He sees Wittgenstein's preoccupation with philosophy as leading words back from the purified metaphysical voice to that of the ordinary, as a project of recovering the human voice, a voice he sees philosophy as having banished (which is not to say that it is a *humanistic* project, as if the notion of the human was transparent). Thus Cavell's account of voice is not that of speech or utterance but as that which might animate words, give them life, so to say. Cavell sees the banishing of the human voice in the register of the philosophical as a suspicion of all that is ordinary, as the fantasy of some kind of purified medium outside of language that was available to us.[10] Words, when they lead lives outside the ordinary, become emptied of experience, lose touch with life—in Wittgenstein, it is the scene of language having gone on a holiday. These are the scenes evoked in the theatrical staging of doubt (surely you cannot have *this* pain), and if skeptical doubt was to be expressed only in such theatricality, then one might be right to suspect that skepticism expresses unnatural doubts. But for Wittgenstein, as Cavell rightly reminds us, the possibility of skepticism is embedded in the ordinary—hence, says Cavell, *Philosophical Investigations* is written in response to skepticism but not as a refutation of it, for the argument with skepticism is one that we are not allowed to either win or lose. I read this as saying that the question is not about knowing (at least in the picture of knowing that much of modern philosophy has propagated with its underlying assumption about being able to *solve* the problem of what it is to know), but of acknowledging. My acknowledgment of the other is not something that I can do once and then be done with it. The suspicion of the ordinary seems to me to be rooted in the fact that relationships require a repeated attention to the most ordinary of objects and events, but our theoretical impulse is often to think of agency in terms of escaping the ordinary rather than as a descent into it.

In the register of literature, Cavell asks whether Shakespearean tragedies might not be a response to (what philosophy identifies as) skepticism: "Yet, might it not well haunt us, as philosophers, that in *King Lear* doubt as to a loving daughter's expressions of love, or in *Othello* doubt cast as jealousy and terror of a wife's satisfaction, or in *Macbeth* doubt manifested as a question about the stability of a wife's humanity (in connection with witches), leads to a man's repudiation or annihilation of the world that is linked with a loss of the power of or the conviction in speech?"[11] As I have suggested elsewhere, this theme of annihilation of the world, or of finding oneself within the scene of world-annihilating doubt, is not necessarily tied to big events—I then located the unknowability of the world and hence of oneself in it in the *ordinary*—for instance, in interactions around witchcraft accusations among the Azande that interrupt the ordinary but are still part of the everyday, or in the pervasive sense that the real could not be authorized in the narratives of health and illness in my ongoing studies of low-income neighborhoods in Delhi.[12] I argued that in these cases we get an intuition of the human as if one of the aspects under which a person could be seen was as a victim of language—as if words could reveal more about us than we are aware of ourselves.

The intimacy between skepticism and the ordinary is revealed in the present work on several sites, as in the panic rumors that circulate and produce the picture of the other as the phantasmal from whom all human subjectivity has been evacuated, or when violence, in the register of the literary, is seen as transfiguring life into something else, call it a form of death, or of making oneself, as it were, into a ghost. But my engagement with the survivors of riots also showed me that life was recovered not through some grand gestures in the realm of the transcendent but through a descent into the ordinary. There was, I argue, a mutual absorption of the violent and the ordinary so that I end up by thinking of the event as always attached to the ordinary as if there were tentacles that reach out from the everyday and anchor the event to it in some specific ways.

I tend to think that while critical and traumatic events of the kind I describe were not simply constituted by forms of the social, they were not wholly its other either. And thus, I find myself attracted to the idea that boundaries between the ordinary and the eventful are drawn in terms of the failure of the grammar of the ordinary, by which I mean that what is *put into question* is how we ever learned what kind of object something like grief, or love, is. This failure of grammar or what we may also call the end of criteria is what I see as the experience of world-annihilating violence—the figure of a brother not being able to decipher whether love consisted in killing one's sister to save her from another kind of violence from the crowd, or handing her over for protection to someone whose motives one could not fully fathom; or a mother's failure to know that her child was safer with her out in the open, in sight of a murderous crowd, rather than hidden in a house with his father.

My interest in this book is not in describing these moments of horror but rather in describing what happens to the subject and world when the memory of such events is folded into ongoing relationships. My wonder and terror is that it is from such fragile and intimate moments that a shared language had to be built and with no assurance that there were secure conventions on which such a language, in fact, could be founded. A possible vicissitude of such fatal moments is that one could become voiceless—not in the sense that one does not have words—but that these words become frozen, numb, without life.[13] Thus there were men and women who spoke, and if asked, they told stories about the violence they had seen or endured on their bodies. My thought was that perhaps they had speech but not voice. Sometimes these were words imbued with a spectral quality, or they might have been uttered by a person with whom I was in a face-to-face encounter, and yet I felt they were animated by some other voice. Contrarily, I describe those who chose to be mute, who withdrew their voice to protect it. Thus, just as I think of the event as attached to the everyday, I think of the everyday itself as eventful.

As the above examples suggest, voice is not identical to speech; nor does it stand in opposition to writing. Voice, as I understand it, is not the same as an utterance, nor is writing only graphic—thus I cannot tie voice to presence and writing to absence as suggested by Jacques Derrida. However, what I find useful in Derrida's powerful analysis of signature is the possibility that words might become untethered from their origin.[14] I try to widen this notion, however, so that we can see not only the new possibilities it offers but also its threats. For example, we may fail to recognize the signature of the utterance we are hearing even in a face-to-face encounter when words are animated by some other voice. This is akin to the possibility of forgery that might put the authoritativeness of a written document into question. Thus, I explore the sense of danger in relation to both oral and written utterances on such sites as rumor or in institutions such as the state that can disengage themselves from their own promise of justice by taking the possibility of signature as forgery and by turning it against those who are suspect in its eyes: the very idea that Derrida finds so attractive as a critique of both presence and intentionality here becomes a tactic of the state to avoid responsibility.

It is not only violence experienced on one's body in these cases but also the sense that one's access to context is lost that constitutes a sense of being violated. The fragility of the social becomes embedded in a temporality of anticipation since one ceases to trust that context is in place. The affect produced on the registers of the virtual and the potential, of fear that is real but not necessarily actualized in events, comes to constitute the ecology of fear in everyday life. Potentiality here does not have the sense of something that is waiting at the door of reality to make an appearance as it were, but rather as that which is already present.[15] The ethnographic task here is to describe how feelings of skepticism come to be embedded within a frayed everyday life so that guarantees of belonging to larger entities such as communities or state are not capable of erasing the hurts or providing means of repairing this sense of being betrayed by the everyday. It will become clear that the sense in which I use the term "community" is not as something already given or primordial (and hence opposed to the state). Rather, community is constituted through agreements and hence can also be torn apart by the refusal to acknowledge some part of the community (e.g., women or minorities) as an integral part of it. This refusal might take the form of voices not heard, or it might reveal itself through a proliferation of words that drown out silences that are too difficult to bear. Thus while voice may give life to frozen words, turned into the plural it can also be lethal as in the case of words floating around in panic rumors without being tethered to a signature.

VIOLENCE IN THE WEAVE OF LIFE

In the years 1973 and 1974 I was engaged in the study of a network of urban Punjabi families with a view to understanding their kinship system.[16] The core of this kinship network was located in Delhi and consisted of ten families who had fled from Lahore at the time of the Partition. Other families in this network were scattered in several cities including Amritsar, Bombay, Calcutta, Ferozepur, Jullundher, Ludhiana, and Simla. In the initial stages of my fieldwork I started by collecting kinship terminologies, making genealogies, recording gift transactions, and tracing the marriage alliances. I was very interested then in the politics of kinship and accordingly attended closely to disputations during weddings and funerals, and to the narratives of relationships that were obsessively discussed and debated. I was even then struck by the fact that the structure of domestic groups did not approximate the typical phases of the developmental cycle that were so dear to the analysts of family and kinship.[17] The most interesting variation was in the number of children who moved between different kinds of relatives in different phases of their lives.

The displacement of the Partition had made it difficult for some of the families to sustain their children because of either the death of a parent or the destitution of the family. Informal adoptions and provision of foster care for short periods, as well as flow of material help in the form of gifts, were essential components of the strategies of survival. The Partition had created significant differences of wealth and income within the network of kinship. Some families in this network had business interests outside of the Punjab that saved them from complete economic devastation. The operation of the "axiom of kinship amity" meant that the more fortunate relatives who had homes on the Indian side of the border gave shelter to those who had escaped from Pakistan.[18] This included help with finding jobs, loans, and shelter for children who had lost a parent. Yet the other side of these kinship relations was the constant allusions to betrayal of trust, infidelities, and the failure to live up to the high moral ideals of kinship solidarity. The manner in which such disappointments in one's relationships were staged, the performance of accusations, and the delicate encoding of references to past favors granted and relationships betrayed made up the aesthetic of kinship. It was not that there was any taboo on the mention of the Partition or that no reference was ever made to the homes that were left behind. Yet violence endured or betrayals of which I was slowly to be made aware seemed to be always on the edges of conversation. These were not spoken in the mode of public performances.

I shall argue in the course of my discussion in the chapters that follow that while the narratives one could glean from state documents used words freely, in the lives of communities the manner in which the violence of the Partition was folded was *shown* (sometimes with words) rather than *narrated*. Words were spoken, but they worked like gestures to show this violence— to draw boundaries between what could be proclaimed as a betrayal, however delicately, and what could only be molded into a silence. The memories of the Partition were then not in the nature of something gone underground, repressed, hidden away, that would have to be excavated. In a way, these memories were very much on the surface. Yet there were fences created around them: the very language that bore these memories had a certain foreign tinge to it as if the Punjabi or Hindi in which it was spoken was some kind of translation from some other unknown language. For the moment, I leave this idea here as a possible way of conceptualizing what many have spoken of as an inner language (as distinct from a private language).

It is important for me to mark one important feature of my fieldwork. I was engaged in the study of kinship among urban families in the context of everyday life. Immersed in the daily life of the women of the households, defined by the temporal rhythms of cooking and eating food, cleaning the house, bathing the children, engaging in the usual conversations in the afternoons when housework was completed—it was easy to be seduced by the idea that the family was encompassed only in the larger generational rhythms of marriages, births, rearing of children, ordinary illnesses, infirmities of old age, and death.[19] The violence of the Partition seemed to have disappeared into a distant past. Even among the children in the families, there was little knowledge of what their parents had gone through during the Partition. Still, within the period of my fieldwork there were dangers—past events of which one had only vague suspicions could suddenly present themselves without any notice. For instance, I witnessed a woman on her death bed saying that her last wish was that her shroud should not come from her brother's house. This refusing of a powerful ritual connection—namely, that the natal family of a married woman acknowledge their connection to the daughter of a house at the moment of her death—hinted at the powerful hold of some past betrayal that had never been explicitly spoken. Yet in the ritual staging of the funeral other relatives persuaded her adult children to disregard her utterance: as the elders said, one could be claimed by all kinds of ghostly forces at the moment of death. The feeling that everyday life as a site of the ordinary buried in itself the violence that provided a certain force within which relationships moved was to become strengthened in my mind as I came to know these families.[20] Yet with one exception I never in fact asked anyone for their stories about the Partition. It is not that if asked people could not tell you a story, but simply that the words had the frozen slide quality to them, which showed their burned and numbed relation to life. I hope that in the descriptions that follow in the book, the nature of this silence will show itself.

Unlike my relation with the displaced families, in which violence was always on the edges, my experience of working with the survivors of the riots in 1984 was of a different nature. The assassination of Indira Gandhi on October 31, 1984, by her Sikh bodyguards was followed by brutal violence against Sikh residents of the resettlement colonies in Delhi. The description of these riots, which received considerable attention in both scholarly and activist writing, will follow in the subsequent chapters. What I want to describe here is the sense that the suddenness of the violence and the imperative force with which I was drawn into the world of the survivors had none of the quality of the slow rhythms with which the violence of the Partition unfolded before me. The violence of the 1984 riots was something *visible* in the colonies in which it had been perpetrated although it was not *acknowledged* in the official pronouncements on the aftermath of Mrs. Gandhi's assassination. The quality of its visibility is best described in my earlier work. Allow me to loop back to my own words on the visual impressions that my first visit to the colony made on me:

> On our first visit to the area we were taken around by a self-styled social worker who attached himself to us and who we later learned was assigned by the local big men to shadow all strangers and keep them informed of events in the colony. We had been able to shake this man off on one pretext or other and had then been shown around by Vakil Singh, who had lost two sons in the carnage. We saw blood splattered on the walls, bullet holes, heaps of ashes in which one could still find bits of hair or skull and bone. But what we encountered in the women was mainly fear. Their men had been killed before their eyes. Their children had been spared but had been threatened with dire consequences if they spoke about the murderers. Yet a sullen resistance formed of anger, fear, and grief was beginning to take shape. They felt surrounded by the murderers, who had established a "camp" in the colony and were ostensibly doing "relief work" to impress the press and social organizations that had come to report the carnage.

My sense that the violence was visible, yet somehow obscured from our view, as if the eye was a camera lens that was being made to focus on a pre-arranged scenery, and as if what we were witnessing was something that had just vanished from view—this was recorded in a diary entry, thus: "As I talked to the women, three or four very old women were wandering around the street in a kind of convoy, each holding the edge of the other's *dupatta* (veil).

Like spirits, they stood in front of each house—mute—but seeing things that were invisible to us. The laments for the dead would not come to their lips. There they stood, before broken doors and scorched walls—unseeing eyes—calling the names of those who had died just two days ago."

In freezing these moments of the funereal landscape, I want to convey the idea of how objects and gestures were stranded, strewn about, torn.[21] The brutal and telescoped violence had blasted out these spaces from their usual normality (which was itself marked by an everyday violence, but which hardly ever made it to the newspapers) and brought them to public attention. Thus, my own "entry" into the field was not marked by any of the slow rituals of initiation through which the anthropologist becomes a part of the everyday life of a community. It was as if a wound had suddenly opened up, slashing through connected tissues. My very presence in the "field" was not that of an anthropologist conducting fieldwork.[22] Along with several others, I had undertaken to act in this emergency for the safety of the survivors and to work toward their rehabilitation. These questions, then, were grounded in the question of how the survivors were to rebuild their lives, to pick up the pieces and find out how and whether to go on, that is, to go on living in this very place of devastation, as of something over.

INTERTWINING

Then there is the question of how and why these events are stitched together, considering the important differences between them. The signature of the Partition in both the literary and popular imagination has been the violation of women, mass rapes and mass abductions, their expulsion from homes, the imperative to court heroic deaths, and the recovery operations staged by India and Pakistan. I do not mean to suggest that there was no violation of male bodies during the Partition. Indeed, it would appear that castration (both literal and figurative) of the enemy was an important mode in which the male body was made to stand for the whole community. Nevertheless, in the discourses emanating from the state (as in the Constituent Assembly debates that I analyze in chapter 2), this fact was always elided. The rhetoric strategy of focusing on abducted and raped women to the exclusion of the sexual violation of men allowed the nation to construct itself as a masculine nation.

In contrast, if we consider the riots against the Sikhs in 1984, the dominant themes were those of humiliation of men. Women were not attacked, though there might have been isolated cases of rape.[23] I had suggested in earlier studies that crowds work with definite ideas of a limit.[24] Subsequent studies of communal violence in other areas suggest that in some cases Hindu and Muslim groups consciously try to avoid rape of women of the other community. In other cases, however, rape still evokes the violence of the Partition. For instance, Deepak Mehta and Roma Chatterji quote their informants from Dharavi in Bombay reporting that Hindu mobs violently attacked a group of Muslim women, dragging them away and shouting, "We are taking away your Pakistan."[25] In contrast, Sudhir Kakar in his study of communal violence in Hyderabad reports that there was an explicit avoidance of rape because those engaging in violence still imagined a future in which they had to live together again. In his words:

> As Mangal Singh remarked "A few days after the riot is over, whatever
> the bitterness in our hearts and however cold our voices are initially,
> Akbar Pehlwan still has to call me and say, 'Mangal Bhai, what do we do
> about that disputed land in Begampet,' and I still have to answer, 'Let's
> get together on that one, Akbar Bhai, and solve the problem peacefully.'"
> Rape makes such interaction impossible and turns Hindu-Muslim
> animosity into implacable hatred.[26]

This is an attractive interpretative move, but it assumes that we know what it means to be living together again. In the case of the Partition, the boundaries drawn around people were national boundaries, were relatively difficult to cross, and were materialized into such symbols of nationhood as border posts, passports, travel permits; the boundaries that come to be drawn around those engaged in collective violence against each other but who continue to inhabit the same space are more subtle.[27] They have to be deciphered in the still waters when life seems quiescent as well as at the more dramatic moments of a crisis, for the boundaries may be drawn between communities, between localities, between members of the family, and even between different regions of the self. It is also the case that stories about violence that circulate during riots include the theme of rape regardless of actual incidences. This does not mean, of course, that the difference between the two situations is insignificant. It does show, though, that in the regions of the imaginary, violence creates divisions and connections that point to the tremendous dangers that human beings pose to each other. How these dangers are mastered, domesticated, lived through is the theme of several of the chapters that follow. Human beings, however, not only pose dangers to each other, they also hold hope for each other. By addressing the theme of social suffering, I try to show in my depiction of ordinary lives that the answer to these dangers is not some kind of an ascent into the transcendent but a descent into everyday life. I think of the delicate task of repairing the torn spider's web, evoked by Wittgenstein in *Philosophical Investigations,* as my metaphor for the engagement with suffering and healing that ordinary life reveals.

FORMS OF LIFE, AGAIN

Let us consider how far Wittgenstein's idea of form of life will take us in thinking about these two events and the lives entangled in these together. Wittgenstein takes language to be the mark of human sociality: hence human forms of life are defined by the fact that they are forms created *by* and *for* those who are in possession of language even as the natural is absorbed within these "social" forms. When anthropologists have evoked the idea of forms of life, it has often been to suggest the importance of thick description, local knowledge, or what it is to learn a rule.[28] For Cavell such conventional views of the idea of form of life eclipse the spiritual struggle of his investigations. In his words:

> The idea [of forms of life] is, I believe, typically taken to emphasize the social nature of human language and conduct, as if Wittgenstein's mission is to rebuke philosophy for concentrating too much on isolated individuals, or for emphasizing the inner at the expense of the outer, in accounting for such matters as meaning, or states of consciousness, or following a rule etc. . . . . A conventionalized sense of form of life will support a conventionalized or contractual sense of agreement. But there is another sense of form of life that will contest this.[29]

What Cavell finds wanting in this conventional view of forms of life is that it not only obscures the mutual absorption of the natural and the social but also emphasizes *form* at the expense of *life.* Now, life is the object of theorizing in powerful ways in the writings of Giorgio Agamben and Michel Foucault, who are both interested in the processes by which management of life becomes an affair of the state, thus inaugurating the biopolitical state: I analyze some of the implications of this in chapter 10. But what interests me most in Cavell's writing is the idea that the vertical sense of the form of life suggests the limit of what or who is recognized as human within a social form and provides the conditions of the use of criteria as applied to others. Thus the criteria of pain do not apply to that which does not exhibit signs of being a form of *life*—we do not ask whether a tape recorder that can be turned on to play a shriek is feeling the pain.[30] The distinction between the horizontal and the vertical axes of forms of life takes us at least to the point at which we can appreciate not only the security provided by belonging to a community with shared agreements but also the dangers that human beings pose to each other. These dangers relate to not only disputations over *forms* but also disputations over what constitutes *life*. The blurring between what is human and what is not human shades into the blurring over what is life and what is not life.

Seen from the perspective of Agamben it is the fact that a biopolitical state can strip someone to what is bare or naked life that produces bodies that are killable with impunity.[31] In Cavell, one glimpses the dangers as if stitched into everyday life when one withholds recognition from the other, not simply on the grounds that she is not part of one's own community but that she is not part of life itself. This is not a question of a reasoned denial but of a denial of accepting the separateness of the other as a flesh and blood creature. Sometimes this announces itself in Cavell's writing in the fear of natality, and the thought that violence may be linked not only to handing out death but also in the refusal to allow another to be born.

The weaving together of both ethnographies of violence as I have done in this book, as if each were shot through with the colors of the other, points to the way in which everyday life absorbs the traumatic collective violence that creates boundaries between nations and between ethnic and religious groups. The difference is that the very fact of my presence near the scene of violence in the case of the 1984 riots, and my relative distance in time from the violence of the Partition, made the relation between spoken words and voices different. The work of time, not its representation, is at issue, for in each case the question of what it is to inherit the legacy of such violence has been different.

THE DARKNESS OF THIS TIME

In the preface to *Philosophical Investigations,* Wittgenstein writes, "It is not impossible that it should fall to the lot of this work, in its poverty and in the darkness of this time, to bring light into one brain or another—but, of course, it is not likely." George Bearn writes that the destructive moment of the *Investigations* threatens the fabric of our daily lives, so it is more destructive than the textbook skepticism of the philosopher or the café skeptic.[32] If in life, said Wittgenstein, we are surrounded by death, so too in the health of our understanding we are surrounded by madness. Rather than a forceful exclusion of this voice of madness, Wittgenstein returns us to the everyday by a gesture of waiting: "If I have exhausted the justifications I have reached bedrock, and my spade is turned. Then I am inclined to say: This is simply what I do."[33] In this picture of the turned spade as indicative of a turned pen, we have the picture of what the act of writing may be in the darkness of this time. For me the love of anthropology has turned out to be an affair in which when I reach bedrock I do not break through the resistance of the other, but in this gesture of waiting I allow the knowledge of the other to mark me.[34] In this sense this book is also an autobiography.

TWO

The Figure of the Abducted Woman

The Citizen as Sexed

WRITING IN 1994, THE WELL-KNOWN HISTORIAN of the subaltern Gyanendra Pandey took the neglect of the Partition in the social sciences and in Indian public culture as a symptom of a deep malaise. Historical writing in India, he argued, was singularly uninterested in the popular construction of the Partition, the trauma it produced, and the sharp division between Hindus, Muslims, and Sikhs it left behind. He attributed this blindness to the fact that the historian's craft has never been particularly comfortable with such matters as "the horror of the Partition, the anguish and sorrow, pain and brutality of the 'riots' of 1946–47." The analytical move in Indian historiography, Pandey further argued, was to assimilate the Partition as an event in the intersecting histories of the British Empire and Indian nation, which left little place for recounting the experience of the event for ordinary people.[1]

In recent years, many writers, including Pandey, have produced impressive testimonial literature on the Partition in an attempt to bring ordinary people's experiences into the story of this event.[2] Corresponding to this development is the scholarly effort to show how anxiety about Hindu-Muslim relations, especially about sexuality and purity of women, circulated in the public domain in the late nineteenth and early twentieth centuries in the popular forms of cartoons, comic strips, posters, and vernacular tracts. Part of the burden of this chapter is to try to understand how public anxieties around sexuality and purity might have created the grounds on which the figure of the violated woman became an important mobilizing point for reinstating the nation as a "pure" and masculine space.[3] At stake, then, is not simply the question of "silence" but also that of the genres that enabled speech and gave it the forms it took. It is instructive that there has been no attempt to memorialize the Partition in the form of national monuments or museums. No attempt was made, for that matter, to use the legal instruments of trials or public hearings to allow stories of mass rape and murder to be made public or to offer a promise of justice to the violated persons.[4] There was no dramatic enactment of "putting history on trial" that Shoshana Felman sees as the particular feature of twentieth-century collective traumas.[5] In fact, the trope of horror was deployed to open up the space for speech in the formal setting of the Constituent Assembly debates and in popular culture, and it gave the recounting of the event a tonality of rumor.

Consider first the numbers and magnitudes as these are cited in official reports. As Pandey argues, numbers are not offered here in the sober register of a judicial tribunal or a bureaucratic report based upon careful collection of data—rather, these function as gestures toward the enormity of the violence. I might add that this mode of reporting was not peculiar to the Partition. It was part of a wider bureaucratic genre that used numbers and magnitudes to attribute all kinds of "passions" such as panic, incredulity, or barbarity to the populace when faced with a crisis such as an epidemic or a riot—thus constructing the state as a rational guarantor of order. We shall see how the figure of the abducted woman allowed the state to construct "order" as essentially an attribute of the masculine nation so that the counterpart of the social contract becomes the sexual contract in which women as sexual and reproductive beings are placed within the domestic, under the control of the "right" kinds of men.

THE ABDUCTED WOMAN IN THE IMAGINARY OF THE MASCULINE NATION

How did the gendering of suffering allow a discourse of the nation to emerge at the time of the Partition? What precise work does the figure of the abducted woman and her recovery do in instituting the relation between the social contract and the sexual contract at the advent of the nation? While I am sympathetic to the question of repression of women's voices in the accounts of the Partition that has animated the work of many feminist historians, I would like to frame this in a different model than that of trauma. Instead of deploying the notion of trauma, I ask what kind of protocols for telling their story might have been imported into the task of making visible (or audible) the suffering of women in the nationalist discourse? I take the figure of the abducted woman as it circulated in the political debates soon after the Partition of the country and ask how this was anchored to the earlier figures that were available through myth, story, and forms of print culture in the early-twentieth-century discourse on this figure. How was the figure of the abducted woman transfigured to institute a social contract that created the nation as a masculine nation?

One of the earliest accounts of the violence of the Partition rendered the story in the following terms:

> The great upheaval that shook India from one end to the other during a period of about fifteen months commencing with August 16, 1946 was an event of unprecedented magnitude and horror. History has not known a fratricidal war of such dimensions in which human hatred and bestial passions were degraded to the levels witnessed during the dark epoch when religious frenzy, taking the shape of a hideous monster, stalked through the cities, towns and countryside, taking a toll of half a million innocent lives. Decrepit old men, defenseless women, helpless young children, infants in arms, by the thousand were brutally done to death by Muslim, Hindu and Sikh fanatics. Destruction and looting of property, kidnapping and ravishing of women, unspeakable atrocities, and indescribable inhumanities, were perpetrated in the name of religion and patriotism.[6]

The government of India set up a Fact Finding Organization on the communal violence. Although the files containing these reports were never made public, G. D. Khosla, who was a justice of the Punjab High Court and was in charge of producing this report, interviewed liaison officers of the Military Evacuation Organization in charge of the large-scale evacuation of the minorities from one dominion to another. Based on this information, Khosla put the figure of loss of life in both warring communities between 200,000 and 250,000 and the number of women who were raped and abducted on both sides as close to 100,000. Some support for this is provided in information given to the House in the context of legislative debates of the Constituent Assembly, where it was stated on December 15, 1949, that 33,000 Hindu or Sikh women had been abducted by Muslims and that the Pakistan government had claimed that 50,000 Muslim women had been abducted by Hindu or Sikh men.

Joint efforts made by the governments of India and Pakistan to recover abducted women and restore them to their relatives led to the recovery of a large number of women from both territories. It was stated on behalf of the government in the Constituent Assembly on December 15, 1949, that 12,000 women had been recovered in India and 6,000 in Pakistan. The figures given by Khosla on the basis of the Fact Finding Organization were that 12,000 Hindu or Sikh women were "recovered" from the Punjab and the frontier regions in Pakistan and 8,000 Muslim women from the provinces of Indian Punjab.

As I said earlier, Pandey makes the subtle point that numbers function here not as forms of reporting in which we can read bureaucratic logic but rather as elements of rumor in which the very magnitudes serve to signal both excess and specificity. He argues that in the official reports as well as in reports by prominent political leaders, the circulation of such stories served to transform hearsay into "truth."[7] What Pandey misses in his analysis, it seems to me, is that the magnitudes established that violence was taking place in a state of exception, which, in turn, opened the way to authorize the state to undertake extraordinary measures by appeals to the state of exception. I argue that the circulation of the figure of the abducted woman, with its associated imagery of social disorder as sexual disorder, created the conditions of possibility in which the state could be instituted as essentially a social contract between *men* charged with keeping male violence against women in abeyance. Thus, the story about abduction and recovery acts as a foundational story that authorizes a particular relation between social contract and sexual contract—the former being a contract between men to institute the political and the latter the agreement to place women within the home under the authority of the husband/father figure.[8] The "foundational" event of inaugurating the nation then is itself anchored to the already circulating imaginary of abduction of women that signaled a state of disorder since it dismantled the orderly exchange of women. The state of war, akin to the Hobbesian state of nature, comes to be defined as one in which Hindus and Muslims are engaged in mutual warfare over the control of sexually and reproductively active women. The origin of the state is then located in the rightful reinstating of proper kinship by recovering women from the other side. If one prefers to put it in the terminology of Lévi-Strauss, one could say that the state reinstates the correct matrimonial dialogue of men. The foundational event of the inauguration of the state brings something new into existence, but the event does not come from nowhere—it is anchored to imageries that already haunt Hindu-Muslim relations.

THE DISCOURSE OF THE STATE

A conscious policy with regard to abducted women and children born of sexual and reproductive violence was first initiated in the session of the Indian National Congress on November 23 and 24, 1946, when delegates expressed grave concern about the fate of women who were violated during the communal riots. Dr. Rajendra Prasad, who was later to become the first president of independent India, moved a resolution that received wide support from prominent leaders of the Congress Party, including Jawaharlal Nehru:

> The Congress views with pain, horror and anxiety the tragedies of Calcutta, in East Bengal, in Bihar and in some parts of Meerut district. The acts of brutality committed on men, women and children fill every decent person with shame and humiliation. These new developments on communal strife are different from any previous disturbances and have involved murders on a mass scale as also mass conversions enforced at the point of a dagger, abduction and violation of women and forcible marriage.

The operative part of the resolution then stated the obligation of the Congress Party toward such women:

> The immediate problem is to produce a sense of security and rehabilitate homes and villages, which have been broken up and destroyed. Women, who have been abducted and forcibly married, must be restored to their homes. Mass conversions, which have taken place forcibly, have no significance or validity and the people affected by them should be given every opportunity to return to their homes and the life of their choice.[9]

This resolution was adopted in November 1946. The situation, however, worsened from March 1947, so that three weeks after India and Pakistan achieved their independence as separate states, the representatives of both dominions met on September 3, 1947, and agreed that steps should be taken to recover and restore abducted persons. Both sides pronounced themselves against recognition of forced marriages.

The All India Congress Committee met in the middle of November and reiterated that "during these disorders large numbers of women have been abducted on either side and there have been forcible conversions on a large scale. No civilized people can recognize such conversions and there is nothing more heinous than abduction of women. Every effort, therefore, must be made to restore women to their original homes, with the co-operation of the Governments concerned."[10]

An interdominion conference followed the Congress session, at which the two dominions agreed to the steps to be taken to recover abducted women and children. The implementation of these decisions led to a recovery of large number of women from both sides—between December 1947 and July 1948, 9,362 women were reported to have been recovered in India and 5,510 in Pakistan. At this time both governments worked toward the creation of a legal instrument for the work of recovery. As a result, appropriate ordinances were issued in India on January 31, 1948, and in Pakistan in May 1948. The ordinance in India was renewed in June 1949. In December 1949 the Constituent Assembly passed the Abducted Persons (Recovery and Restoration) Act of 1949, which remained in force until October 31, 1951.

The events outlined above point to the manner in which the state took cognizance of the sexual and reproductive violence directed against women. To some extent this obligation was generated by the expectations of the affected population. The devastated refugees who had lost their homes, their families, and their possessions in the bloody riots and were housed in refugee camps in Delhi thought it appropriate to address the leaders of independent India as appropriate recipients of their laments. In this manner, they were not only creating a framework for the state to legitimately take up the task of recovery of abducted women but also learning that claiming entitlements over women of one's own community could be seen as a legitimate affair of the state.

Khosla reported that refugees in distress made loud and frantic appeals to all departments of government. Pandit Nehru received letters in the months of August, September, and October seeking his personal intervention to save a relative left behind or to recover a piece of property or a precious possession abandoned in Pakistan. People wrote to him, accusing him of enjoying a victory that had been won at the expense of the Hindus of the west Punjab. Khosla quoted a letter by a retired schoolmaster addressed to Pandit Nehru: "What has compelled me to write this to you is the fact that in casting about my eyes I fail to find anyone in the world except you who can help me in my calamity."[11] How was the nation to respond to such investment of both despair and hope in its leaders?

THE QUESTION OF NATIONAL HONOR

For the new nation state of India, the question of the recovery of abducted women and children then became a matter of national honor. There was a repeated demand, publicly enunciated, that the state must take the responsibility of the recovery of women and children upon itself. The new government in India tried to reassure the people of its intention in this regard through several press releases. For instance, Rajashree Ghosh cites a press release published in *The Statesman* of November 4, 1947, that "forced conversions and forced marriages will not be recognized and that women and girls who have been abducted must be restored to their families."[12] Various administrative mechanisms for the recovery of women were operative in the early stages of the recovery operations including the Office of the Deputy High Commissioner, the Military Evacuation Organization, the Chief Liaison Officer, and the Organization for Recovering Abducted Women, consisting of social workers and other officials. All these efforts culminated in an interdominion agreement signed on September 3, 1947, and finally the Abducted Persons (Recovery and Restoration) Act of 1949. Through these legal instruments, each country provided facilities to the other for conducting search and rescue operations. Both agreed that the exchange of women should be equal in number. Wide powers were given to the police to conduct the work of recovery, and arrangements were made for housing the recovered women in transitory camps. Disputed cases were to be referred to a joint tribunal for final settlement.

In terms of procedure, the Indian government set up Search and Service Bureaus in different cities in the Punjab where missing women were reported. This information was then passed on to the relevant authorities, and a search for these women and children was mounted. The Indian government accepted the help of several women volunteers, especially those with a Gandhian background, to help in the recovery process. Prominent among these women were Mridula Sarabhai, Rameshwari Nehru, and Kamlabehn Patel. In her memoirs of this period Kamlabehn Patel reports that "in those days it wasn't prudent to trust any male, not even policemen as far as the safety of women was concerned."[13] Several transit camps were set up, such as the Gangaram Hospital Camp in Lahore and Gandhi Vanita Ashram in Amritsar. Kamlabehn herself was in charge of the transit camp in Lahore to which recovered women and children were brought. They were then transferred to India or Pakistan, as the case might be, under police escort. A woman or child who was claimed by a close relative in the case of an Indian citizen could be handed over to the relative only at Jullundher in the presence of a magistrate.

Taken at face value it would appear that the norms of honor in the order of the family and the order of the state were mutually supportive. The families with whom I worked related stories of a generalized nature in which the heroic sacrifices made by women were lauded, but to speak in the first person on the facts of abduction and rape was not easy. Later chapters will show the specific ways in which stories were framed in the first person, and especially the place of silence in the "telling." Here I am interested in the logic of the state of exception with regard to the way that law was instituted to shape the nation as a *masculine* nation, so that the social contract became a contract between men conceived as heads of households. As so many statements that I have quoted show, normality was seen as restoration of women "to their families." Men appear here as heads of households rather than as individuals sprung from the earth, as in the famous mushroom analogy favored by Hobbes in conceptualizing the makers of the social contract.

It is my contention that once the problem of abducted women moved from the order of the family to the order of the state (as in the demand for legislation), it sanctified a sexual contract as the counterpart of the social contract by creating a new legal category of "abducted person" (applicable, however, only to women and children) who came within the regulatory power of the state. There was an alliance between social work as a profession and the state as *parens patriae,* which made the official kinship norms of purity and honor much more rigid by transforming them into the law of the state.

The discussion on the Abducted Persons (Recovery and Restoration) Act of 1949 in the Constituent Assembly focused on three issues.[14] The first was the definition of a civilized government and especially the responsibility of the state to women on whom violence had been unleashed. The second was the definition of an abducted person, and the rights of women abducted by men. The third issue was the rights of children born of "wrong" sexual unions and the obligations of the state toward them. The connecting thread between these three issues is the notion of national honor and preservation of purity of the population through which the sexual contract is made the grounds for a social contract that institutes the nation as a masculine nation.

In introducing the bill, Shri N. Gopalaswami Ayyangar, the then Minister of Transport and a distinguished lawyer, stated that there were experiences associated with the partition of the country in regard to which "most of us will have to hang our heads down in shame." He went on to say that "among the many brutalities and outrages which vitiated the atmosphere . . . none touched so low a depth of moral depravity as these mass abductions of women on both sides. . . . Those of us who think of civilized government and want to conduct the government on civilized lines should feel ashamed."

As is clear from this statement, the state distanced itself from the "depths of moral depravity" that the population had shown and took upon itself the task of establishing a civilized government. Part of the definition of this civilized government was to not only recover women defined by the new nation as "our" women but also to restore to the opposite side "their" women. The interest in women, however, was not premised upon their definition as citizens but as sexual and reproductive beings. As far as recovery of women held by the "other" side was concerned, what was at stake was the honor of the nation because women as sexual and reproductive beings were being forcibly held. This was explicit in the demands made by several members that not only should the recovery of women on both sides be more or less equal but also that women in their reproductive years should be "recovered." Shri Gopalaswami Ayyangar especially referred to this criticism, saying that several critics alleged that "while in India we have recovered women of all ages and so forth, in Pakistan they had recovered for us only old women or little children." He went on to counter this criticism by citing figures to show that the distribution by age of recovered women from both dominions was, in fact, roughly equal. Of the total women recovered, he said, girls below the age of twelve from Pakistan and India were 45 and 35 percent, respectively. In the age group 12 to 35 years old, the recovery was 49 percent in Pakistan and 59 percent in India, while the percentage dropped to about 10 percent for women older than 35. This discussion clearly shows that national honor was tied to the regaining of control over the sexual and reproductive functions of women. The social contract that would legitimate both nations was seen as one instituted by men in which they were capable of recovering their own place as heads of households by placing the sexuality and reproductive powers of women firmly within the family.

Thus the figure of the abducted woman signals the impossibility of the social contract because the sexual contract that would place men as heads of households (not as a matter of kinship but as matter *for the state*) was in jeopardy. Pandit Thakur Das Bhargava explicitly drew on this figure when he stated during the debates, "You will remember, Sir, how when one Ellis was kidnapped by some Pathans the whole of Britain shook with anger and indignation and until she was returned Englishmen did not come to their senses. And we all know our own history, of what happened at the time of Shri Ram when Sita was abducted. Here, where thousands of girls are concerned, we cannot forget this. We can forget all the properties, we can forget every other thing but this cannot be forgotten."[15]

Then there was the question of whether Muslim women needed to be returned to their own families. It is interesting to note the particular tonality that crept into Pandit Thakur Das Bhargava's statement that "I don't suggest for a moment that the abducted Muslim girls should be kept here because I believe that not only would it be good for them to be sent away but it is equally good for us to be rid of them. I don't want immorality to prosper in my country."

It is important to note here that to be a citizen as a head of the household demands that men's own sexuality be disciplined, oriented to the women who have been placed "correctly" within the family, and that children who would claim citizenship are born of the right kind of union of men and women. Elsewhere I have analyzed courtroom talk in the cases of rape in Indian courts of law to argue that "male desire" is construed as a natural need in the judicial discourse on rape, so that whenever the cultural and social constraints are removed, men are seen as falling into a state of nature in which they cannot control their appetite for sex. I quote here from an earlier paper, where I argued that

> it is male desire which is considered as "natural," hence "normal," and the female body as the natural site on which this desire is to be enacted. Women are not seen as desiring subjects in the rape law—as wives they do not have the right to withhold consent from their husbands, although the state invests its resources in protecting them from the desires of other men. Paradoxically, women defined in opposition to the wife or the chaste daughter, i.e. women of easy virtue, as the courts put it, also turn out to have no right to withhold consent. . . . A reading of female desire as interpreted by the courts demonstrates, that while men are seen to be acting out their "natural" urges when engaging in "illicit" sex, women who show any kind of desire outside the confines of marriage are immediately considered "loose." By escaping the confines of male-centered discourses of sexuality and alliance, these women are

then castigated by becoming the objects of any kind of male desire. Rape is not a crime but is reduced to an act that she herself deserves or seeks.[16]

Clearly, the deeply rooted assumptions about the husband/father figure continue in the juridical unconscious even when the figure of the abducted or raped woman appears in the singular in post-Independence India.

Let us consider the next question—Who is an abducted person? According to the bill, "An 'abducted person' means a male child under the age of sixteen years or a female of whatever age, who is, or immediately before the 1st day of March 1947 was, a Muslim and who, on or after that day, has become separated from his or her family and is found to be living with or under the control of a non-Muslim individual or family, and in the latter case includes a child born to any such female after the said date."[17]

We shall take up the question of children defined as "abducted" under the provisions of the bill later. As for the women, it was clear that the bill failed to make any provision for ascertaining whether a woman wished to return to her original family or not. This question was raised by several members. The sharpest criticism came from Thakur Das Bhargava, who stated, "You want to take away the rights of a major woman who has remained here after the partition. . . . My submission is that the law of nations is clear, the law of humanity is clear, the Indian Penal Code is clear, the Constitution we have passed is clear, that you cannot force a woman who is above 18 to go back to Pakistan. This Bill offends against such a rule."

In addition to the manner in which the rights of a woman to decide her future course of action were taken away by the state to protect the honor and purity of the nation, there was also the question that the bill gave wide powers to the police to remove a woman forcibly if she came under the definition of an abducted woman under its clauses. This, as Shri Bhargava pointed out, took away the rights of habeas corpus from a person who was treated as an abducted person even if she were mistakenly so labeled.

When several members of the House pointed to the increasing evidence that many women were refusing to go back to their original families and were practically coerced by social workers to return, Shrimati G. Durgabai, speaking on behalf of both the social workers and the women's movement, defended the social workers on the grounds that they knew best what the women's true preferences were. Durgabai's statement is worth quoting in detail:

Questions are also asked: Since these women are married and settled here and have adjusted themselves to the new environment and to their new relatives here, is it desirable that we should force them to go back? It is also argued: These women who have been able to adjust themselves to their new surroundings are refusing to go back, and when they are settled, is it desirable that we should force them to go back? . . . These are the questions we have to answer. May I ask: Are they really happy? Is the reconciliation true? Can there be a permanent reconciliation in such cases? Is it not out of helplessness, there being no alternative that the woman consents or is forced to enter into that sort of alliance with a person who is no more than the person who is a murderer of her very husband, her very father, or her very brother? Can she be really happy with that man? Even if there is reconciliation, is it permanent? Is this woman welcomed in the family of the abductor?

Paradoxically the authority of the woman social worker was used to silence the voice of the woman as subject and to put upon her an obligation to *remember* that the abductor to whom she was now married was the murderer of her husband or her father. The disciplining of sentiment according to the demands of the state collapsed the duty to the family with duty to the state. The women themselves seem to have been caught in the impossible situation where the obligation to maintain a narrative continuity with the past contradicted the ability to live in the present. Durgabai herself testified to the apprehensions of the women at the prospects of returning to their original homes: "Sir, we the social workers who are closely associated with the work are confronted with many questions when we approach a woman. The women say, 'You have come to save us; you say you have come to take us back to our relatives. You tell us that our relatives are eagerly waiting to receive us. You do not know our society. It is hell. They will kill us. Therefore, do not send us back.'"

Yet at the same moment that these apprehensions were expressed, the authority of the social worker was established by the statement that "the social workers associated with this work know the psychology of these abducted recovered women fully well. They can testify to it that such a woman only welcomes an opportunity to get back to her own house." The refusal of many women to go back and the resistance that the social workers were encountering in the field was explained away by an attribution of false consciousness or a kind of misrecognition to the women. The appropriate sentiment in all such cases was coercively established as a desire for the original home that allowed men on both sides of the border to be instituting the social contract as *heads of households* in which women were "in their proper place."

CHILDREN AND REPRODUCTIVE FUTURES

We come now to the category of children defined as abducted. As stated earlier, the bill defined any child born to a woman after March 1, 1947, as an abducted person if its mother came under the definition of an abducted person. These, in short, were children born through "wrong" sexual unions. The discussion in the Constituent Assembly focused on several issues. First, how were rights over a child to be distributed between the male and the female in terms of their relative contributions to the process of procreation? Second, what legal recognition was to be given to children whose parents were not considered to be legally married since the bill held all forcible marriages to be null and void? Third, was there a contradiction between the legality established by the state and the customary norms of a community regarding the whole question of determining the legitimacy of a child? Finally, if only one parent was entitled in these cases to transmit filiation as a basis for establishing citizenship, was it the relationship with the mother or the father that was to be considered relevant for creating the necessary credentials for citizenship?

Although there was no explicit enunciation of a theory of procreation and the relative contributions of the male and the female to the procreative process, analogies drawn from nature were sometimes used. For instance, Pandit Thakur Das Bhargava stated at one point in the discussion that he did not understand how a general rule could be formulated by which the child was to be handed over to the mother rather than the father: "It takes only nine to ten months gestation during which the child has to remain in the mother's womb. . . . It should not be made a rule that in every case the child is to be given over as a matter of rule. It is something like the rule that when you plant a tree it grows on the ground; therefore the tree goes with the land and the fruit of the tree goes with the tree. A child is the fruit of the labour of two persons. There is no reason why the father should be deprived in each case. Why should we make this rule?"

Analogies from nature, especially from the activities of agriculture or horticulture to conceptualize procreation, are part of the repertoire of ideas contained in Hindu texts and in the popular ideas regarding procreation.[18] What is important here is that a theory about the "labor" of reproduction enters into the state's repertoire of ideas even as it is articulated in opposition to the provisions of the bill. Although Durgabai did not pose the question in these terms, she questioned the rights of the male on the grounds that he was an abductor. Men who had forcibly abducted women, sold them, and used them for commercial purposes, she argued, could not claim rights over the children born to these women. In contrast to the earlier argument, Durgabai's interpretation would be that it was not the joint labor of a man and a woman that had created such a child but the plunder by men of women's bodies. Hence, "What right has the abductor to keep the child? The child has to go with the mother."

Another member, Shri Brajeshwar Prasad, also evoked the notion that in nature there was no question of illegitimacy or legitimacy of a child, and that it was only the conventions of society that made children legitimate or illegitimate. In his words, "Sir, I do not know how a child born of a man and a woman can ever become illegitimate. This is a notion I have not been able to grasp, but still knowing full well the attitude of the present Government, knowing full well the attitude of the Hindu society, we have to take the facts as they are and the illegitimate children if they are to live in India, they will remain as dogs, as beasts."

In the above discussion it was clear that the question of the legitimacy or illegitimacy of the children was related to the fact that it was the provisions of the bill that had made all unions that may have started with abduction and ended with marriage illegal and thus the children born to such unions illegitimate. As one member, Shri Brajeshwar Prasad, put it, even if a natural attachment had developed between the abductor and the abducted woman, the law did not recognize such marriages. Therefore, a woman could continue to stay with her abductor "only as a prostitute and a concubine," while her children could only remain in the country as illegitimate children who would be a "standing blot on Hindu society."[19]

A contradiction between state-defined legality and community-based legality was pointed out by Chaudhari Ranbir Singh, at least as he saw the matter, for he thought it would be a mockery to the country if children born to Muslim women were sent away on the grounds that they would be mistreated as illegitimate children here. "There is a general custom in our Punjab," he stated, "particularly in the community to which I and Sardar Bhupinder Singh Man belong, that, regardless of religion or community of the woman one marries, the offspring is not regarded as illegitimate, and we give him an equal share." Clearly a wide variety of customary norms regarding children born to women through proscribed sexual unions existed that were now standardized into one single law by which illegitimacy was defined.

How are we to understand this moment as foundational in terms of the relation between the social contract and the sexual contract in defining the nation-state? I suggested earlier that the figure of the abducted woman had circulated in the late nineteenth and early twentieth centuries as the site of anxiety for defining the place of men as heads of households.[20] It is important to note that the question of a father's rights over his children after his conversion to another religion was not a new question—it had legal precedents. For instance, whether a man who had converted to Christianity could continue to claim conjugal rights over his wife had been debated before the colonial courts as well as the issue of whether a man's "natural" rights over his child overrode the dissolution of marriage after conversion. I have argued elsewhere that although the courts were reluctant to apply English common law to these cases, arguing that the legal imagination must contend with people of one faith living under a political sovereign who owes allegiance to another faith, the general consensus was that the father's right could not be denied.[21] It now became possible to set aside the legal precedents on these questions and to take away custody from the father in the case of children born to women who had been forcibly possessed, precisely because the foundational event was located within an imagination of a state of emergency when normal rules were set aside. In the next section I discuss these issues briefly and then conclude with the question: Why is the state interested in women as sexual and reproductive beings?

ANCHORING THE FIGURE OF THE ABDUCTED WOMAN

Recent work on the nexus between ideas of sexuality, obscenity, and purity shows that the images of lustful Muslim males and innocent Hindu women proliferated in the propaganda literature generated by reform Hindu movements such as the Arya Samaj and political organizations such as the Hindu Mahasabha and the Rashtriya Sevak Sangh.[22] Charu Gupta has recently marshaled impressive material from the vernacular tracts published in Uttar Pradesh in the late nineteenth and early twentieth centuries to show that mobilization of the Hindu community, especially by new forms of religio-political organizations such as the Arya Samaj and the Hindu Mahasabha, drew upon the image of the lustful Muslim as a threat to Hindu domesticity. Consider the following passage from a speech delivered by Madan Mohan Malviya in 1923 on the subject of kidnapping, cited by Gupta:

> Hardly a day passes without our noticing a case or two of kidnapping of Hindu women and children by not only Muslim *badmashes* and *goondas,* but also by men of standing and means, who are supposed to be very highly connected. The worst feature of this evil is that Hindus do not stir themselves over the daylight robbery of national stock. . . . We are convinced that a regular propaganda is being carried on by the interested party for kidnapping Hindu women and children at different centers throughout the country. It is an open secret that Juma Masjids at Delhi and Lahore are being used as headquarters of these propagandists. . . . We must do away with this mischievous Muslim propaganda of kidnapping women and children.[23]

References to the lustful Muslim and appeals to innocence of Hindu women who could be easily deceived by Muslim men were plentiful. In some cases, harshness of Hindu customs against widows was evoked to explain why Hindu women fell into the traps of seduction laid by wily Muslims. Gupta is surely correct in concluding that evocation of these fears provided an emotive basis for arguments in favor of Hindu "homogeneity and patriarchy."[24] I think we can go further—for the story of abduction has implications for the very staging of sovereignty, such that when this story appears magnified at the time of the Partition, it becomes the foundational story of how the state is instituted and its relation to patriarchy. It invites us to think the story of the imaginary institution of the state in Western theory from this perspective rather than the other way around.

It should be obvious that the line of argument proposed here does not see the family simply as the institution located in the domain of the private but proposes that sovereignty continues to draw life from the family. The involvement of the state in the process of recovery of women shows that if men were to become ineffective in the control they exercise as heads of families, thus producing children from "wrong" sexual unions, then the state itself would come to be deprived of life. The figure of the abducted woman acquires salience because it posits the origin of the state not in the mythic state of nature, but in the "correct" relations between communities. Indeed, the mise-en-scène of nature itself is that of heads of households at war with other heads of households over the control of the sexual and reproductive powers of women rather than unattached "natural" men at war with each other. There is an uncanny address here to Lévi-Strauss's notion of the original state as one in which men are posited as relational beings and exchange of women is the medium through which this relational state is achieved.[25] The disturbance of proper exchange then comes to be construed as a disturbance in the life of the state, robbing it of the sources from which it can draw life. Does this story located at the particular juncture of the inauguration of the nation-state in India tell us something about the nature of sovereignty itself?

In an acute analysis of the relation between fatherly authority and the possibility of a woman citizen, Mary Laura Severance argues that in Hobbes we have a predication of fatherly authority based on consent rather than something that is natural or originary, as claimed by Sir Robert Filmer.[26] But, as she notes, the consent of the family to be ruled by the father is, in effect, a neutralization of his power to kill. By grounding the power of the father in the consent of the family, Hobbes is able to draw a distinction between fatherly and sovereign authority as two distinct but artificial spheres. However, this is done within the framework of the seventeenth-century doctrine that women are unfit for civil business and must be represented (or concluded) by their husbands. The sexual contract and the social contract are then two separate realms. As Severance notes, however, the idea of the state of nature as that in which every man is in a state of war with every other man should be modified to read that every *father*, as the head of the family, is at war against every other *father*. In her words, "the members of each individual family 'consent' not to the sovereign's but to the father's absolute rule; they are not parties to the 'contract' that brings the commonwealth into existence."[27] I would claim that this war of "fathers" is what we witness in the acts of abduction and rape. The state's commitment to the recovery of women is the acknowledgment of the authority of the father as the necessary foundation for the authority of the state. I find it useful to think of Rousseau's analysis of the figure of the woman in the discussion on sovereignty in *Émile* to show that the notion of the sexed individual as the basis of the political has a deep linkage with the idea of the life of the sovereign.[28]

As I have argued elsewhere,[29] the figure of the woman in Rousseau is introduced not so much as the symmetrical opposite of the man but rather as the obligatory passage through whom the man moves along the road of marriage, paternity, and citizenship. While the scene of seduction is necessary for the pupil in *Émile* to be inserted into the social, his capability to be a citizen is proved by learning how to renounce the very lure of the woman who was his passage into sociality. The parable of Sophie, whom

Émile must both learn to love and through whom he must learn to overcome his fear of death, points to the close relation for a man between learning how to inhabit society through the engagement with sex and how to become a good citizen by overcoming the fear of separation and death. It is worth pausing here to reflect on this.

It is from Émile's journey into citizenship that we learn the multiple chains of signification in which the figure of Sophie is inserted. She is the chimera who is inserted into the text—figure of seduction, the future mother of a family, and one through whom Émile learns that to be a good citizen is to overcome his fear of death by giving a law to the desires of his heart. Hence, she is the seductress in the present, the maternal in the future, and the teacher of duty and code of conduct. Without her, he can overcome physical ills, but with her and then despite her, he will become a virtuous citizen: "When you become the head of a family, you are going to become a member of the state, and do you know what it is to be a member of the state? Do you know what government, laws, and fatherland are? *Do you know what the price is of your being permitted to live and for whom you ought to die?*" [30]

There are two thoughts here. The first is that to be a citizen of the state, you must be the head of a household; the second is that you must know for whom you ought to die. For the woman, the duty as a citizen is confounded with her duty to her husband. A woman's comportment must be such that not only her husband but also his neighbors and friends must believe in her fidelity. When she gives her husband children who are not his own, we are told, she is false both to him and to them and her crime is "not infidelity but treason." [31] Thus, woman as seductress holds danger for the man, because she may use her powers of seduction to make the man too attached to life and thus unable to decipher who and what it is worth dying for. In her role as mother, she may deprive him of being a proper head of the household by giving him counterfeit children. That this is treason and not infidelity shows how the mother, who was completely excluded as a figure of thought in Hobbes, comes to be incorporated into the duties of citizenship. For Rousseau the individual on whose consent political community is built is, no doubt, a sexed individual, but the woman has the special role of not only introducing the man to forms of sociality but also teaching him how to renounce his attachment to her in order to give life to the political community. [32]

Within this scheme, women's allegiance to the state is proved by their role as mothers who bear legitimate children (recall the remark about the crime of bringing illegitimate children into the world being not about infidelity but about treason); and men learn to be good citizens by being prepared to die to give life to the sovereign. Once the individual is recognized as social because he is sexed, he is also recognized as mortal. In Rousseau, we saw that man is said to receive life from the sovereign. Political community as population is dependent on reproduction: thus, the citizen's investment of affect in the political community is attested by his desire to reproduce and to give the political community legitimate "natural" children. A corollary is that a woman's infidelity is an offense not only against the family but also against the sovereignty of the state.

We can see now that the *mise-en scène* of abduction and recovery places the state as the medium for reestablishing the authority of the husband/father. It is only under conditions of ordered family life and legitimate reproduction that the sovereign can draw life from the family. Gupta's work allows us to see that the earlier imagination of the Hindu woman as seduced or duped by the Muslim man is complemented by the idea that her attraction to Muslim practices is an offence against the patriarchal authority of the Hindu man, imagined within the scene of colonialism. Thus, for instance, Gupta gives examples from many vernacular tracts in which the practice of Hindu women praying to the Muslim *pirs* (holy men given the status of saints, especially among Shi'a Muslims), a common religious practice of Hindus and Muslims alike, is construed as a betrayal of the Hindu man—a mocking of his potency—that to my ears sounds remarkably akin to the act of treason that Rousseau attributes to women who bring "wrong" children into the world. The following quotation from a vernacular tract offers a particularly telling example:

> God believes in the worship of only one husband for women, but they
> pay service to Ghazi Mian for many years. . . . Where before Hindu
> women worshipped their husband for a lot of love and produced a
> child, today they leave their husband and go to the dead Ghazi Mian
> and at his defunct grave ask for a child. It is not women but men who
> are to be blamed for this hateful act. Even when they are alive, instead
> of asking their wife to become a true *pativrata* [a woman devoted exclu-
> sively to her husband, regarding him as a god], they allow her to go to
> the dead grave of a Turk to ask for a child and become an infidel.[33]

In the introduction to this chapter, I juxtaposed the problem of the silence on the Partition with the excess of speech in the mode of rumor—encountered not only in popular imagination but also at the heart of the official documentation of the event. The analysis offered here takes the legal and administrative discourse on the abducted woman as an important site for understanding how the social contract was grounded in a particular kind of sexual contract. The trope of horror through which this space of (excess) enunciation and action was opened up under the sign of the state not only drowned out the voices of women but also recognized their suffering as relevant only for the inauguration of sovereignty. The repression of voice and what is it to recover it—not through the speech generated in collecting oral history or in the process of psychotherapy, but as part of everyday life in which women give an expression to their violation—this is what the cases presented later will try to show. But before that I turn to the register of the literary in the following chapter, for don't we often look to the poets to give us the gift of language when we are left simultaneously with a loss of voice and its appearance as simulacrum? How else are we to overcome the taint of the official discourses that could see the suffering of women who were abducted and violated, but only for establishing the correct order of the family and the state?

THREE

Language and Body

Transactions in the Construction of Pain

IN AN EARLIER VERSION OF THIS CHAPTER, I wrote, "In repeatedly trying to write the meaning(s) of violence against women in Indian society, I find that languages of pain through which social sciences could gaze at, touch or become textual bodies on which this pain is written often elude me."[1] I felt compelled then to look toward the transactions between language and body in the work of mourning, and especially in the gendered division of labor by which the antiphony of language and silence re-creates the world in the face of tragic loss. In the previous chapter, I tried to give an account of how it is that the imagining of the project of nationalism in India came to include the appropriation of bodies of women as objects on which the desire for nationalism could be brutally inscribed and a memory for the future made. As I tried to argue, the imagination of a social contract that would inaugurate the nation-state saw men as heads of households—husbands and fathers—who became authorized to initiate the advent of the nation-state only after they had shown themselves capable of offering protection to women defined as "their own women" from men of the enemy community, who themselves agreed to forego violence against the women of the other community. Despite the frequent references to the suffering of women, however, what the Constituent Assembly debates showed was the substitution of authoritarian forms of speaking in the absence of any standing languages through which the pain could be addressed.

One might recall Foucault here: "Nothing is more inconsistent than a political regime that is indifferent to the truth: but nothing is more dangerous than a political system that claims to prescribe the truth."[2]

If I cannot claim to know the pain of the other, unlike the social workers who *knew* what women who were abducted *wanted*—what is it to relate to such pain? The absence of any standing languages of pain is perhaps symptomatic of the fact that I cannot separate my pain from my expression for it—another way of saying this is that my expression of pain compels you in unique ways—you are not free to believe or disbelieve me—our future is at stake. I want to reenter this scene of devastation to ask how one might inhabit such a world, one which has been made strange through the desolating experience of violence and loss. Cavell describes this as the Emersonian gesture of approaching the world through a kind of mourning for it.[3]

Some realities need to be fictionalized before they can be apprehended. I shall allow myself three scenes of writing as opening paths for understanding how one might allow such pain to happen to oneself and intersperse this move with thoughts on violence and pain. In these three scenes I call upon the words of the philosopher Wittgenstein, the poet-novelist-essayist Rabindranath Tagore, and the short story writer Sa'adat Hasan Manto as persons who responded to the call of the world in the register of the imaginary. Tagore and Manto are important to me, for they responded in sounds and senses of the Indian languages to the scenes of devastation; Wittgenstein, because he showed the possibilities of the imagination of pain within a rigorous philosophical grammar. In placing their texts within mine, I hope I shall be evoking the physiognomy of their words not in the manner of a thief who has stolen another's voice, but in the manner of one who pawns herself to the words of the other.

SCENE ONE

The first scene is from Wittgenstein's *Blue and Brown Books* on the question of how my pain may reside in another body:

> In order to see that it is conceivable that one person should have pain
> in another person's body, one must examine what sorts of facts we call
> criteria for a pain being in a certain place. . . . Suppose I feel a pain

which on the evidence of the pain alone, e.g. with closed eyes, I should call a pain in my left hand. Someone asks me to touch the painful spot with my right hand. I do so and looking around perceive that I am touching my neighbor's hand. . . . This would be pain *felt* in another's body.[4]

In this movement between bodies, the sentence "I am in pain" becomes the conduit through which I may move out of the inexpressible privacy and suffocation of my pain. This does not mean that I am understood. Wittgenstein uses the route of a philosophical grammar to say that this is not an indicative statement, although it may have the formal appearance of one. It is the beginning of a language game. Pain in this rendering is not that inexpressible something that destroys communication or marks an exit from one's existence in language. Instead, it makes a claim on the other—asking for acknowledgment that may be given or denied. In either case, it is not a referential statement that is pointing to an inner object.

What is fascinating for me is that in drawing the scene of the pathos of pain, Wittgenstein creates language as the bodying forth of words. Where is my pain? In touching you to point out the location of that pain, has my pointing finger—there it is—found your body, which my pain (our pain) can inhabit, at least for that moment when I close my eyes and touch your hand? And if the language for the inexpressibility of pain is always falling short of my need for its plenitude, then is this not the sense of disappointment that human beings have with themselves and the language that is given to them? But also, does the whole task of becoming human, even of becoming perversely human, not involve a response (even if this is rage) to the sense of loss when language seems to fail? Wittgenstein's example of my pain inhabiting your body seems to me to suggest either the intuition that the representation of shared pain exists in the imagination but cannot be translated into concrete ways that could be put into the world—in which case, one would say that language is hooked rather inadequately to the world of pain—or, alternately, that the experience of pain cries out for this response of the possibility that my pain could reside in your body and that the philosophical grammar of pain is an answer to that call.

If I might be allowed, I would like to draw out the meaning of my repeated (and even compulsive) reliance on Wittgenstein by braiding my words with those of Cavell. In generously agreeing to augment my reflections on pain, Cavell offered what to me was a philosophical friendship in which he was able to hear what I was stuttering to say. I quote:

This seems to me a place Veena Das finds company in work of mine, especially that on Wittgenstein. So, I will testify to my conviction in two moments in which she finds her ground: first, in her appeal to her own experience (e.g., "In my own experience the question of how good death and bad death is to be defined by the act of witnessing is a more complicated one"), an appeal in her writing that I unfailingly place confidence in and am grateful for; second, in her use of Wittgenstein's example of "feeling pain in the body of another," a passage that no one, to my knowledge, has put to more creative, nor sounder, use. I take Wittgenstein's fantasy in that passage as a working out of Descartes's sense that my soul and my body, while necessarily distinct, are not merely contingently connected. I am necessarily the owner of my pain, yet the fact that it is always located in my body is not necessary. This is what Wittgenstein wishes to show—that it is conceivable that I locate it in another's body. That this does not in fact, or literally, happen in our lives means that the fact of our separateness is something that I have to conceive, a task of imagination—that to know your pain I cannot locate it as I locate mine, but I must let it happen to me. My knowledge of you marks me; it is something that I experience, yet I am not present to it. . . . My knowledge of myself is something I find, as on a successful quest; my knowledge of others, of their separateness from me, is some-thing that finds me. . . . And it seems reasonable to me, and illumi-nating, to speak of that reception of impression as my lending my body to the other's experience. The plainest manifestation of this responsive-ness may be taken to be its effect on a body of writing.[5]

SCENE TWO

The second scene I call forth is from Rabindranath Tagore. The invest-ment of sexuality into the project of nationalism is prefigured in three of his novels—*Gora, Ghore Baire,* and *Char Adhyaya.* Here I want simply to draw out certain passages from *Ghore Baire (Home and the World)*—a novel that is set in the context of the *swadeshi* movement against the British Raj.[6]

The nature of a spiritual struggle for Tagore seems to announce itself as a struggle to make the self that has become frozen in language mobile and free again. It is this frozen self that reads itself as if it were a script dra-matized in the character of Sandip. It produces a magnification of the images of both nation and sexuality, and in Tagore's reading, it is the pursuit of such magnified images that can make one blind toward the concrete-ness of human beings, their being flesh and blood creatures, and thus to their suffering.

The story of *Ghare Baire* is well known. The narrative device is to relate the story through interspersed accounts of the three main characters, Nikhil, the local *zamindar* who is bound to his *praja* (subjects who include both Hindus and Muslims) by ties of patronage and love; his wife Bimala, whose desire moves from Nikhil to Sandip and then returns to Nikhil; and his friend Sandip, the fiery nationalist revolutionary. I reproduce only some root metaphors from each character.[7]

Bimala

When inspired by Sandip's passionate speech in favor of the *swadeshi* movement, which she has heard in the company of other women from behind the curtains, Bimala tells her husband that she wishes to serve a meal to Sandip with her own hands. Serving food by a woman to a man is a sensuous gesture, hovering between the maternal and the sexual in Bengali imagery. This is the first time Bimala will enter any male presence except that of her husband, for, according to convention, women of the feudal household do not step outside the women's domestic space.

Listen here to Bimala's self-reflection: "I shall speak the truth. That day I felt—why has not god made me unbelievably beautiful. . . . Today as this great day dawns, let the men of the nation see in its women—the form of the goddess Jagaddhatri [the goddess who holds the earth]. . . . Will Sandip be able to see that awakened power of the country in me? Or will he think that I am an ordinary woman, merely the wife who lives in his friend's house?"

Sandip

The magnification of her image in Sandip's eyes that Bimala desires finds an answering chord. But before I describe that, how does Sandip construct himself? Listen to the opening line, when the reader first hears the voice of Sandip: "When I read my own account, I reflect, is that Sandip? Am I simply constructed in language? Am I just a book constructed of flesh and blood?" And then Sandip responds to the desire for the magnification of the image of Bimala that would merge with the image of the nation—a desire, however, that is read as need:

Unless they can behold the nation with their own eyes, our people will not awaken. The nation needs the icon of a goddess. . . . It will not do if *we* construct the icon. It is the icons that have been transmitted by tradition that will have to be transformed into the icons of our nation. The path of worship is deeply transcribed in our country—traversing that path we shall have to direct the devotional stream toward the nation.

When I saw Bimala, I said *that* god(dess) for whose worship I have come to the earth after a hundred thousand *yuga* (ages), till (s)he revealed her form to me, till then could I have believed in her with all my body and soul? If I had not been able to behold you, then I could not have seen the whole country as one, this I have told you many times. I do not know if you understand this. It is very difficult to explain that the gods in their heaven remain invisible, only in the world of death do they show themselves.

And then we see this desire as reported speech in Bimala's story:

Sandip then got up and said, Man reaches such a state when the whole world comes to be concentrated in one small place.[8] Here in your salon I have seen my world revealed. . . . I worship you. . . . After seeing you my *mantra* [sacred formula] has changed. Not *vande matram* [I worship the nation as mother] but *vande priyam* [I worship the nation as beloved], *vande mohinim* [I worship the nation as the enticing one]. The mother protects us . . . the beloved destroys us. Beautiful is that destruction. You hear the tinkling of the bells of that dance of death. This delicate, luminous, fruit bearing, the one cooled by the Malay mountains[9] —this earth of Bengal—you have altered its image in the eyes of your devotee in the fraction of a second [literally, in the blinking of an eye]. You, oh, Mohini [the enticing one, a female form that the god Vishnu took to entice the demons to drink poison]—you have come with your vessel of poison—I shall either die after drinking this poison or shall become the one who has conquered death.

Nikhil

In an argument with Sandip, Nikhil says: "I am willing to serve my country but not to worship it. To offer worship to anyone else except that which should be worshipped is to destroy it." In an argument with Sandip on the nation as icon (as reported speech in Sandip's voice) we hear:

But all this is very difficult to explain to Nikhil. Truth is now like a prejudice in his mind. As if there is a special substance called truth. I have said to him often that where falsity is truth, there falsehood *alone* is truth. That falsehood shall be superior to truth. Those who can think of the icon of the nation as a truth, that icon will do the work of truth. We as a people cannot visualize the idea of a nation with ease, but we can see the icon as the nation easily. . . . Those who want to accomplish the project of nationalism will have to work with this understanding.

Nikhil suddenly got very agitated and said, You have lost the power to serve the truth, therefore you want a sacred formula to drop from the skies. This is why when for hundreds of years the work of the nation has remained undone, you now want to make the nation into a god so that you can stretch your palms in supplication and receive a blessing as if by magic.

And finally Nikhil accepts his defeat, in that his wife and beloved Bimala saw him as a diminished human being in comparison to Sandip, but refuses to accept this as the extinguishing of the self:

Today I shall have to see myself and Bimal[10] completely from the outside. I am greedy. I wanted to enjoy that Tilottama [a mythic woman created by the gods so that every particle of her being was perfect] as my mental creation. The Bimal who had an external existence had become a pretext for that. But Bimal is what she is—she does not have to become Tillottama for me—there is no reason for that.

Today I have understood this clearly—I am just a contingency in Bimal's life. That person with whom Bimal's whole being can merge, that person is Sandip. But it would be a great lie if I were to say that it means I am nothing, for my manhood was not simply a means to capture the women of the interior.

An Interlude

Let us bring together the movements that run through these three voices for a tentative weaving together at this moment. Each of the two men has found his destruction in Bimala, but in different ways. Sandip began his account by voicing the idea that he was just a script—someone who had no existence outside of language. In the only moment of authenticity that is permitted to him, which comes when Bimala has turned away from him, she responds to a passionate plea by saying, "Sandip Babu, have you got several speeches written in your exercise book—so can you produce an appropriate one for each occasion?" Sandip's own fear is finally confirmed in the reflection in Bimala's speech—he exists only in language as if signifying a will to emptiness. His words do not *falsify* an inner life or draw a veil over it—they are indeed functioning to hide the fact that there *is* no inner life to hide. His search for the nation is a search for an icon, his desire for the other is for a magnification of image in which the lack of individual self may be hidden by a collectivization of desire. I would have been tempted to draw an analogy with the idea of certain kinds of ghosts in folklore whose identity is revealed in a mirror by the fact that they cast no reflection. Rabindranath himself, who appears in the voice of a schoolmaster, compares him to the new moon (*amavasyar chand*)—simply an absence.

As distinctions dissolve and the nation becomes a magnified image of the beloved worshipped in the abstract, it becomes possible to inflict all kinds of violence on all those who resist this or who create counter-images, equally enlarged. The desire for icons allows the nation as an absent object to be made magically visible through an investment in this magnified sexuality. The potential for violence is written in this construction. The story ends with a communal carnage that the reader does not gaze at directly but that is happening outside the immediate frame, waiting as it were, as the double of the nationalist ideology that has been propounded.

Nikhil may seem to have won since Bimala returns to him. But in their last exchange of intimacies, Bimala falls on his feet and begs him to let her worship him. Is this traditional slippage between husband and god not what he has tried to resist in their relationship all along? He does not try to stop her from this disastrous identification anymore: "Who am I to stop her—after all it is not I who am the recipient of this worship." Nikhil's defeat is the realization that the everyday life embodied in tradition lives as much in the worship of icons (the husband as god) as the new transformations that Sandip is trying to bring (nation as god). We see Nikhil riding away from us into the heart of the carnage, offering himself as either a sacrificial victim or a martyr (but never being named as such)—the very magnification of the image of nation and the investment of sexual desire in it has made it into a monster. We know only that, as the voice of the schoolteacher tells us, it won't do for him not to go there, for what is being done to the women is unspeakable. Toward the end he is brought back, injured, in a carriage. The news, says the person who has rescued him, is not good. We do not know if he will live or die.

Tagore does not permit himself a closure. Nikhil is the truth seeker who can find comfort neither in the psychological clichés of tradition (husband is god) nor in those of modernity (nation is god). He sees the potential of violence in both. Tradition is what diminishes women and permits a subtle everyday violence to be perpetrated upon them. Thus when Bimala once comments that women's hearts are ungenerous, small, Nikhil replies, "Yes, like the feet of Chinese women that are tied and never allowed to grow." In the modern project of building a nation, the image is not diminished, but enlarged. Its dramatization means that bodies of women are violently appropriated for the cause as nationalism gives birth to its double—communalism. If one deified women so that the nation could be imagined as the beloved, the other makes visible the dark side of this project by making the bodies of women the surfaces on which their text of the nation is written.[11]

Body and language both function as simulacra in which collective desire and collective death meet. Nikhil, the truth seeker, prefigures the image of the martyr who must offer himself in an unheroic mode so that the magnified images of gods and demons have a chance to be humanized again. I think this is the task Tagore sets his reader—to hear the unfinished nature of this story of the transformations of the projects of tradition and modernity.

SCENE THREE

The third scene I want to evoke is from a story entitled *Khol Do* by Sa'adat Hasan Manto, which I first analyzed in 1986.[12] The setting is the Partition of India and the communal carnage, though we never gaze at the violence directly. An aged father and his daughter take a journey from one side of the border to another. On reaching his destination, the father cannot find the daughter. He goes berserk searching for her. He comes across some young men who are acting as volunteers to help trace lost relatives of refugees who are pouring in. He tells them about his daughter and urges them to find her. They promise to help.

The young men find Sakina, the daughter, hiding in a forest, half crazed with fear. They reassure her by evoking the name of her father and how he had asked them to find her and bring her safely back to him. She climbs into the jeep with them (because we assume that she is assured of their good intentions). One of them, seeing how embarrassed she is because she does not have her *dupatta,* gives her his jacket so that she can cover her breasts.

We next see a clinic. A near-dead body is being brought in on a stretcher. The father, Sarajjudin, recognizes the corpse. It is his daughter. Numbly he follows the stretcher to the doctor's office. Reacting to the heat and suffocation in the room, the doctor points to the window and says, "*khol do—*open it." There is a movement in the dead body. The hands move toward the tape of the *salwar* (trouser) and fumble to unloosen (literally, open) it. Old Sarajjudin shouts in joy "My daughter is alive—my daughter is alive." The doctor is drenched in sweat.

As I understood this story in 1986, I saw Sakina condemned to a living death. The normality of language has been destroyed as Sakina can hear words conveying only the "other" command. Such a fractured relation to language has been documented for many survivors of prolonged violence, for whom it is the ordinariness of language that divides them from the rest of the world. I noted that even Sakina's father cannot comprehend the nonworld into which she has been plunged, for he mistakes the movement in the body as a sign of life whereas in truth it is the sign of her living death. Only the doctor—as the off-the-center character in the story—can register the true horror, I said.

Upon deeper meditation on this story, I think there is one last movement that I did not then comprehend. In giving a shout of joy and saying "My daughter is alive," the father does not speak to give voice to a scripted tradition. In the societal context of this period, when ideas of purity and honor densely populated the literary narratives as well as family and political narratives, so that fathers willed their daughters to die for family honor rather than live with bodies that had been violated by other men, *this father wills his daughter to live even as parts of her body can do nothing else but proclaim her brutal violation.*

In the terms set by the example from the *Blue and Brown Books,* one may ask if the pain of the female body so violated can live in a male body. One can read in Manto a transaction between death and life, body and speech, in the figures of the daughter and the father. In the speech of the father, at least, the daughter is alive, and though she may find an existence only in his utterance, he creates through his utterance a home for her mutilated and violated self. Compare this with hundreds of stories in accounts purporting to be based on direct experience in which the archetypical motif is of a girl finding her way to her parents after having been subjected to rape and plunder and being told, "Why are you here—it would have been better if you were dead." As I have argued elsewhere, such rejections may not have occurred as often as they were alleged to have happened in narratives. But the widespread circulation of such narratives and their truths, the normativity attributed to the idea of sacrificing the daughter or the wife to maintain the unsullied purity and honor of the family—these proved the power of stories. To be masculine when death was all around was to be able to hand death to your violated daughter without flinching one bit—to obliterate any desire for the concreteness of this human being who once played in your family's yard.[13] In the background of such stories, a single sentence of joy uttered by old Sarajjudin transforms the meaning of being a father.[14]

In Tagore's reading of Sandip, he was capable of constituting himself as subject only as a linguistic cliché. In Manto, the sentence "My daughter is alive" is like Wittgenstein's "I am in pain." Although it has the formal appearance of an indicative statement, it is to beseech the daughter to find a way to live in the speech of the father. And it happens not at the moment when her dishonor is hidden from the eyes of the world but at the moment when her body proclaims it. This sentence is the beginning of a relationship and not its end.

At this moment I want to present a glimpse of a later argument. I have written elsewhere that in the gendered division of labor in the work of mourning, it is the task of men to ritually create a body for the dead person and to find a place in the cosmos for the dead. This task, which is always a very difficult one for the mourner, may even become repulsive, as when members of the Aghori sect who live on cremation grounds state that in the cases when someone has died an unnatural or violent death, they have to consume parts of the dead body so as to free the dead person from living the fate of a homeless ghost.[15] I wonder if Sarajjudin performed this terrifying task of accepting the tortured relationship with the daughter whom other fathers may have simply cast away as socially dead. And whether instead of the simplified images of healing, which assume reliving a trauma or decathacting desire from the lost object and reinvesting it elsewhere, we need to think of healing as a kind of relationship with death.

INHABITING THE WORLD IN MOURNING

Nadia Serematakis has put forward the powerful idea of the ethics of antiphony to describe the structure of Greek mourning rituals. She shows how the interaction between acoustic, linguistic, and corporeal orientations serves to give a public definition to a "good death" and to distinguish it from a "bad death." "The acoustics of death embodied in "screaming" and lamenting and the presence or "appearance" (*fanerosi*) of kin construct the "good death." The silent death is the asocial "bad death" without kin support: "Silence here connotes the absence of witness."[16] Thus, it is the special role of women to "witness" death and to convert silence into speech.[17] In the rendering of this issue Serematakis seems to slip into the assumption that what is at stake is physical death.

What happens to the work of mourning when women have been abducted, raped, and condemned to a social death? The classical ritualistic solution in this case is for the social body to cut itself completely off from the polluted individual. This symbolic death is objectified and made present by the performance of symbolic mourning for the "dead" person, by such ritualistic devices as the breaking of a pot that comes to stand for the person who is socially dead but is physically alive. This is the sentiment underlying the stories I described earlier of kinsmen refusing to accept women who had been abducted or violated, or of men construing their kinship obligations in terms of the obligation to kill a beloved sister or wife rather than let her fall into the hands of men of the other community. Such women who were violated and rejected may be said to be occupying a zone between two deaths, rather than between life and death. Let us take a step backward toward mourning in everyday life as it occurs in the case of "normal" deaths and ask if it was possible to deploy cultural codes to represent the kind of social death I have described. It does not seem an easy matter to transform these "bad deaths" into "good deaths."

In an earlier paper I described the division of labor between women and men, between professional mourners and close relatives, and between kin and affine in giving structure to the work of mourning in Punjabi families.[18] It is through the ritual work performed by the professional mourners (usually women of the barber caste who have specialized roles in the death rituals) that grief was objectified in the form of a portrait. We can glean from descriptions of death rituals given in several accounts that women would form a circle around the dead body and move in circular forms, all the time beating their breasts and inflicting injuries upon their own bodies. In the frenzy of this "grief" they would tear at their clothes and their hair, improvising various mourning laments to make the loss that has occurred public and utterable. They gave a lead to the mourning laments of the other women who were closely related to the dead person. The laments articulated what the loss meant for each person, now bereaved. The address was to the dead person, to the living, to their own bodies as well as to the gods. I give a brief example of each kind of address from my own ethnography:

(To the dead son)—Open your eyes just once my beloved jewel (*mere lal*)— you have never turned back any request I made of you.

(To the men who are going to take the dead body of her husband to the cremation ground)—Do not let the fire touch him—I fold my hands before you—he could never bear the heat.

(To one's own body)—Are you made of stone that you do not break when you see this calamity?

(To the family goddess, referring to the fact that the goddess is a virgin; address is by the mother of a dead son)—You call yourself a goddess—you were just jealous of the good fortune of my *bahu* (son's wife)—you had to make her a widow because you have yourself never found a husband—you call yourself a goddess—you are a demoness.

I could give extensive examples of statements that are close to blasphemy in the laments, on how women rage against the idea that gods are *just* beings, rather than callous, small-minded beings who play with the happiness of mortals. They rage against their bodies, which have to bear pain within, rather than disintegrate in the face of such tragedy. But since the mourning laments also have a dialogical element, soon other women begin to punctuate this by the counsel to get on with the work of living and by assurances to the most deeply affected mourners that the support of the community is with them. It is not that grief is seen as something that shall pass with time. Rather, the representation of grief is that it is metonymically experienced as bodily pain and that the female body will carry this pain forever within itself. A mimesis is established between body and language, but it is through the work of the collectivity that this happens rather than at the level of individual symptom. A mourning lament from rural Greece recorded by Loring Danforth[19] bears the same grammar as the mourning laments in Punjabi families:

> My child, where can I put the *ponos* I feel for you?
> If I toss it by the roadside, those who pass will take it.
> If I throw it in a tree, the little birds will take it.
> I will take it in my heart so that it will take root there
> So that it will cause me *ponos* while I walk.
> So that it will kill me as I stand.

So, in a sense, it is the objectification of grief on the body taken as surface and as depth, as well as in language, that bears witness to the loss that death has inflicted. According to Seremetakis, it is this witnessing that can make the performance of death public and even convert a bad death into a good death. In my own experience the question of how good death and bad death are to be defined by the act of witnessing is a more complicated one, and I shall return to it a little later.

The excess of speech in the mourning laments and the theatrical infliction of harm on the body enacted by women stand in stark contrast to the behavior of men. While in the course of everyday life, men dominate the public domain in terms of the control over speech, in the case of death they become mute, as it were. While the corpse is in the house, all the preparations, including the bathing and dressing of the dead body, are performed by the women. Women cling to the dead body imploring the dead person not to leave them. It is the men who have to disengage the dead body from the weeping and wailing women, to carry it on their shoulders to the cremation *ghats* and to give the sacred fire to the dead person. It is they who gather the bones on the fourth day and perform the ritual of immersing these into the sacred river. For a period ranging from ten to thirteen days the dead person hovers between the living and the dead in the form of a ghost, and it is through the gift of a body ritually created for him or her by the chief mourner (usually the husband or the son) that the ghost finally becomes an ancestor. Thus if women perform the task of bearing witness to the grief and the loss that death has inflicted (otherwise people will say was it a dog or cat that died, one woman told me), it is men who must ritually create all the conditions so that the dead too can find a home.

But if the good death is defined by the bearing of witness on the part of women so that grief can move between the body and speech can be publicly articulated, as well as the performance of rituals for the dead so that they do not have wander in the world of the living as a ghost, how is bad death to be represented? Seremetakis formulates this by saying that it is death that is unwitnessed and kinless that is bad and gives some very moving examples of how women's speech might convert such a bad death into a good death. In my own experience, the relation between women's speech and their silence is a very complicated relation. It involves the question of the agency of a bad death. In a sense every death except that of a very old person introduces disorder in personal and social life. But in the flow of everyday life this is understood as caused by events beyond the control of the living community. Indeed, one of the underlying tensions of mourning rituals is to absolve the living from taking responsibility for the death that has occurred. If a woman has died in her husband's home, efforts will be made immediately to get her natal kin before the body is taken for cremation so that her kin can mourn her properly but also to ensure that they do not suspect the affines of neglect or worse. In the case of a man who has died, the piety of the widow would be attested in the mourning laments so that she does not blame herself for the death of her husband. A common refrain in mourning laments is to say that the ostensible cause of the death (for instance, a particular disease) is only the pretext for death to do its appointed job. Of course, when death is seen as caused by the willful action of others, then a great tension prevails as to what definition of the situation will come to prevail through the control of mourning laments.[20]

All this is reversed when the normal flow of life is seen as disrupted by the violence of men. In that case women bear witness to this disorder by a new construction of speech and silence. A woman recalled to me a mourning lament that witnessed the defeat of the Sikhs at the hands of the British troops in the Anglo-Sikh wars:

> The crowns on the heads of the young wives—
> The flowing laps of the mothers—
> The swagger of sisters protected by brothers—
> Wiped out in a moment—
> Oh, from seven seas across came the white man to fight.

She went on to say that although everything was wiped out, it was possible for the women to wail since their men had died heroically in war. The men had died as husbands, sons, and brothers. But in the case of all who died in the Partition, there was nothing but silence—for the men who inflicted such violence on women were not only strange men but also men known and deeply loved.[21] It is to an elaboration of this statement that the next section is devoted. It is an amplification that I have constructed—for it was never possible for me to get an exegesis of such statements from the women themselves.

AN AMPLIFICATION

In the literary imagination the violence of the Partition was about inscribing desire on the bodies of women in a manner that we have not yet understood. In the mythic imagination in India, victory or defeat in war was ultimately inscribed on the bodies of women. The texts on the *vilap*— mourning laments of Gandhari in the Mahabharata or of Mandodari in the Ramayana, whose kin were all slain in the epic battles—are literary classics.[22] This is a metaphoric transformation of the role of witnessing death in everyday life.

The violence of the Partition was unique in the metamorphosis it achieved between the idea of appropriating a territory as nation and appropriating the body of the women as territory. As we saw earlier, a prefiguration of this is found in Tagore's rendering of the idea of the magnification of the image of nation, which draws its energy from the image of magnified sexuality.

However, this image of sexuality and its intimate connection with the project of nationalism not only has a genealogy in the Indian imagination, but it was also an important narrative trope in the representation of the violation of the project of empire. The image of the innocent white woman who was brutally raped by the barbaric sepoys was an important narrative trope for establishing the barbaric character of the natives in 1857, when the first large-scale rebellion against the British took place. Jenny Sharpe has analyzed the image of helpless women and children being cut to pieces by leering sepoys as establishing the "truth" of the "mutiny." As she says, "Commissioners and magistrates entrusted with investigating the rumors could find no evidence of systematic rape, mutilation and torture at Cawnpore or anyplace else. The official reports, however, came too late, as the sensational stories had already done their work. Rebels were seen as sadistic fiends, and Nana Sahib was especially vilified for the unforgivable crime of desecrating English womanhood. Barr exhibits a predictable understanding of the Cawnpore massacre when she writes that there 'one of the most revered of Victorian institutions, the English lady was slaughtered, defiled and brought low.' When the massacre of women is reported as the destruction of an institution, we know that the sacred image of English womanhood has outlived the story of women's lives."[23]

Thus we have the interweaving of two strands. First, the idea that women must bear witness to death, which is found in the classical Indian literature and in everyday life, gets transformed into the notion that the woman's body must be made to bear the signs of its possession by the enemy. The second strand seems to come from a narrative trope established at the time of the mutiny that equates the violation of the nation with the violation of its women. It is not very clear whether during the riots nationalist slogans were actually imprinted upon the private parts of women, although the most horrific stories about such violations are commonly believed.[24] The figures given in the Legislative Assembly during the Constituent Assembly debates in 1949 confirm that a large number of women were abducted and raped. It is also affirmed that processions of women who were stripped naked were organized to the accompaniment of jeering crowds in cities like Amritsar and Lahore. Family narratives abound telling of men who were compelled to kill their women to save their honor though they often lack specificity. Such sacrificial deaths are beatified in family narratives, while women who were recovered from their abductors and returned to their families or who converted to the other religion and made new lives in the homes of their abductors hardly ever find a place in these narratives, although they occur frequently in the literary representations.

When women's bodies were made the passive witnesses of the disorder of the Partition in this manner, how did women mourn the loss of self and the world? It is in considering this question that we find startling reversals in the transactions between body and language. In the normal process of mourning, grievous harm is inflicted by women on their own bodies while the acoustic and linguistic codes make the loss public by the mourning laments. When asking women to narrate their experiences of the Partition, I found a zone of silence around the event. This silence was achieved either by the use of language that was general and metaphoric but that evaded description of any events with specificity so as to capture the particularity of their experience, or by describing the surrounding events but leaving the actual experience of abduction and rape unstated. It was common to describe the violence of the Partition in such terms as rivers of blood flowing and the earth covered with white shrouds right unto the horizon. Sometimes a woman would remember images of fleeing, but as one woman warned me, it was dangerous to remember. These memories were sometimes compared to poison that makes the inside of the woman dissolve as a solid is dissolved in a powerful liquid (*andar hi andar ghul ja rahi hai*). At other times a woman would say that she was like a discarded exercise book in which the accounts of past relationships were kept. At any rate, none of the metaphors used to describe the self that had become the repository of poisonous knowledge emphasized the need to give expression to this hidden knowledge. Or rather, containing it was itself the expression of it.

This code of silence protected women who had been brought back to their families through the efforts of the military evacuation authorities after they were recovered from the homes of their abductors or who had been married, by stretching norms of kinship and affinity since the violation of their bodies was never made public. Rather than bearing witness to the disorder that they had been subjected to, the metaphor that they used was of a woman drinking the poison and keeping it within her: "Just as a woman's body is made so that she can hide the faults of her husband deep within her, so she can drink all pain—take the stance of silence." And as one woman told Ritu Menon and Kamla Bhasin, "What is a woman? She is always used,"[25] or to me, "What is there to be proud of in a woman's body—everyday it is polluted by being consumed." The sliding of the representations of the female body from everyday life into the body that had become the container of the poisonous knowledge of the events of the Partition perhaps helped women to assimilate their experiences into their everyday life.

Just as the relation between speech and silence is reversed in the act of witnessing here, so is the relation between the surface and depth of the body. In the fantasy of men, the inscription of nationalist slogans on the bodies of women (Victory to India, Long Live Pakistan), or proclaiming possession of their bodies (This thing, this loot—*ye mal*—is ours), would create a future memory by which men of the other community would never be able to forget that the women as territory had already been claimed and occupied by other men. The bodies of the women were surfaces on which texts were to be written and read—icons of the new nations. But women converted this passivity into agency by using metaphors of pregnancy—hiding pain, giving it a home just as a child is given a home in the woman's body. Julia Kristeva's description of pregnancy—it happens but I am not there—may also be used to describe such violence.[26] But the subsequent act of remembering only through the body makes the woman's own experience displace being from the surface to the depth of the body. The only difference is that unlike the child, which the woman will be able to offer to the husband, this holding of the pain inside must never be allowed to be born. This movement from surface to depth also transforms passivity into agency.

It was once again Sa'adat Hasan Manto who was able to give literary expression to the body as a receptacle of poisonous knowledge. In his story *Fundanen*[27] (Tassels), a woman is sitting in front of a mirror. Her speech is completely incoherent, but like many strings of nonsense used in rhymes or musical compositions, its phonetic properties are like theatrical or musical representations. Interspersed between the strings of nonsense syllables are meaningful sentences with precise information such as the bus number that brought her from one side of the border to another. The woman is drawing grotesque designs on her body, registering these only in the mirror. She says she is designing a body that is appropriate for the time: in those days, she says, women had to grow two stomachs—one was the normal one, and the second was for them to be able to bear the fruits of violence within themselves. The distortion of speech and the distortion of body seem to make deep sense. The language of pain could only be a kind of hysteria—the surface of the body becomes a carnival of images, and the depth becomes the site for hysterical pregnancies—the language having all the phonetic excess of hysteria that destroys apparent meanings.

When Tagore's Bimala said that she wondered if Sandip could see the power of the nation in her, she seems to have prefigured Manto's women in whom one could see the completion of that project of making the nation visible by a surrealist juxtaposition of images.

So if men emerged from colonial subjugation as autonomous citizens of an independent nation, then they emerged simultaneously as monsters. What kind of death rituals could have been performed for these wandering ghosts to be given a place in the cosmos? Intizar Hussain described this in his story "The City of Sorrow," in which three nameless men are having a conversation. The story opens with the first man saying, "I have nothing to say. I am dead." The story then moves in the form of a dialogue on the manner of his dying. Did he die when he forced a man at the point of his sword to strip his sister naked? No, he remained alive. Then perhaps when he saw the same man forcing another old man to strip his wife naked? No, he remained alive. Then when he was himself forced to strip his own sister naked? Then too he remained alive. It was when his father gazed at his face and died that he heard in his wife's voice the question, "Don't you know it is you who are dead?" and he realized he had died. But he was condemned to carry his own corpse with him wherever he went.

It appears to me that just as women drank the pain so that life could continue, so men longed for martyrdom by which they could invite the evil back upon themselves and humanize the enormous looming images of nation and sexuality. But it was not the political discourse that achieved this. The debates in the Constituent Assembly on the issue of abducted women were full of the imagery of restoring national honor by recovering the women who had been abducted from the other side and returning "their" women back to the Muslims. Mahatma Gandhi, writing about the exchange of women and of prisoners on the same page of his Delhi diary, said that it had pained him to learn that many Hindu men were reluctant to return the Muslim women. He urged them to do so as a form of repentance. Nehru urged Hindu men to accept the women who were recovered and to not punish them for the sins of their abductors. In this entire discourse of exchange of women from both sides, it was assumed that once the nation had reclaimed its women, its honor would have been restored. It was as if you could wipe the slate clean and leave the horrendous events behind.

It was on the register of the imaginary that the question of what would constitute the passion of those who occupied this unspeakable and unhearable zone was given shape. The zone between two deaths that the women had to occupy did not permit of any speech, for what "right" words could have been spoken against the wrong that had been done them? Hence Manto's Sakina can proclaim the terrible truth of this society by a mute repetition of a *gesture—murde mein kuch jumbish hui* (there was movement in the corpse). The task for men was to hear this silence and to see the gesture, to mold these into something else by their presence. Hence the joyful cry by the father that his daughter was alive. This being alive in the zone of two deaths and witnessing the truth of the woman's violation is how mourning in this zone could be defined. Hence the issue is not that of an Antigone, mourning for her dead brother in defiance of the law of Creon, proclaiming that the register of someone who has been named must be preserved, as Lacan makes us witness it in his interpretation of Antigone's famous passage that she would not have died for a husband or a child but that this concerned her brother, born of the same father and the same mother (the product of criminal desire and criminal knowledge).[28] Here it is the issue of the women drinking poisonous knowledge and the men molding the silence of the women with their words. Truth does not need here the envelope of beauty as Jacques Lacan would have it, but rather a renouncing of beauty, as Tagore's Nikhil came to state it.

It is often considered the task of historiography to break the silences that announce the zones of taboo. There is even something heroic in the image of empowering women to speak and to give voice to the voiceless. I have myself found this a very complicated task, for when we use such imagery as breaking the silence, we may end by using our capacity to "unearth" hidden facts as a weapon. Even the idea that we should recover the narratives of violence becomes problematic when we realize that such narratives cannot be told unless we see the relation between pain and language that a culture has evolved. I have found it important to think of the division of labor between men and women in the work of mourning as a model for thinking about the relation between pain, language, and the body. Following Wittgenstein, this manner of conceptualizing the puzzle of pain frees us from thinking that statements about pain are in the nature of questions about certainty or doubt over our own pain or that of others. Instead, we begin to think of pain as acknowledgment and recognition; denial of the other's pain is not about the failings of the intellect but the failings of the spirit. In the register of the imaginary, the pain of the other not only asks for a home in language, but also seeks a home in the body.[29]

It is not that there is a seamless continuity between the distant shore and the everyday shore in which violence and grief are met, but one can understand the subtle transformations that go on only as we move from one shore to the other, if we keep in mind the complex relation between speaking and hearing, between building a world that the living can inhabit with their loss and building a world in which the dead can find a home. It worries me that I have been unable to name that which died when autonomous citizens of India were simultaneously born as monsters. But then I have to remind myself and others that those who tried to name it such as Manto themselves touched madness and died in fierce regret for the loss of the radical dream of transforming India. Those who found speech easily as in the political debates on abducted women in the Constituent Assembly continue to talk about national honor when dealing with the violence that women have had to endure in every communal riot since the Partition.

FOUR

The Act of Witnessing

Violence, Gender, and Subjectivity

MANY RECENT CONTRIBUTIONS TO THE THEORY of the subject have argued that the experience of becoming a subject is linked to the experience of subjugation in important ways.[1] The violations inscribed on the female body (both literally and figuratively) and the discursive formations around these violations, as we saw, made visible the imagination of the nation as a *masculine* nation. What did this do to the subjectivity of women? We need to ask not only how ethnic or communal violence was enacted through specific gendered acts of violation such as rape, but also how women may have taken these noxious signs of violation and reoccupied them through the work of domestication, ritualization, and renarration. I argued earlier that the discursive formations through which the nation-state was inaugurated attributed a particular type of subjectivity to women as victims of rape and abduction. Yet women's own formation of their subject positions, though mired in these constructions, was not completely determined by them. The previous chapter argued that women spoke of their experiences by anchoring their discourses to the genres of mourning and lamentation that already assigned a place to them in the cultural work of mourning, but they spoke of violence and pain *within* these genres as well as *outside* them. Through complex transactions between body and language they were able to both voice and *show* the hurt done to them as well as to provide witness to the harm done to the whole social fabric—the injury was to the very idea of different groups being able to inhabit the world together.

In this chapter I hope to explore the meaning of being a witness to violence—to speak for the death of relationships.[2] In the literary imagination of the West, the figure of Antigone as witness provides a kind of foundational myth that explores the conditions under which conscience may find a voice in the feminine. Hegel, as is well known, saw a conflict of structures in this story. In his reading, Creon is opposed to Antigone as one principle of law is opposed to another—call it the opposition between the law of the state and the law of the family:[3] "The public law of the state and the instinctive family-love and duty toward a brother are here set in conflict. Antigone, the woman, is pathetically possessed by the interest of family: Creon, the man, by the welfare of the community. Polyneices, in war with his own father-city, had fallen before the gate of Thebes, and Creon, the lord thereof, had by means of a public proclamation threatened everyone with death who should give the enemy of this city the right of burial. Antigone, however, refused to accept this demand, which merely concerned the public weal, and constrained by her pious devotion for her brother, carried out as sister, the sacred duty of interment."[4]

As long as we are with Hegel looking at the dialogue as constituting the arena of the play, it is difficult to find other meanings in this tragedy except in the conflict of these two discourses. In contrast, Lacan invites us to shift our gaze to the *tragic setting* of Antigone.[5] What is the nature of the zone that Antigone occupies in this setting? Lacan specifies it variously as the *limit*, as a happening between two deaths, as the point at which death is engaged with life. The scene of Antigone's death is staged in this particular zone from which alone a certain kind of truth can be spoken.

Lacan rejects Hegel's interpretation that Creon is opposed to Antigone as one principle of law is opposed to another. Instead, he is more sympathetic to Goethe's view that in striking Polyneices, Creon had gone beyond the limit. The issue, Lacan feels, was not that of one law versus another, but whether the law of Creon could subsume everything, including the funerary rites to the dead. For Lacan, it was never a question of one right versus another, but a wrong against something else that is not easily named. Lacan insists that Antigone's passion is not for the sacred rights of the dead—it is not that she speaks for the rights of the family against the claims of law. Instead, he draws attention to the famous passage in Antigone's speech that has caused much discussion among commentators. This is the speech Antigone makes after every move has been made—her capture, her defiance, her condemnation, her lamentation. Antigone is facing the tomb in which she is to be buried alive when she makes this speech paraphrased thus by Lacan: "Understand this. I would not have defied the law of the city for a husband or a child to whom a tomb has been denied because after all if I had lost a husband I could have taken another and even if I had lost a child I could have made another child with another husband. But it concerned my brother, born of the same father and the same mother."[6]

It appears that there are two points here—the first that Antigone has moved toward the limit at which the self separates into that which can be destroyed and that which must endure, and the second that her brother, though a criminal by the laws of the city, is, for her, a unique being. Antigone is making that speech when she can imagine herself as already dead—and yet she endures this awesome play of pain to affirm not her own desires but the nonsubstitutability of her brother. Lacan, taking the voice of Antigone, says, "My brother may be a criminal, she is saying, but from my point of view my brother is my brother, the register of someone who has been named must be preserved."[7]

To Lacan, it appears that it is Antigone speaking from this zone between two deaths who can voice the truth of the uniqueness of being. The truth whose name she speaks goes beyond the laws of the state, and one may say that in affirming the uniqueness of her criminal brother, her passion evokes the crime underlying the law of the city. This is an important formulation on the emergence of voice—it emphasizes that voice emerges at the moment of transgression. What distinguishes Lacan's formulation though, from the hundreds of papers appearing every year on desire, pleasure, transgression, and location of agency, is that the affirmation of uniqueness of being against the scripting of law is not located in submission to immediacy of need or desire. Instead, the zone between two deaths is identified as the zone from which the unspeakable truth about the criminal nature of the law might be spoken. Why is it Antigone who must affirm the uniqueness of the person whom the law of the state has condemned as a criminal and whom it wishes to consign to an eternal forgetfulness?

For Lacan, the unbearable truth that Antigone speaks is too terrible to behold. For, in questioning the legitimacy of a rule that would completely efface the uniqueness of a being even in death, she shows the criminality of the social order itself. This truth, says Lacan, needs the envelope of beauty to hide it and yet make it available to the gaze. While there is a sense in which one can find the suspicion of vision, which many authors have noted in Lacan,[8] the relation between voice and vision is a complicated one in the articulation of this unbearable knowledge.

The theme of the woman who finds voice when she is occupying the zone between two deaths is an important one in the Indian imaginary: it builds on but also separates itself from the gendered division of speech and silence in mourning laments.[9] But the truth articulated from this zone is rarely enveloped in beauty or splendor as even the well-known female figures of Indian mythology, such as the goddess Kali or the goddess of smallpox, Sitala, would testify. Instead of looking at this contrast at the level of the imaginary as articulated in mythology and literature, however, I want to take the argument in a different direction. What is it to bear witness to the criminality of the societal rule that consigns the uniqueness of being to eternal forgetfulness through a descent in everyday life—to not simply articulate loss through a dramatic gesture of defiance but to inhabit the world, or inhabit it *again,* in a gesture of mourning? It is in this context that one may identify the eye not as the organ that sees but the organ that weeps. The formation of the subject as a gendered subject is then molded through complex transactions between the violence as the originary moment and the violence as it seeps into the ongoing relationships and becomes a kind of atmosphere that cannot be expelled to an "outside." I want to evoke at this point Wittgenstein's sense of there being no outside and the image of turning back that he offers, as thinking of a humble way of using words: "The ideal, as we think of it, is unshakable. You can never get outside it; you must always turn back. There is no outside; outside you cannot breathe."[10]

This image of turning back evokes not so much the idea of a return, as a turning back to inhabit the same space now marked as a space of destruction, in which you must live again. Hence, the sense of the everyday in Wittgenstein as the sense of something recovered. How you make such a space of destruction your own not through an ascent into transcendence but through a descent into the everyday is what I shall describe through the life of one woman, here called Asha.[11] If the figure of Antigone provided one way in which we could think of voice as a spectacular, defiant creation of the subject through the act of speech, the figure of Asha shows the creation of the gendered subject through engagement with knowledge that is equally poisonous, but is addressed through the everyday work of repair. In the case of Asha, as we shall see, the originary moment of the violence of the Partition got woven into the events of her life because she was already vulnerable as a widow in a kinship universe of Hindu upper-caste ethos.

But to be vulnerable is not the same as to be a victim, and those who are inclined to assume that social norms or expectations of widowhood are automatically translated into oppression need to pay attention to the gap between a norm and its actualization. The idea of presenting a "case" here is not so much to offer an example of a general rule or an exception to it, but rather to show how new norms emerge in experiments with life, in spiritual self-creation. How do individuals set norms for themselves, and how are these related to the way in which societal norms are imagined?

WIDOWHOOD AND VULNERABILITY

Asha was fifty-five years old when I came to know her. Married into an affluent family of the trader caste, she had lived with her husband and his two elder married brothers in the ancestral home in Lahore. She was widowed at the age of twenty in 1941 when her husband was infected with typhoid and died within three weeks of the onset of his illness. He was the youngest brother in a fraternally joint family. In addition, he had been very close to his two older married sisters, who had virtually brought him up since their mother had died in childbirth. She said that the grief of her husband's sisters had been as fierce as her own grief.

Asha recalled the earliest period of her bereavement as one in which she had received enormous affection and support from her affinal family. She continued to live with the family of her husband's elder brother. The fact that she was childless weighed heavily upon her. She said that she had lost all interest in life—her heart did not engage in anything.[12] To reawaken her interest in life, her husband's younger sister gave her own son in "adoption" to her. The child stayed with his own mother, but it was presumed that as he grew into adulthood, he would take the responsibility of caring for Asha, as his second mother, as it were. Such arrangements were common within a kinship group even thirty years ago, for women often treated their children as "shared" (*Bache te ji sajhe honde hain*—literally, children belong to all). It was not unusual for various combinations of relationships to evolve over a single child. This was one way for a community of women to take care of a bereaved member. One might say that women evolved cultural subtexts that were anchored upon the dominant patriarchal texts of the society, yet created spaces for new and caring relationships. In this case, for example, it would have been out of the question to let the widow adopt a child outside the kinship group—by marking one child from within the kinship group as especially hers, the women hoped that a special relationship would develop between them. In the women's understanding and construction of human nature, a woman, it was felt, experienced the lack of motherhood most acutely—hence her husband's sisters tried to fill this emptiness in Asha's life. One may argue that this very construction of female "need" constrains women to invest desire in maternity rather than, let us say, sexuality. Hence, it constructs the female self in accordance with the dominant cultural paradigms. This is true—yet we shall see that the cultural representations do not become completely mapped upon the self. If the social context alters suddenly, the woman herself or others in her social world might evoke a different definition of female "need." Thus, individual lives are defined by context, but they are also generative of new contexts. The turbulent period of the Partition became such an event for Asha as it pried open the relation between social norms and new forms of subjectivity. It is not that older subject positions were simply left behind or abandoned—rather, there were new ways in which even signs of injury could be occupied. In that sense, the question of how one makes the world one's own was re-posed for her, and she moved between different ways in which she could find the means to re-create her relationships in the face of the poisonous knowledge that had seeped into these relationships.

During the Partition Asha's conjugal family lost everything and had to escape from Lahore empty-handed. Her husband's elder sister died in the riots. It was never clear whether she had killed herself or whether she had been abducted. In all the narratives about Lahore that I heard in this family, there was a blanking out of this period. For instance, I have seen photographs of the whole family in which, this woman—now dead—appears in various happy contexts. These occasions usually evoked narratives of the event portrayed in the photograph, but no reference was ever made to her present absence. A question such as "What happened to her?" was met with a cursory answer—"She died in that time."

As I have explained in the first chapter, in the months just preceding and following the Partition, residential arrangements were very unstable with people moving from one place to another in search of jobs, houses, and ways to remake their existence. Asha's natal family lived in Amritsar, the nearest town to the border on the Indian side—so they became the first source of support for her conjugal family. At one time, she recalled, forty persons received shelter in their house. Slowly, within months, as other relatives in Simla, Delhi, and Ferozpur came forward to help, her conjugal kin began to scatter to different places. Asha stayed with her "adopted" son in her father's family. But while her parents were supportive, her brother and his wife did not want to take this extra burden upon themselves. They never stated this directly but perhaps communicated it through veiled speech and an aesthetic of gestures. As with any utterance that gets its meaning from the context (which is not to say that it cannot be itself generative of context), the fragments of her speech that I shall quote are bristling with words not fully stated, performative gestures, and a whole repertoire of culturally dense notions that surround the utterances. Thus, while I do not wish to suggest an objectified idea of meaning (here a word, there a meaning, as Wittgenstein put it), it appears to me that filling out the repertoire to which each fragment points allows us to construct meaning as a process in which the spoken utterances derive their meaning from the lifeworld rather than from the abstract notions of structural semantics. I am obviously aware that the rules of structural semantics render the meaning of utterances as linguistic entities, but these remain disembodied utterances. The introduction of the subject as the maker of this speech necessitates an introduction of context, not only linguistic context but also lifeworld as context. Yet I am hesitant to introduce the idea of intentionality here, because the *givenness* of language as *parole* requires a certain forgetfulness to the act of speech, as Gadamer suggests.[13] The fact that Asha was not explicitly engaged in telling me the story of what happened during the Partition but was rather narrating here and there, as the occasion arose, certain fragments of her world makes this forgetfulness an important part of what was said.

Robert Desjarlais, commenting on how we may attend to words so that we can grasp the dynamics of language, time, and political agency as these operate within life, says the following: "All this is in the words themselves. More often than not, though, it's in the words as Yolmo listeners might hear them. If non-Yolmo readers were presented with Kisang's utterances alone, they would, I think, miss a great deal—the intonations of her voice, what her words implied, how they related to other words and situations in Yolmo lives."[14] With these reflections, I now turn to Asha's words as she philosophized on what she construed as her brother's reluctance to give her a home: "A daughter's food is never heavy on her parents, but how long will one's parents live? When even two pieces of bread are experienced as heavy by one's own brother, then it is better to keep one's honor—make one's peace—and to live where one was destined to live." Asha's formulation— an indicative utterance—also constitutes her reproach to life. I offer an exegesis by taking different phrases and filling up the dense cultural encoding that will, I hope, provide the context for understanding her reproach.

I am reminded here of several performative genres in India, especially in dance, in which a small phrase can be augmented through facial and eye gestures for anywhere up to an hour.

First Fragment

A daughter's food is never heavy on her parents. (Beti di roti ma pyo te kadi pari nahin hondi.) Asha is evoking the cultural idea here that even though the norms of kinship orient a daughter toward her affines, the natal kin have some residual obligations toward married daughters who may have met with some misfortune. A woman can always lay claims on her father and mother for support in case of trouble—parents do not consider the obligation to provide the daughter with support as a burden because of their love for their daughter (but one should note that the emphasis is only on support for survival; if they try to provide more to their daughters, it would create resentment among their sons, who think of themselves as legitimate heirs). Hence what the daughter claims as food from the father's house is not experienced as *heavy* (i.e., burdensome) by them. Clearly there is a form of subjectivity here attributed to parents when Asha takes the voice of the daughter to claim entitlement: yet the most wounding idea in Punjabi life is that this entitlement can rarely be realized, making the daughter into a permanent exile.[15]

Second Fragment

But how long will one's parents live? (Ma-pyo kine din rehenge?) When a married daughter makes a claim on her parents because she is facing misfortune in her husband's house, she tends to forget time's effacement of relationships. There will inevitably come a time when parents will not be there to offer her welcome—power will pass into the hands of her brother and his wife. Then the two pieces of bread she is laying claims on in her parental home will become *heavy* on her brother and his wife. A daughter must always keep the ephemeral nature of her claim on her parents' home in mind. The concept of time as a destroyer of relationships occurs as a constant refrain in Punjabi life and accounts for the fact that at the moment in which one is living, the actual is imaged in relation to the eventual. Thus the subject is conceived as a plural subject, inhabiting the present moment but also speaking as if she were already occupying a different moment in the future. This has important implications for understanding the temporal depth in which the subject is constituted and the manner in which traumatic memory[16] opens up time to construe the blindness of the present already from a projected point in the future.

Third Fragment

When even two pieces of bread are experienced as "heavy" by one's own brother . . . (Jad do rotiyan wi apne hi pra nun pari pein lagan . . .)   In Punjabi society, the relation between brothers is acknowledged as fraught with tensions stemming from their coparcenery status. There is a further tension between the principle of hierarchy by which the elder brother is to be treated as a father, for he inherits the moral obligation to look after his younger siblings, and the principle of equality by which all brothers have equal rights over the ancestral property and are to be treated as equals. In contrast, the relation between the brother and sister is valorized as a sacred relationship in which the sister provides spiritual protection to the brother. In exchange, she is the honored gift receiver in her brother's house.[17] A married sister who visits on ritual occasions, carries gifts for her brother's children as is appropriate, and receives gifts given freely and lovingly from the brother's house is said to bring honor to both families. But a destitute married sister who has been compelled to leave her affinal home and make a place for herself in her brother's house comes to be an object of mistrust, especially by the brother's wife, who suspects that she may use her position as a beloved daughter to usurp a share of the brother's property. Many of the women's songs capture this sense of the married daughter being an exile—her desire to visit her father's home is being seen by the brother as an excuse to demand a share in the father's property. This is why *the two pieces of bread that the sister consumes come to be seen as heavy*—they point to a time when the anguish of the sister will not be *heard* anymore in the natal home. The framing of the future in these terms makes it unbearable for Asha to imagine her transfiguration from a beloved daughter and sister to a burden on the family. It is important to note that Asha is not complaining of neglect that she has already experienced but imagining where her story might go within a possible societal emplotment of such stories.

Fourth Fragment

. . . it is better to keep (protect) your honor . . . (. . . apni izzat bacha ke rakho . . .)   Asha knows that in the altered circumstances, her affinal kin were hard pressed to support her. Yet it is better to keep your honor, she says, by putting up with humiliations in the affinal home—that is considered to be a woman's lot. In contrast, the parental home is imagined as a

place where she is *entitled* to receive honor. Thus, if she fails to anticipate the inevitable souring of relations and claims what is her right, she will lose her honor. Yet there is more than a hint of disappointment here in that the individual story could not rise above the culturally given plot in which the temporality of the brother-sister relation is imaged.

. . . and make your peace . . . (. . . shanti banaye rakho . . .) Making your peace does not have the sense of a passive submission here but of an active engagement—the constant doing of little things that will make the affinal family see you in a different aspect than that of a widow who is a burden. For example, while Asha must completely efface her sexuality, she must be always available for chores that others shrink from—rolling *papads* for hours, cleaning a young child's bottom, grinding or pounding spices. Similarly, expression of affect has to be managed carefully. As a widow Asha's face must always portray the constant presence of grief—the parting of the hair being emptied of the auspicious red vermilion, she told me, was symbolic of all that is in the nature of a void in the cosmos. The performance of the gendered identity of widowhood has the force of a compulsory social ritual. Yet, if grief is too flamboyantly displayed, it makes everyone uncomfortable, as if they were betraying a departed brother, or an uncle, by laughing or enjoying a special snack. There is a special aesthetic of the senses here. A widow, especially a young childless widow, understands her vulnerability, for she must incorporate in her behavior the culturally held belief that she is inauspicious—all the outward criteria by which her inauspicious status is conveyed are present in her embodiment—yet her own relation to her body is not simply a mapping of this exterior onto an interiorized self. She reminds everyone in the family of a much beloved brother whom they have lost to untimely death, and yet whose memory must not be allowed to come in the way of other tasks of getting ahead in life. Her face and her body must constantly enact this aesthetic. Again, I do not mean to say that there are feelings, thoughts, and sensations that are "inner" and behavior that is "outer." But the whole deportment of the body as providing external criteria through which others may read the "inner" is an important cultural move that is embedded, in this case, in the grammar of widowhood in Indian society. I am inclined to say that the body becomes almost too expressive to bear.

. . . and live where one is destined to live (literally, where fate has written, there you stay). (. . . jithe kismet which likhya hai othe hi raho.) Here is the evocation of the cultural idea that a woman's destiny lies in the husband's house. This theme is constantly reiterated for girls, whose socialization

emphasizes their future in the husband's house. Older women often express the idea that a girl goes into her husband's house in the bridal palanquin (*doli*)—and should come out as a corpse carried on the shoulders of four men.

The exegesis of this single statement makes clear how much of Asha's voice was shaped by the cultural, patriarchal norms of widowhood—yet it must be remembered that before the Partition she did not have to consider these choices. It was not that the norms were different earlier, but that the composition of the family and especially the close relations she had with her husband's sister did not invest these norms with the force that they later acquired. Though a widow, Asha had felt loved and had been given the familial support that made her feel that she had a rightful place within her affinal family.

With the Partition came an enormous decline in the family's fortunes. Each unit of the previously joint family was facing new and what appeared to be insurmountable problems. Where would they live? Where would the children go to school? One of the children was ready for medical school. How was his father going to raise money for his education? Under the new kinds of tensions to which families were now daily subjected, Asha found a subtle change in others' attitudes toward her.[18] Whereas earlier the death of her husband was seen as a great misfortune for her, now blame came to be attached to her for his death. She was slowly being pushed into the position of a scapegoat. Sometimes her female affines, that is, her husband's brother's wife and her husband's sister, would suggest by innuendo that she had been unable to lure her husband from the edge of death back into life. As Asha described it: "They began to hint that he had been very disappointed in my looks. He was such a handsome man, and I was such an ordinary woman. They said that perhaps he lost interest in life because he did not really like me. This made me so guilty and remorseful that I often thought of killing myself." Asha moved between her natal family, her husband's brother's family, and her husband's sister's family for the next four years:

> Everywhere I tried to make myself useful. I would work from morning to night. I was so fond of the children that I was prepared to put up with anything for their sake. Soon the taunts became worse. And then, what was unbearable was the fact that my *jija ji* [literally, sister's husband, but here used as a term of address for her husband's sister's husband, who was now a widower] began to make sexual passes at me (*ched chad*) that became very difficult to resist. I was torn between loyalties to my dead

husband, his sister whom I had loved very much, and the new kinds of needs that seemed to be aroused by the possibility of a new relationship. I began to see that I would always be the person who was available for experiments. He never suggested marriage, which would have created a scandal since I had lived in their house for so long. [The implication is that there would be gossip that they had a long-standing sexual relationship that was now simply being formalized.]

Finally, I wrote to a very dear friend of my husband's who lived in Poona. He suggested that I come to visit his family. When I went to Poona, he persuaded me that I had long life stretching ahead of me and that if I did not wish to be constantly degraded, I should get remarried. There was a wealthy man in Poona. His wife had left him. He was much older than I was, but this friend arranged a marriage between us. I then wrote both to my natal family (*peke*) and to the members of my conjugal family (*saure*) that I had been remarried. There was a complete furor, and they swore never to see me again. They said I had disgraced them with my behavior. And, indeed, I had disgraced them. They had showered me with so much love until their own lives had become disrupted, and I had responded by sullying their white turbans (*pagdis*).[19] They would not be able to show their face in the community. But I was helpless.

Then what followed was a period of great tension for Asha. Although she remarried and in the next four years had two children, she seemed unable to forget her connections with her earlier conjugal family. Her new husband also appeared disinclined to sever his own ties with his first wife, who visited them from her village often to reiterate the rights of her children over the property and affection of their father. In fact, one of her sons came to live with his father and seemed to consider himself as the proper heir to the father's property. My impression, after many informal talks with Asha in which this topic would come up, was that she regarded herself more as a concubine of her new husband than his wife. For instance, when I asked her how she felt as a young woman when her husband's previous wife visited their house, she looked a little surprised and said, "But she had the right to visit him."

This way of forming a new relationship but never quite giving up the older conjugal ties may be an expression of the strong religious commitment to the conjugal relationship that Gananath Obeyesekere argues is the core of Brahmanical values.[20] What struck me, however, was that the first husband did not seem to preoccupy Asha in the same manner as did his surviving sister or the child who had been "given" to her. Always referring to it as "that house," she did everything possible to reestablish the broken links with the family of her first husband. This was remarkable, considering that these relationships could have been easily obliterated from her life, for they were the source of painful memories. Though she never spoke about it, it appears to me that it may not have been easy for her to explain her continued attachment to that family to anyone in light of her much disapproved remarriage. During the first five years of her marriage to the second husband, she continued to write letters to the surviving sister of her husband. She heard from her that there was no possibility of rapprochement. Her first husband's sister, as I said, had died under circumstances that were never made clear. The sexual interest shown by the dead woman's husband toward Asha and her struggle over this relationship had perhaps put him on the defensive toward her. As a result, he was virulent in his attacks on her morality. But the husband's younger sister continued to make attempts toward rapprochement, and finally after eight years of her new marriage she was invited to come from Poona and visit the family.

I was curious as to why it had been so important for her to continue her relationships with her earlier conjugal family. Her own answer was that she felt an extreme attachment to the husband's sister who had given her young son to Asha. She also felt that by going away she had made the child feel that he was of no importance in her life, whereas the fact was that she felt she owed her very life to the child and his mother. Then there was the temporal depth in which she saw her relationships.

"When I married," she said "my husband's sister was very young and she became very attached to me. We made up all kinds of games as a sign of our special relationship—for example, we always exchanged our *dupattas*. When we sat down to eat, we ate from the same plate. She would feed me one [mouthful], and then I would feed her one. Everyone in the family used to laugh but we really had fun." She did not articulate her relation to her husband's young sister as an *individuated relationship* but tended to derive it from the relationship with her dead husband. Thus we could say that the relations between the women were conducted under the shadow of patriarchy, for they could acknowledge their love only through the mediation of a dead brother/husband: "I don't know. I had such little time with my husband. It was almost as if a flower that was to blossom was picked off a branch. But I had so many desires that in some other time, some other place they are bound to bear fruit. The only important thing is that I must keep my connections with that house alive."[21] One is bound to ask, what was the meaning of the second marriage to her? That marriage had, after all, borne fruit. There were two lovely daughters to whom she seemed much attached. In one rare moment of explicit formulation of her relationships, she said:

> I have been very happy, very lucky that I found someone so good to marry me. He has really looked after me. To the best of my own conscience, I have provided him with every comfort. But I was drawn to this marriage because of this wretched body—it has needs, it has an existence over which I have no control. I don't mean just my needs. I could not help it when men looked at me with lust in their eyes. It was not I—it was this body that attracted them. If *jija ji* had not begun to make passes at me (*ched chad na karde*), I might have lived an ascetic life, appropriate to a widow, in my husband's house. But after what happened between us, how could I have faced my sister-in-law? How could I have faced my husband in my next life? With him it is a connection for eternity. With my present husband—it is as if two sticks were brought together in a stormy sea—the union of a moment and then oblivion. I want all accounts settled with him in this life—all give and take (*lena dena*) must be completed. Then I can depart without sorrow. After all, he has another wife, and in god's eyes, it is she and not I who will stand with him. I am a sinner (*papin*).

It may seem from the above account that Asha had a deep attachment to her dead husband. Yet in conversations with her it often appeared to me that her husband was a very shadowy character to her. She once remarked that when she saw old photographs of herself with her husband, she felt that she was looking at two strangers. It is also remarkable that it is memories of her husband's sister that appear to be far more concrete and vital in her narrative as it was the first husband's sister who slowly overcame the objections of the men to allow Asha back into their lives.

I would suggest that for many women such as Asha the violence of the Partition lay in not only what happened to them in the riots and the brutal violation of their bodies but also what they had to witness—namely, the possibility of betrayal coded in their everyday relations. Think for a moment about what was taken to be the givenness of life in Asha's account and how that involved a form of concealment of which she was to be made aware only in the unfolding of events. Who could have predicted that a major political event would show the concealed side of kinship relations to be made of the possibility of betrayal? There are other cases of such betrayal that I encountered in my fieldwork—the point is that the horrendous violence of communal riots solidifies the membership of a group at one level, but it also has the potential to break the most intimate of relations at another level. The obverse of this is that people are moved to offer support beyond all normal expectations (e.g., neighbors belonging to the other community are given shelter at the risk of one's own life)—hence, the heterogeneous experience one has of these events is not only of hate and violation, but also an experience of sympathy that can display heroic virtues, cutting short the lengthy chains of claims and responses of everyday life. However, how these passionate moments are carried forward into everyday life requires a different kind of story to be told, and my uneasiness with many such accounts of passionate hatred or heroic moments is that we don't see how such moments are then carried into everyday life.

I have elsewhere described the case of Manjit, whose story I take up further in the next chapter.[22] Some of the memories of the Partition for her were of a brother leaving a packet of poison with her while he went out every day, with the instructions that she should not hesitate to swallow the contents if Muslim mobs came to the house. Manjit, then barely thirteen years old, had the vague sense that while he himself indulged in unspeakable deeds with gangs of young men that had been formed, he expected her to die rather than court dishonor.[23] This was an experience as frightening as the experience of waiting every day expecting to be attacked or the experience of being rescued by the army. In Asha's case, it was when the protector of yesteryear became the aggressor of today that her life's projects had to be reformulated. In all this, it was the solidarity forged between the women who helped her to not only escape a suffocating situation but also connect the present with the past. Yet she was unable to acknowledge that it was the community of women that healed, framing this relationship itself within the dominant male-female relationships. Perhaps this suggests that even when a woman has broken the most important taboos as Asha did, she may not feel that she has really transgressed against the idealized norms: Asha did not feel that she had become another person—only that she had entered into temporary arrangements while her true relationships remained suspended for a while.

I propose that Asha's way of telling her story also tells us something important about the hyphenated relation between legislation and transgression. It is not that first there is a law and then a transgression—first an individual who is completely defined by the norms and then one who transgresses. Rather, in breaking the taboo on widow remarriage and earning censure for it, Asha felt that she had preserved the integrity of the norms and yet not succeeded in following them. This is testified in her statements that divide her against herself—"I am a sinner"—and then "But after what happened between us, how could I have faced my sister-in-law? How could I have faced my husband in my next life? With him it is a connection for eternity."

In Lacan's rendering of the passion of Antigone, she spoke from the experience of that limit in which she could see her life as already lived. In juxtaposing the far less dramatic mode of speech that Asha used with the dramatic speech of Antigone, I hope to have shown that in their descent into the everyday, women such as Asha occupied a different zone by descending into the everyday rather than ascending toward a higher plane. In both cases, however, we see a woman as witness not just in the sense that she is within the frame of events, but that she is marked by these events. The zone of the everyday within which Asha spoke had to be recovered by reoccupying the very signs of injury that had been marked to forge continuity in that space of devastation.

WITH THE EYES OF A CHILD

Until now I have described the events of Asha's life primarily in her voice. I want to give one vignette of how her first visit (after she was remarried) had appeared to her "adopted son" (Suraj), who was then about eight years old. At the time of this exchange with me Suraj was an adolescent, but he still remembered how bitterly everyone would talk about her after news came of her remarriage. They talked about how they had showered affection on her but she had betrayed them. For instance, her (first) husband's brother would say, "We had clasped her to our heart thinking she was the only sign of our dead brother, but she wanted to carry out a different meaning/purpose" (the phrase *matlab kadna* in Punjabi can refer to a manipulative use of others for self-serving purposes). A common genre of family conversations among urban Punjabis is to address an absent person as if he or she is present. In this case she was made the subject of taunts,[24] for example, "Kudos to you, oh, queen—you truly preserved our honor" (*vah ni rani - tu badi laj rakhi sadi*). Her adopted son said that his own mother would mutter to herself sometimes in his presence, "What is the life of a woman?"

Suraj had been very tense at the prospect of seeing her, his "other" mother. The family conversations had built her image as a shameless woman who had betrayed the family and especially betrayed a special trust by abandoning him, her "special" son. When she came she looked well and clearly had lots of new clothes and some jewelry. Her body was not a proclamation of her widowhood—Suraj had wanted to avoid looking at her, as if she were too dazzling. But she did not display her newly found wealth; she settled into helping in the domestic chores as she used to. Suraj remembered one particular occasion, for he had become adamant that they should all go out to eat ice cream. The whole family had been gathered together, and the elders were not particularly encouraging. But, he said, he wanted his will to prevail—he wanted to claim that he had special claims over her against everyone else. Conceding to his demands, she went in to change and came out wearing a colorful sari. A *tonga* was called to take them to the market, and as they—Asha, Suraj, and a cousin—were going to embark, his uncle (the same man who had subjected her to sexual advances) said, "There is no need to show the stylized charms (*nakhre*) of a *sethani*." The term literally means the wife of a *seth* or a rich trader, but is used among Punjabis to refer to a woman who is lazy, does not perform household chores, and is interested only in dressing up and displaying her wealth. Asha's eyes filled with tears, and as they sat in the *tonga* she put her arm around Suraj and said, "See, for your sake I have to listen to such derision" (*boliyan sun-ni paindiyan hain*).

REFLECTIONS

The writing of history and anthropology in recent years has been strongly influenced by the literary analyses of narratives. As Byron Good has noted in the context of illness narratives, though, the narrator of an autobiographical story is relating a story that is not yet finished; or, as Desjarlais says, there is a narrated I and a narrating I, so that there are two temporalities that are braided together in the telling.[25] In the context of the Partition, historians have often collected oral narratives formulated to answer the question: What happened? I have chosen not to frame the question in these terms. Instead, seeing how the violence of the Partition was folded into everyday relations has animated my work. Another way to put this is to say that I am not asking how the events of the Partition were present to consciousness as past events, but how they came to be incorporated into the temporal structure of relationships, especially remaining mindful of the projecting character of human existence.

In the case of Asha we saw that she defines relationships of kinship much more through ideas of care, and in her story the brutality of the Partition lay in what violence could do to alter the ways in which kin recognize or withhold recognition from each other. Thus, the memory of the Partition cannot be understood in Asha's life as a direct possession of the past. It is constantly interposed and mediated by the manner in which the world is being presently inhabited. Even when it appears that some women were relatively lucky because they escaped direct bodily harm, the bodily memory of being-with-others makes that past encircle the present as atmosphere. This what I mean by the importance of finding ways to speak about the experience of witnessing: that if one's way of being-with-others was brutally damaged, then the past enters the present not necessarily as traumatic memory but as poisonous knowledge. This knowledge can be engaged only through a knowing by suffering. As Martha Nussbaum puts it:

> There is a kind of knowing that works by suffering because suffering is the appropriate acknowledgement of the way human life, in these cases, is. And in general: to grasp either a love or a tragedy by intellect is not sufficient for having real human knowledge of it. Agamemnon *knows* that Iphigenia is his child all through, if by this we mean that he has the correct beliefs, can answer many questions about her truly etc. But because in his emotions, his imagination and his behaviour he does not acknowledge the tie, we want to join the Chorus in saying that his state is less one of knowledge than one of *delusion*. He doesn't *really know* that she is his daughter. A piece of true understanding is missing.[26]

As for Asha, she was also *known* in her role as the widow of a much loved brother—her body was incorporated, not only ritually, but also in everyday interactions in the family, in the body of her dead husband. This was the only *acknowledged* aspect of her being. Yet there might have been other subtexts operating—the love between her husband's younger sister and herself, the recognition that she was a sexual being whose sexuality had been forcibly effaced by the death of her husband and the demands of family honor. It appears to me that these were the subtexts that came to be articulated because of the turbulence of the novelty that was born during the Partition.

Once her sexual being was recognized in the new kind of gaze—someone in the position of a surrogate brother revealing himself to be a lover—she was propelled into a choice.[27] Would she wish to carry on a clandestine relation and participate in the "bad faith" on which Pierre Bourdieu recognizes the politics of kinship to be based?[28] Or would she accept the public opprobrium to which she subjected the family honor for a new definition of herself, which promised certain integrity, though as an exile, to the life projects she had earlier formulated for herself? In the process of this decision the subject may have become radically fragmented and the self a fugitive, but I think what I have described is the formation of the subject, a complex agency made up of divided and fractured subject positions. This becomes evident not necessarily at the moment of violence, but in the years of patient work through which Asha and her first husband's sister repaired the torn shreds of relations. There was the poisonous knowledge that she was betrayed by her senior affinal kin, as well as by her brother, who could not undertake to sustain the long-term commitment to a destitute sister. What was equally important for her was the knowledge that she may have herself betrayed her dead husband and his dead sister by the imagination of infidelity and made a young child, her "special" adopted son, feel abandoned. It was not any momentary heroic gestures but the patient work of living with this new knowledge—*really knowing* not just by intellect but through the passions—that made the two women's work described simply as *ais ghar nal sambandh bana rahe*—let the relation between these two houses continue—an exemplary instance of agency seen as a product of different subject positions—perpetrator, victim, witness.

At this point my analysis of what it is for Asha and her (first) husband's sister to work to overcome this poisonous knowledge joins some reflections of Cavell's on the sense of being cursed or sickened by the fact of knowing itself—that is, of knowing more than his fellows about the conditions of knowing. The context of this reflection in Cavell's writing is the inability of the father in *The Winter's Tale* to acknowledge the son as his, as caused by him. Shakespeare's expression of knowledge as infected, of a spider steeped in a cup, speaks to the whole theme of the skeptic's distrust in relations, his demands for more and more proof—and yet what would cure this condition is not more knowledge but acknowledgment that some doubts are normal and that the cure for suspicion cannot come from within suspicion. Cavell sees this as the question of owning or disowning knowledge.[29] However, just as Cavell repeatedly points to the condition of the *modern* subject within skepticism (signaled by the death of God within philosophy), showing that the issue is historically located, so it seems to me that the coming to doubt of relationships that the Partition amplified has a specificity of its own. It could be repaired only by allowing oneself a descent into the ordinary world but as if in mourning for it. Recovery did not lie in enacting a revenge against the world, but in inhabiting it in a gesture of mourning for it.[30]

The relation between the formation of the subject and the experience of subjugation was captured by Michel Foucault in his analysis of the discipline of the body by an imprisoning metaphor, "the soul is the prison of the body."[31] In the context of the prison, Foucault argued, the discipline of the prison is not just one that regulates the behavior of the prisoner but invades the interior and in fact produces it. Though reversing the relation of interiority and exteriority, of body and soul, does manage to produce a shock, Foucault seems to me to be still caught within the standing languages of inner and outer.

In coming to understand the complicated relationships between the folding of an originary political violence into the ongoing relations of kinship through the life of Asha, I have found the models of either power/resistance or metaphors of imprisonment to be too crude as tools to understand the delicate work of self creation. Instead, I have found that in exploring the temporal depth in which such originary moments of violence are lived through, everyday life reveals itself to be both a quest and an inquest, as Cavell puts it.[32] Thus, instead of imprisoning metaphors to capture the relations between outward criteria and inner states, one may think of these as lining each other, of having a relation in which they are next to each other but joined in the way in which legislation and transgression are joined.

It is this relation of nextness between norm-setting legislation and transgression that seems to have allowed Asha to have experienced herself as laying claims to the very culture and the relationships that had subjugated her. Clearly the terrible violence of the Partition signaled the death of her world, as she had known it. It also provided a new way by which she could reinhabit the world. From some perspectives her attachment to the past might be read through the imprisonment metaphor—something she is incapable of breaking out of. From another perspective, though, the temporal depth in which she constructs her subjectivity shows how one may occupy the very signs of injury and give them a meaning not only through acts of narration but through the work of repairing relationships and giving recognition to those whom the official norms had condemned. I see that as an appropriate metaphor for the act of witnessing, which is one way to understand the relation between violence and subjectivity.

FIVE

Boundaries, Violence, and the Work of Time

IN CONTEMPLATING FURTHER MUCH RECENT WORK on violence I am struck by the sense voiced by many scholars that, faced with violence, we reach some kind of limit in relation to the capacity to represent. Often this argument is staged through the trope of "horror." We are then invited to consider how human beings could have been capable of such horrific acts on such large scales, as in Rwanda or the former Yugoslavia. As we saw, the violence of the Partition provides a similar trope of horror in the historiography of India. It appears to me that we render such acts as shocking and unimaginable only when we have a given picture of how the human subject is to be constructed. Thus, these descriptions serve to reaffirm the boundaries between civilized and savage, while allowing our picture of the human subject to remain intact.[1] In contrast to this plenitude of speech, I would like to offer a picture of poverty, especially poverty of words, and to reflect on this very poverty as a virtue. One may say of anthropology what Henri Lefebvre said of philosophy: "The role of philosophical thought is to eliminate premature explanations, those limitative positions which could prevent us from penetrating and possessing the formidable content of our being."[2] This image of holding back also recalls, for me at any rate, Cavell's sketch of philosophy as that which does not speak *first*, its virtue lying in its responsiveness: tireless, awake, when others have fallen asleep.[3] The image of wakefulness to the occurrence of violence, of responsiveness to wherever it occurs in the weave of life, leads one to ask whether acts of violence are transparent. How does one render the relation between possibility and actuality, and further, between the actual and the eventual? If violence, when it happens dramatically, bears some relation to what is happening repeatedly and unmelodramatically, then how does one tell this, not in a single narrative but in the form of a text that is being constantly revised, rewritten, and overlaid with commentary? As in the case of Asha and her work of repairing, one may think of stories not as completed but as in the process of being produced. Though we often fall into the image of a story as if it were a text, one may better speak of some stories as an engagement in the everyday with creation of boundaries in different regions of the self and of sociality. The *work* of time, not its image or representation, is what concerns me here as I describe these processes.

As I argued in the last chapter it was through the act of witnessing that Asha and her female relatives turned this poisonous knowledge as transfigured into recognition of the being of the other, thus constituting a knowing by suffering. But stories of discord and betrayals do not disappear, for they remain suspended and can break into the present without notice. This is well recognized in Punjabi life so that narratives of betrayal between kin have to be managed carefully on the occasions of weddings and deaths, as well as in gatherings of kin. Despite this potential of stories to disrupt, I continue to be struck by the silence on the violence that was done to and by people in the context of the Partition. As I stated, it is not that, if asked, people will not tell a story—but that none of the performative aspects or the struggles over the control of the story, a mark of storytelling in everyday life, are present. In contrast, there is the quality of frozen slides in the accounts of the violence of the Partition. In everyday conversations of the generation that left Lahore, references to the *puris* (fried bread) and *lassi* (yoghurt drink) of Lahore, the *zari* (brocade) embroidery, the sweetness and freshness of vegetables, the contributions of the Lahore Government College to intellectual life, shopping in the Anar Kali Bazaar, and the myths of Hira Mandi were made liberally. Yet any spontaneous reference to atrocities done, witnessed, or suffered during the Partition was not allowed to surface. What is the relation between the elaborate managing and staging of narratives that speak of violence, betrayal, and distrust within the networks of kinship and the thick curtain of silence pointing to an absconding presence?

Writing on violence and narrative in Lebanon, Michael Gilsenan has written: "The rhetoric that life was a tissue of calculated performance, aesthetic elaboration of form, artifice, and downright lies behind which one had to look for true interests and aims of others was common to all. In this sense a violence that was not physical coercion but was of a more diffuse kind and integral to accounts of human relations was common to all."[4] A similar way of defining human relations pervades accounts of masculinity in the feud narratives among the Jat Sikhs that my colleague R. S. Bajwa and I have described elsewhere.[5] The Hindu Punjabi families considered the Jat Sikhs to be simply "hotheaded." Their own notions of masculinity were those of prudent management of public occasions through restraint. Yet the idea that life was a calculated performance and that one's honor (*izzat*) had to be preserved by careful management of the narratives about one's family in public spaces was, indeed, part of the rhetoric of life. *Duniya ki kayegi?*—What will the world say? *Logan di zaban kis ne pakadi hai?*—Who has caught the tongues of people? *Apni izzat apne hath hondi hai*—One's honor is in one's own hands—all these exhortations that spiced everyday conversations referred not only to culturally appropriate behavior but also to the control over one's own narrative. Yet such is the uncertainty of relations within families and within kinship groups that appear to have solidity from the outside that there is always a precarious balance around issues of honor and shame.

In 1974 I attended a grand wedding in one of these families. The father of the groom had risen from the destruction of his economic life in Lahore to establish a flourishing business in Delhi. All weddings are an occasion for great tension for the bride's family that something may go wrong. For example, the groom's family may come up with an unforeseen demand for a higher dowry, or a sudden death may lead to postponement or even cancellation of the marriage; hundreds of other obstructions (*badhas*) may arise that no one had even imagined. In this case the tension among the close kin of the bride and the groom was at a truly high pitch though masked from the guests. I want to tell the story of this tension moving both backwards and forwards.

The mother of the groom, Manjit, had been abducted during the Partition and then rescued by the Indian army, though this was not known to many.[6] Her parents had died in the riots. She came to live with her mother's brother (*mama*). Apprehensive that he would not be able to fulfill all the new responsibilities that had fallen on his shoulders, he soon arranged a match for Manjit with a much older man who was a distant relation. Such matches were tolerated after the Partition both because of the economic ruin (a flower garland, people said, was all that a girl could be married with) and because there was the perception of a shared misfortune of having been unable to protect the honor of the girls.[7] Her kin did not disown Manjit, unlike stories of many other girls that one hears, but neither was her story widely known. The community seemed to have offered protection by silence.

After her marriage, though, Manjit faced continuous hardships. Her husband was consumed by suspicions that she had been raped—that he might have been tricked into marrying a "spoiled" girl—that she may have had a Muslim lover. No one verbalized this except in "taunts"[8] when her husband was drunk, or in quarrels between Manjit and her husband's mother. "*Chupchap sundi gayi, sahendi gayi*" (Quietly I went on hearing, went on bearing) is how Manjit described her stance, elongating the first word—thus giving the past a sense of continuous work of hearing:

> I stitched up my tongue, I did not even protest when they said good-bad things (*bura bhala kya*)[9] about my parents and my *mama*. But, one thing, he never lifted his hands to me.
>
> My *saas* [husband's mother] said to me that I am inordinately proud— "What is there to be proud of in a woman's life?" she said. "A woman eats the dung of the man" (*aurat da ki hai—aurat te admi da gun khandi hai*).
>
> "*Manji, asi tan roti khande haan*" (Mother, but we eat bread), I said. She was so angry with me that she did not speak to me for two days.

This small exchange shows the great battle over words that goes on in families every day. By using the plural "we," Manjit had managed to suggest a difference between the kind of community of women to which she belonged—women who ate bread—and the kind of woman her husband's mother was, who claimed that women ate dung. The cultural picture of women's subordination through sex is turned on different axes here. This is not a matter of the powerless having hidden scripts, as Scott suggests,[10] but of the danger to the authority of the powerful, danger of losing face because they do not know how to wield words.

Manjit's husband and his mother seemed to have turned their anger against her into resentment against her first-born son, Jagat, whom they saw as having closer affinity to his mother than anyone else. Her second son suffered from Down Syndrome, but he never faced any aggression from his father—only indifference. Her husband would direct his anger against his elder son in all kinds of ways. "Everything was a struggle," said Manjit. If he sat down to study, his father would send him for an errand. If he needed money for books, Manjit would have to steal from her husband to buy him books. But because of the boy's determination and the support of his mother he was able to complete his studies. At that point, his father wanted him to join his business, "work at his shop." The boy simply refused. He never confronted his father directly, but told his mother that he would beg in the streets or go hungry rather than work at his father's shop.

Since Jagat had acquired a reputation of being a good person and the family business was flourishing, many offers of marriage started pouring in. The father wanted his son to marry a girl from a rich house—he wanted a *kunba* (extended kin or affines) in which men were like him and would drink, gamble, and visit women. On the other hand, Jagat had said clearly that his only condition for the marriage was that the girl should be educated. For a while there was no solution to this impasse. Then a retired colonel whose daughter was a graduate approached them. The family was the kind that Manjit's son liked, but they had very little money to offer as dowry. Acting as a mediator, Manjit's mother's brother's son fixed a meeting between the girl's parents, Manjit, and her *mama*. "We did not hide the true situation from them, you know, about the way that the head of the family was behaving," Manjit told me, "but the girl's father said, 'Our concern is with the boy'" (*sanu tan ji munde nal matlab hai*). But how to manage the boy's father's consent?

After much debate the subject was approached by Manjit's *mama*, in the presence of some other older kin of the recalcitrant father. As a reasonable "outsider," I was invited to come along. "After all we cannot turn down every offer. People will begin to wonder whether there is something wrong with your family"—this was the refrain of the discussions. Manjit's husband sat in a corner in a chair. Manjit sat on the floor, her head covered, refusing to lift her eyes up to anyone. Her husband seemed like he was tied in knots. Everyone had expected that he would shout and rage. But he simply nodded, looking sullen, and said "*jo twadi marzi*—whatever you wish."

"You do not have to do anything, we will run around, make all the arrangements," Manjit's *mama* stated.

"Yes, do what you will."

"But he must give his word that he will stand in the ceremony as the boy's father; he will not shame us," Manjit demanded, suspicious of this capitulation without any resistance on her husband's part.

The preparations began. Then came the much feared "obstacle"—a fortnight before the actual event, Manjit's husband completely denied that he had given consent. "That was just an act," he claimed. At this stage, Manjit and her son were truly fed up. They declared that the wedding would take place anyway. If he, as the father, refused to stand with them, then they could not possibly shame him by having a big wedding, but they would go to a *gurudwara* (a Sikh temple) or to an Arya Samaj (a Hindu reform sect) priest and have a simple religious ceremony performed. When her husband saw how determined they were, he again gave in. This time though his sullen acquiescence was replaced by an inexplicable enthusiasm. The wedding was to be on a scale no one in the kin group could rival. Money was poured out like water, said everyone. Manjit said her heart trembled: "What could be the meaning of all this?" She expected some new catastrophe to arise at any moment. But the wedding went off peacefully.

Within a month of the marriage ceremony, the troubles started. Sardar Ji, Manjit's husband, insisted that the bride must be sent away.[11] "I did not consent to the marriage," he said. "That was only an act." All those who had negotiated the agreement with him were called for a meeting, including myself. He was adamant. So was Manjit. The bride was someone's daughter, someone's sister; you could not trample on their honor like this. People would say that the bride was sent home because she did not bear a good character. Who knows? Some enemies might say that the boy was impotent, unable to consummate his marriage. Had Sardar Ji thought of all the implications? He simply laughed. He had staged a drama—it was theater, couldn't you all see it? What else was the meaning of getting the bride home not even in a decorated car but in a *palaki* (palanquin) on the shoulders of four *kahars* (a caste group with one of the ritual functions of carrying the bridal palanquin on their shoulders on behalf of their patron caste—a custom hardly ever followed in urban contexts now)? Do marriages take place like that any more? No, it was a scene designed by him, literally lifted out of a scene from a Hindi film, but the film was over—the heroine must go back.

Manjit refused to send the girl to her parents' place. Then began the daily struggle to protect the bride from the wrath of her husband's father. He would get drunk, call her into his room, and beat her. Neighbors would sometimes see her running out from the house in a disheveled condition. Rumors were beginning to spread that he fancied her. Once when I was in their house and saw what was happening, I threatened to call the police, but he threatened me in turn. Manjit begged for peace. The girl simply refused to talk.

Sometimes a kindly neighbor would call the young bride into their house when it became obvious that she was standing in the street waiting for the drunken abuses to stop. An elaborate pretence of hearing and not hearing would be maintained on these occasions while the neighbor offered tea, the girl politely declined, and small talk was carried on frantically to cover the obvious and dirty abuses pouring into the house for everyone to hear. Finally, with the consent and encouragement of Manjit, against all the cultural norms of a joint family, her son set up house separately with his wife.[12]

Manjit was separated from her son, his wife, and their two children for five years. They would meet secretly, and when her husband came to know of these meetings, he would abuse Manjit, occasionally slapping her, which he had never done before. Manjit's stance was as if she was turned to stone. No reaction showed on her face. She did not abuse him; she did not abuse his family. "I could not bear that he lift a hand against another's daughter, but as for me, I was now in the habit of enduring. Regularly I did my *puja* (worship) and *path* (recitation of sacred texts). I served him as much as I could, but I could never sit and talk to him."

In time Manjit's son grew in prestige as he became established in his own business. His father grew progressively frail. Heavy drinking, intemperate eating, and "something that seemed to eat at him from the inside," as one of his relatives put it, made him prone to several chronic diseases. His strength failed. After six years, Manjit's son came back to the family home with his own wife and two sons, and clearly the household reins passed into his hands. By that time his father's eyesight had gone, his kidneys were failing, and he was completely bedridden.

I would not say that there was no vengeance exacted on the father. Although he was kept in comfort, no member of the household ever spoke to him except when necessary. Manjit found a lot of joy in her grandchildren. Reflecting on her life, she does not feel she had anything to complain about. I continued to visit her over the years. "You know everything," she would say. "It was a bad time, but by the grace of God it passed. Never have I had to bear any dishonor from my son or his wife."

A SKETCH OR A FRAGMENT

Manjit's patience in biding her time—shadowing time to seize particular moments when she could impose her vision of the truth of her family—makes her more of a stalker than a rebel. Indeed, her conversations were always peppered with statements about time. *Vakat di mar hai, vakat ne bade sitam dhaye, vakat kadna si*—that is, it is how time strikes, time showered great cruelties, the time had to be made to pass: the vision of time in all these statements was one of a cruel perpetrator. She as a woman had the duty to show patience (*sabar*); one could very well imagine that she appears here as passive, simply waiting for things to change. Yet I would suggest that there is a tremendous struggle to escape from the narrative positioning that is assigned to her by the more powerful actors—her husband and his mother. Overtly it is her husband who is aggressive, violent, but who seems to have lacked the resources to truly "author" his story. This is the reading of the situation if we take the standing that different actors have acquired within the kinship network. The narrative, however, does not reveal itself in an elegant linear movement. It is rather like a text that has been scratched through and written many times. Further, while at the time of the ethnography there was a merging of the narrative voices of Manjit, her son, and her son's wife, one cannot be certain that violence done to the young bride would remain inert. Punjabi life was full of incidents in which the power of narratives that had lain inert in the times of the fathers came alive and started a new cycle of injury, violence, or revenge in the time of the sons.[13] I do believe, though, that what I have described in the case of Manjit is a picture of culture and a form of life as it is created in the conflicts of generations and of the sexes.

What is evident is that there are narrative, symbolic, and societal forms in which this diffused violence is woven. In the process of being articulated and sometimes practiced, violence seems to define the edges at which experimentation with a form of life as a *human form of life* occurs. "Can one keep one's standing if the male head of the household refuses to stand as the 'head' of the family that is entering into marriage negotiations?" "Is beating a girl who is of another family and is a bride of the house to be tolerated in silence?" "Shall I let go of my son now rather than maintain the form of a joint family that is crumbling?" In Manjit's case each of these questions was worked through engagement with violence. There are other households in which the experimentation with violence in these kinds of edges happens not through physical violence but violations of other kinds. But what is significant is that these are part of the speech through which, even in the face of violation, one asks for recognition from one's culture, and in turn recognizes this culture. This experimentation with the making of culture is quite different from the other kind of violence to which Manjit was subjected but of which she could never speak. It is to this thick curtain of silence that I now turn.

The violence that I have described here forms a pattern that occurs with different variations in the weave of Punjabi life—in the interior of families and kinship groups. The interior here is not that which is completely hidden, but that which shows itself or is shown, in the performative techniques actors deploy to make the conflict and violence present on public occasions. The ability to speak the violence is within the recesses of this culture of performance and storytelling, within the domains of family and kinship. Time is not purely something represented but is an agent that "works" on relationships—allowing them to be reinterpreted, rewritten, sometimes overwritten—as different social actors struggle to author stories in which collectivities are created or re-created. Within this context the violence of the Partition is folded into the experimentation with different voices and the different modalities in which narratives of families develop.

Let us contrast this with the frozen slide quality of the narrations or rather the "non-narrations" of the violence of the Partition itself. Manjit herself, when she agreed to talk to me about the events of the Partition, decided to produce a one-page written document that was full of gory metaphors like "rivers of blood flowing" and "white shrouds covering the landscape as far as the eye could see." General stories of the events of the Partition made references to some famous instances—for example, a village in which the menfolk killed all the women when they suspected that an attack by a crowd of Muslims was imminent, or a village in which there was no room in the well for more bodies after all the young women had thrown themselves into it.[14] Such stories emplotted the incidents within a heroic narrative in which ordinary women behaved like the famous mythological figures of Padmavati or Krishnadevi, for they chose heroic death over dishonor.[15] Such stories frame the violence in a manner that can be assimilated into the culture's experimentation with the edges of human experience. Even in the face of horrific death, men know how to behave according to norms of masculinity—women know what it takes to preserve the honor of their men.

One step further from this edge are the stories of the Partition for which all authorship is lost. For instance, I heard the story of a woman who had been gang-raped by a group of men from the same *biradari,* or kin group. Left naked and unconscious in the inner courtyard, she was brought to consciousness by the efforts of the women of the same *biradari* and urged to bathe and wear some clothes. She refused to get up, rolling on the floor and saying she would die, *would die* on that very *dalhiz* (threshold), hungry and naked. Or there was the bizarre story of Muslim women in Delhi who were abducted and marched naked to the river to the accompaniment of a band as if in a wedding procession, and made to bathe in the Yamuna amidst Sanskrit chants to purify them so that they could be "reconverted" to Hinduism. All such stories were framed by the anonymous collective voice "It was heard those days" or "Strange were the stories one heard." No one ever authored these stories—they were only heard.

Although Manjit herself did not ever speak to me or by all accounts to anyone of what happened to her between the time that she was abducted and recovered by the army, I feel that the widely circulated general stories of the brutalities done to women during the Partition created a certain field of force within which her later narrative moved. Consider, for instance, her husband's anger that as a poor relative and a much older man, he may have been made into a sacrificial scapegoat in marrying a "spoiled" girl. Then there was Manjit's own sense that she could not speak, or her husband's mother's veiled references to women who eat the dung of men: these allusions pointed to the fact that the family remained within the field of force of the original story of abduction and rape. Yet all emotion pertaining to that original event was deflected to other stories that were "sayable" within the kinship universe of Punjabi families.

I have tried to conceptualize the violence that occurs within the weave of life as lived in the kinship universe as having a sense of the past continuous, while the sudden and traumatic violence that was part of the Partition experience seems to have been frozen. Time cannot perform its work of writing, rewriting, or revising in the case of the second kind of violence. Let me attempt to relate this difference to the double register on which one can read the idea of the "form of life" in Wittgenstein's *Philosophical Investigations*.

The idea of the form of life is usually taken to emphasize or underscore the social nature of language and of human conduct. As Stanley Cavell suggests, however, if all that Wittgenstein meant to do was to dismantle the idea of isolated individuals in their use of language, then the concept does not have very much to offer us. Cavell argues that when Wittgenstein talks about human beings agreeing to the language they use, this agreement is not to be understood as an agreement in opinions, or even as a contractual agreement as in the notion of shared ideas and beliefs. Rather, there are two ways in which the notion of agreement can be read: the first is the agreement in the *forms* that life may take, and the second is the idea of what distinguishes *life* itself as human.

As for the forms that life may take, there are numerous examples in the *Investigations* that within the notion of the human there may well be disputation between the generations and that culture is inherited over these disputations. Thus, there are what Cavell calls horizontal differences in the forms that human life takes—differences, for instance, in the institution of marriage or property. Agreement over forms of life in this sense is what constitutes different forms—it is not agreement over what constitutes life itself. Cavell captures this kind of distinction by drawing attention to the difference in meaning between such neighboring terms as inauguration and convocation, on the one hand, and eating, pecking, or pawing, on the other.

The latter set of terms point to the way in which the idea of forms of life may be read with emphasis this time upon the term *life*. This especially pertains to the idea that specific strengths and scale of the human body and the human senses and the human voice are not fixed in advance. Thus testing the limits of the human takes the notion of evolving the criteria to be applied to the condition of being human itself. For example, the criteria of *pain* do not apply to the realm of the inorganic or to machines. Similarly, according to Wittgenstein, we may say that an animal expresses fear or joy, but can we say that it expresses *hope?* Just as the difference between inauguration and coronation expressed the idea of horizontal differences, of differences in form, so for Cavell the linguistic expressions of, say, eating, pecking, and pawing express vertical differences, differences in life— between being a human being, a bird, or an animal. The limits of the idea of the human seem to evoke the sense that life itself has been put into question, as if one cannot fall from being human without bringing this larger sense of life into jeopardy.

It is this notion of form of life, that is, its vertical sense of testing the criteria of what it is to be human, that I think is implicated in the understanding of Manjit's relation to the non-narrative of her experience of abduction and rape. Men beat up their wives, commit sexual aggression, shame them in their own self-creations of masculinity—but such aggression is still "sayable" in Punjabi life through various kinds of performative gestures and through storytelling.[16] Contrast this with the fantastic violence in which women were stripped and marched naked in the streets, or the magnitudes involved, or the fantasy of writing political slogans on the private parts of women. This production of bodies through a violence that was seen to tear apart the very fabric of life was such that claims over culture through disputation became impossible. If words now appear, they are like broken shadows of the motion of everyday words. Can one say, after all, of such mutilation that *os di izzat lut gayi*—her honor was robbed, as one says of rape in the singular? Or *aurat tan roz varti jandi hai*—a woman is used/exchanged/consumed every day? Such words were indeed uttered and have been recorded by other researchers, but it was as if one's touch with these words and hence with life itself had been burned or numbed. The hyperbolic in Manjit's narration of the Partition recalls Wittgenstein's sense of the conjunction of the hyperbolic with the groundless.

I suggest, therefore, that what becomes the non-narrative of this violence is what is unsayable within the forms of everyday life. I suggest, further, that it is because the range and the scale of the human that is tested and defined and extended in the disputations proper to everyday life move through the unimaginable violence of the Partition into forms of life that are seen as not belonging to life proper. That is to say, these experiments with violence raise certain doubts about life itself, and not only about the *forms* it could take. Was it a man or a machine that plunged a knife into the private parts of a woman after raping her? Were those men or animals that went around killing and collecting castrated penises as signs of their prowess? These are not, however, simply places of doubt about the human—for the terror of the violation of the Partition was precisely that victims *knew* their perpetrators to be human: that is what puts life itself into question. There is a deep moral energy in the refusal to represent some violations of the human body, for these violations are seen as being "against nature," as defining the limits of life itself. The precise range and scale of the *human* form of life is not knowable in advance, any more than the precise range of the meaning of a word is knowable in advance. But the intuition that some violations cannot be verbalized in everyday life is to recognize that work cannot be performed on these within the burned and numbed everyday.

Have I come perilously close to arguing either that pain is intrinsically incommunicable, or that there is a givenness to human nature that provides limits to ways of being human? On both of these accounts let me say that an encounter with pain is not a one-shot, arm's length transaction. As I have argued earlier, to deny someone's claim that she is in pain is not an intellectual failure, it is a spiritual failure—the future between us is at stake. Those violations of the body cannot be spoken, for they create the sense in oneself that one is a thing, a beast, or a machine; these stand in contrast to the violations that can be scripted in everyday life when time can be allowed to do its work of reframing or rewriting the memories of violence.

In the case of Manjit, one may say that her capacity to engage in everyday life was directly related to the fact that as far as the events of the Partition were concerned, language just left her. The lack of sociability of the texts she may have spoken or heard at the vertical boundary, when life itself was being redefined, her silence, also constitutes her reproach. I believe it is this quality of reproach that is buried in the narrative performances of Manjit in relation to the other violence that is speakable in her life.

Perhaps I might draw on the difference Heidegger suggests between that which has the mode of being of things and that which has the mode of being of work. The oscillation between the extraordinary violence and the everyday violence is clearly not the oscillation of the tick-tock of a clock. The contrast between the mode of things and the mode of work points to the difference I have been struggling to articulate. In the lives of women like Manjit, it is the mode of work that defines their relation to the violence in everyday lives. Conversely, the abduction and possible rape she experienced cannot be subjected to work within the contours in which her life has been lived. But we must remember that although crystallized narratives of the Partition celebrate the lives of only those women who offered themselves up for heroic sacrifice, there were countless men and women who carried on the work of everyday life in the midst of riots and afterwards. Women who made their peace with those who had abducted them, who resisted being "recovered" and sometimes mourned the loss of the humanity of their abductors with them rather than against them, are not inscribed in the stories of heroic sacrifice. Consider the haunting story of two Muslim women, abducted and made pregnant by a Sikh man. They had been recovered by the military authorities and placed in a camp while waiting to be returned to their relatives in Pakistan. They disappeared one night. When they returned the next day and were interrogated by the authorities, they confessed that they had wanted to set eyes on the father of their unborn children one last time.[17] The anxiety that comes to the fore in the literature and cinema on the Partition as to whether one is human, whether what one has encountered is the limit of life itself, is overcome, even if only momentarily, by the insertion of the everyday and by the very poverty of words that constitutes its responsiveness to the violence.

I am reminded here of the attention Deleuze asks us to pay to what might be *a* life.[18] For him, no one has described *a* life better than Charles Dickens if we take the indefinite article as an "index of the transcendental." Deleuze goes on to recount the story of a disreputable man held in contempt by everyone. But when he is thought to be dying, those taking care of him show respect and even love, but as soon as it becomes clear that he is not going to die, they go back to their earlier dispositions of contempt toward him. Deleuze asks us to contemplate that moment between his life and death when everyone around him senses that it is a moment characterized only as *a* life playing with death. As Deleuze says, "The life of the individual gives way to an impersonal and yet singular life that releases a pure event freed from accidents and external life, that is from the subjectivity and objectivity of what happens."[19]

This moment for Deleuze is not that of individualization but of singularization. What I found compelling in my relations with Manjit was her recognition that her violation was of an order that the whole principle of life stood violated and that to put it back into words could not be done except with extreme hesitation. Hence the boundaries she had created between saying and showing could not be crossed by careless invitations to conversation such as: Tell me what happened.

WOMEN AND DEATH

The anthropological portraiture of women and death has shown the intimacy of tasks that women perform in relation to death. I have argued throughout this part of the book that the existential status of death in relation to life is not a simple given. I did not learn this from textbooks but from the way men and women I worked with attended to their relations, their obstinate turn toward the ordinary. There is a complex relation between *a* life and life so that how one lives in relation to one's own and others' deaths turns out to be a project of how one protects not only a *form* of life over disputations, criticisms, and recognition in the fact of change— but also how one protects the institution of *life as lived in the singular.*

In choosing to bring the singularity of the lives of Asha and Manjit into soft focus, I am not proposing that they are somehow representative of Hindu women, but that in the delicate task of finding voice and withholding it in order to protect it, they show the possibilities of a turn to the ordinary. The realization of the spiritual in their lives is not simply a living out of a script of a Hindu wife or widow, but it is finding a voice in challenging the kind of simulacrum of voice that emerged in the Constituent Assembly debates.

One of the films that Cavell has studied most is Max Ophuls's *Letter from an Unknown Woman,* in which he shows how the death of a woman and the appearance of her voice in the form of a letter takes away the man's taste for existence.[20] This is not the place to recount the entire argument—I am interested in one aspect of it. In opening his discussion of the film, Cavell says, "When the man in Max Ophuls's film *Letter from an Unknown Woman* reaches the final words of the letter addressed to him by the, or by some, unknown woman, he is shown—according to well-established routines of montage—to be assaulted by a sequence of images from earlier moments in the film. This assault of images proves to be death-dealing."[21] Why so? It is worth hearing Cavell's own words on this point:

> Of course, they must make the man feel guilt and loss; but the question is why, for a man whose traffic has been the sentiments of remorse and loss, the feeling this time is fatal. Surely, it has to do with the letter itself, beginning as from the region of death ("By the time you read this I may be dead") and ending in the theme of nostalgia ("If only . . . if only . . . "). And of course, it has to do with the fact that there is a double letter, the depicted one, the one bearing the title *Letter from an Unknown Woman*, this film that ends soon but distinctly after, narrated from the beginning, it emerges, by the voice of a dead woman, ghost-written.[22]

Cavell here is depicting how, in receiving this film, we, as audience, might feel the force of coming to know that the film is ghost-written—the second time we see the images, we are enclosed in a temporality of the already past, the voice of the woman is already that of a ghost. I must confess that in reading many scholarly accounts of "Partition narratives" this is the feeling I had—as if the accounts were ghost-written. Cavell was not perhaps thinking of ethnography. Yet as ethnographers we must surely be haunted by the thought that our texts might just have words whose touch with life has been lost or numbed—ghost-written? I hope that the singularity of lives depicted here might take us in the ethnography of the ordinary to that moment when we say, "My spade is turned"—and to recognize that as a spiritual moment.

In *Philosophical Investigations*, Wittgenstein writes:

> But how is *telling* done? When are we said to *tell* anything?—What is the language game of telling?
>   I should like to say: you regard it much too much as a matter of course that one can tell anything to anyone. That is to say: we are so much accustomed to communication through language, in conversation, that it looks to us as if the whole point of communication lay in this: someone else grasps the sense of my words—which is something mental: he as it were

takes it into his own mind. If he then does something further with it as well, that is no part of the immediate purpose of language.[23]

Here as well as elsewhere in the text, Wittgenstein draws attention to the limits of a model of language that assumes that the only thing language does is to communicate. We saw in Manjit's case that there is a boundary between what is being told and what is being shown. The distinction between saying and showing, though, is not simply the distinction between word and gesture. Words can show one's numbed relation to life just as gesture can tell us what forms of life, what forms of dying, become the soil on which words can grow or not.[24]

SIX

Thinking of Time and Subjectivity

THIS CHAPTER IS A REFLECTION ON ISSUES of temporality that surface from the first part of the book as well as a bridge to the next set of chapters in which I try to capture my sense of adjacency to the violence among the survivors in Delhi in 1984. My arguments are not a comprehensive review of notions of time in anthropology—they stem from a very specific issue in the ethnography of the two events under consideration. In the last chapter we saw how Manjit made frequent references to the agency of time. Time is what could strike one, time is what could heal one, she said. I was further interested to note that references to specific kinds of events during the Partition, ones that came to condense the horrors of the Partition in collective memory such as trains arriving at stations with loads of people who were killed or severely wounded as they made their way from one part of the divided country to another, or references to magnitudes reappeared in panic rumors during communal riots. Thus I became interested in questions of temporality, not as representation but as work. What is the work that time does in the creation of the subject? What is the relation between structure and event here?

There is a venerable history of thinking about time in anthropology that is structured around the relation between natural rhythms and social rhythms, synchrony and diachrony, cyclical time and linear time, and repetition and irreversibility.[1] Issues of cultural variability have been addressed through the literature on calendars asking which calendars are geared toward practical activities (seasons for sowing or harvesting, making time schedules, etc.) and which provide a means of representing abstract concepts such as those of the auspicious and the inauspicious around which members of a given society might orient themselves.[2] Are ritual calendars or genealogies about representing the *passage* of time, or are they about *suppressing* the idea of duration? These are, indeed, important questions, but they address the relation between time and subjectivity only in an oblique manner. A couple of observations relevant for framing the latter part of the argument may be in order here.

One way to think of subjectivity is to think of the differences between phenomenal time and physical time that have engaged both philosophers and anthropologists. The attempt to give a structure to these differences often revolves around the difference between the time of occurrence and the time of telling, sometimes conceptualized as the difference between historical truth and narrative truth.[3] For example, Alfred Gell's laudable attempts to clear up certain metaphysical clouds in anthropological discussions around time are basically a restatement of this difference. Gell bases his discussion of temporality on McTaggart's distinction between what he calls an A series and a B series.[4] An A-series notion of time, he argues, is a categorization of events according to past, present, or future, whereas a B-series categorization refers to their occurrence before or after in relation to *each other*. Gell's basic thesis is that "Very roughly, A-series temporal considerations apply in the human sciences because agents are always embedded in a context of situation about whose nature and evolution they entertain moment-to-moment beliefs, whereas B-series temporal considerations also apply because agents build up temporal 'maps' of their world and its penumbra of possible worlds whose B-series characteristics reflect the genuinely B-series layout of the universe itself."[5] It seems to me that despite the way in which Gell uses propositional logic to clarify these points, his discussion is basically pointing to the fact that we can put a date on events such as, say, the death of Mahatma Gandhi on January 30, 1948, even though we might debate whether suspicion of the Hindu Right in Indian politics happened before or after. I agree that some kinds of events can be fixed in time by putting a date on them, so long as we realize that there are other kinds of events for which to be dateable means something quite different (namely, that they are not timeless and eternal). For example, could one put an exact date on when one fell in love or out of love, although when such events become public as in a wedding, they can be "fixed" on an objective calendar? At one level this distinction might be contrasted as public time and private time. At a deeper level, though, there are publicly observable events for which we cannot name an observable "now." For example, in Wittgenstein's rendering of time as transfiguration, who can say when a walk becomes a skip or speaking becomes transfigured into singing? The point is not that there are moment-to-moment beliefs and then there are stable temporal maps, but rather that the particular mode in which the subject is immersed in the temporal shapes the contour of the event. At this stage let me call Nelson Goodman to my aid in stating why issues around phenomenological renderings of time and subjectivity ask for a different sensibility than that which assumes that these differences can be grounded in a sharp separation between physical time and phenomenal time. Goodman says:

> Even though phenomenal time and physical time do not move with respect to each other, the relationship between them is far from simple. Physical time divides into particles too small to be perceived; some events in physical time lie outside phenomenal time; some physically simultaneous events are not phenomenally simultaneous. Indeed, phenomenal time may cut across physical time in amazing ways; at one moment, I may see a leaf fall, hear a word that was spoken a few seconds earlier, and see a stellar explosion that occurred some centuries before that. Moreover, a brief physical event may occupy considerable phenomenal time, while a longer physical event may occupy only an instant of phenomenal time.[6]

In other words, the simultaneity of events at the level of phenomenal time that are far apart in physical time make the whole of the past simultaneously available. We will see how this particular feature of time as past, present, and future gives a certain force to rumors and accounts for the lethal quality of language in the phenomenology of panic.

FEELING OF PASTNESS

In the first part of the book I suggested that although the Partition was of the past if seen through homogeneous units of measurable time, its continued presence in people's lives was apparent in story, gesture, and conversation.[7] Though of the past, it did not have a *feeling* of pastness about it. Such questions did not pose any dilemmas at the time of my work with survivors of 1984, for the presence of violence and its immediacy was palpable through every sense—seeing, hearing, smelling, touching. Also, at the time I worked with the survivors, the danger of their being violated or killed was not yet in the past. The sense of the present then was marked by a fearful anticipation. The survivors in the locality were living not only with memories embodied in the walls of houses, on the charred doors, in the little heaps of ashes in the street, but also with threats embodied in words and gestures as the perpetrators of the violence continued to live in the same neighborhoods as the victims. The blind complexity of the present made it difficult to draw boundaries around the event of Mrs. Gandhi's assassination. When did the event begin and when did it end? I try to reflect on these issues by thinking of the relation between time and subjectivity and what counts as the past. I am not interested in logical puzzles arising from the solipsism of the present moment but rather in the fact that I, the ethnographer, was present to the violence in 1984 in ways that were quite different from the way that the events of the Partition left their tracks in my ethnography.

Is there one duration or are there many? The question is a haunting one. In a famous passage on time, Bergson says, "When we are sitting on the bank of a river, the flowing of the water, the gliding of a boat or the flight of a bird, the uninterrupted murmur of our deep life, are for us three different things, or a single one, at will.[8] As Gilles Deleuze observes in his insightful reflections on this passage, Bergson endows attention with the power of appropriating without dividing and thus of being both one and several. The simultaneity of one and many becomes possible only because Bergson thinks of duration as having the power to encompass itself. In Deleuze's words, "The flowing of the water, the flight of the bird, the murmur of my life form three fluxes; but only because my duration is one of them, and also the elements that contain the two others."[9] Duration then is not simply one of the aspects of subjectivity—it is the very condition of subjectivity.

Of various anthropologists writing on questions of subjectivity and time, Desjarlais has perhaps best captured the sense of multiplicity of time as experience and not simply as different ways of bending or deforming Newtonian time.[10] The Yolma Buddhist woman Kisang, who offered ongoing reflections on her living and dying to Desjarlais, made constant references to time much as Asha and Manjit evoked time as sometimes a cruel perpetrator, sometimes a healer. Thus, Desjarlais offers the idea that Kisang was living and dying within several culturally recurrent engagements with time. The presence of death within the lives of the living, he says, often brings the passage of time and the effects of time in sharp relief. He identifies several ways Kisang had of thinking of time and how she thought these might contribute to the actual timing of her death. Desjarlais talks of the *effects of time* as in the erosion of the body, the *person in time* as living in anticipation of death, the *time of dying,* as in Kisang's awareness that sometimes this would entail a specific and sometimes a stretched-out period of waiting for death, *unknown time* as in not being able to specify the exact moment in which death would occur, *fated time* as in the moment of death having been written on the forehead . . . and so on.[11]

Much as I admire the meticulous attention that Dejarlais has given to this multiplicity and how it was woven into the way Kisang reflected on her experience of living in a dying space, it appears from this description as if these various temporal fluxes reside on some flat surface and the eye can move from one kind of time to another as if moving in space.[12] Manjit and Asha, I feel, instruct us otherwise. In Manjit's case the difference between the past that is preserved as if frozen and the past as the passage of events of her life after her marriage, her motherhood, and the constant work she performs on her relationships invites reflections on the modalities in which the past becomes present in our lives. What is the meaning of her frequent reiteration of time being the true agent of her life? In Asha's case her sense of being in two temporalities—one that connected her past to her projected "some future life" and the second in which her present relationships were like "two sticks meeting in the middle of the sea"—gave the present a particular hue. I want to try and see if Bergson's notion of the past as given all at once might help us to think of the nature of temporality in question here.

One particular passage in Bergson that Deleuze quotes is particularly striking: "Memory, laden with the whole of the past, responds to the appeal of the present state by two simultaneous movements, one of *translation,* by which it moves in its entirety to meet experience, thus *contracting* more or less, though without dividing, with a view to action; the other of *rotation* upon itself, by which it turns toward the situation of the moment, presenting to it that side of itself which may prove to be the most useful."[13] Deleuze evokes this paragraph with regard to a particular question—that is, how can pure reflection take on a psychological existence? How can the virtual coexist with the actual?[14] Deleuze suggests that for Bergson, the present makes an appeal according to the requirements or the needs of the present situation. In making this leap we place ourselves not generally in the elements of the past as such but in a particular region of the past. For certain purposes we can make analogies between space and time, between temporal duration and spatial extent. Yet if time is not to be imagined as if it were another dimension of space, then this region of the past is not to be compared with, say, a part of a picture that was in darkness and that we have made to appear by shining a light on it. Rather, each level corresponds to a contraction of the past. Deleuze explains the process as follows:

> And Bergson adds: There are also dominant recollections, like *remarkable points,* which vary from one level to another. A foreign word is spoken in my presence: given the situation this is not the same thing as wondering what the language in general, of which this word is a part, could be or what person said this once, said this word or a similar one, to me. Depending on the case, I do not leap into the same region of the past; I do not place myself on the same level; I do not appeal to the same essential characteristics.[15]

Thus memory is, for Bergson, laden with the whole of the past, but it can respond to the appeal of the present only through certain processes—these he identifies as processes of translation and rotation. The former involves contraction and the latter orientation. As I see it, in the former case we move from a general past to the level of contraction that can meet the appeal of this moment, as, for instance, in the example of identifying a particular foreign word that I try to recall. In the case of rotation, it is as if the past itself turns to present its most useful facet to us. My purpose here is not to give a detailed exposition of Bergson (with whose work I am not fully conversant) but to extract from his work two points of interest to me. The first is that the past is not remembered as a succession of "nows"—rather, it is because the whole of the past is in some ways given all at once that it can be actualized in a contracted form. Second, although the process of actualization might involve translation that appeals to the present, there is also the process of rotation in which, independent of my will, certain regions of the past are actualized and come to define the affective qualities of the present moment.[16] In my fieldwork I experienced the latter in the regions of rumor in which the past was present as whole—contracted in response to appeals of a collective kind, which we will see elaborated in the next chapter. Here language acquired an infectious quality—words were not reined in, but they spread, as the popular saying goes, like wildfire. Similarly, the presence of rumor in the life of Manjit lived as that unspoken past that remained virtual—surrounding her relationships yet never given direct expression in speech. This is what gives language its lethal power.

I saw the work of translation in the manner in which ideas of hope were not seen in transcendence or in escaping to a different future but in being able to descend into the ordinary by what I would call a temporality of second chances.[17] In the first chapter I drew attention to the idea that what it is to inhabit the same space of devastation *again,* to make your dwelling with the broken pieces of rubble, to stalk time, to inhabit the world in a gesture of mourning—all this gives everyday life a quality of something recovered. This is not some kind of oriental fatalism but an acceptance of finitude in a gesture that assumes that hope is always hope against the evidence (otherwise it might be expectation?). In the next part of the book I am also compelled to attend to the possible failures of such a project when the turn to the ordinary is blocked.

TURNING INTO STONE

The pressure to interpret violence through a model of trauma is evident in a wide range of disciplines, ranging from literary theory to psychoanalysis. At the same time, many scholars have pointed out the dangers of a pathological public sphere brought into existence in a popular culture that seems mesmerized by stories of suffering and the spectacle of wounded and dismembered bodies.[18] I do not deny that there is a paradox in that communities created around suffering might become communities of ressentiment, yet at the same time it seems to me that everything might be at stake or nothing might be at stake in the question of whether social sciences become complicit in participating in the silencing of suffering. Here, simply as a gesture toward discussions to come later, I visit this question through two different theoretical stances toward violence.

The first stance is in theories of trauma in which drawing from a wide variety of literary sources and individual case histories, it is argued that the wound inflicted on the self (unlike physical wounds) is not something that simply heals with time. Drawing upon the works of Freud (or at least one interpretation of them), the literary critic Cathy Caruth has argued that the "wound of the mind—the breach in the mind's experience of time, self, and world" is like an event that is experienced too soon and too unexpectedly to be fully assimilated as experience.[19] It is only when it imposes itself again on consciousness in the form of nightmares or repetitive compulsions that the survivor can take account of this experience. In Caruth's summary of the problem:

What the parable of the wound and the voice tells us, and what is at the heart of Freud's writing on trauma, both in what it says and in the stories it unwittingly tells us, is that trauma is much more than a pathology, or the simple illness of a wounded psyche: it is always the story of a wound that cries out, that addresses us in an attempt to tell us of a reality or truth that is not otherwise available. This truth, in its delayed appearance and its belated address, cannot be linked only to what is known, but also to what remains unknown in our very actions and our language.[20]

The notion of trauma as bearing witness to some forgotten wound is a trope that is often used in Indian historiography and in public pronouncements on the problem of sectarian violence. Such violence is often rendered as stemming from the originary wound of the Partition, which was never fully acknowledged in Indian society and polity. Individual trauma in such literary accounts as those of Caruth and Felman slides into collective trauma,[21] and the notion of literary voice provides the connection between these two. Thus, for instance, Caruth argues that since traumatic experience is not fully assimilated as it occurs, questions about witnessing cannot be asked in a straightforward way—these must be spoken in a language that is somehow literary and that cannot be reduced to the thematic content of the text. As Caruth states it, beyond what we can know or theorize, the literariness of the language "persists in bearing witness to some forgotten wound."[22]

I have argued elsewhere that witnessing is not a matter of all or nothing,[23] and I trust that the previous chapters have shown a different picture of witnessing—as in engaging everyday life while holding the poisonous knowledge of violation, betrayal, and the wounded self from seeping into the sociality of everyday life. Caruth and other trauma theorists make a direct transition between individual experience and collective processes, whereas I have suggested that the idea that the reenactment of the past at the collective level is a *compulsion to repeat* seems to short-circuit the complex ways in which we might understand how particular regions of the past are actualized through mediums of rumor, or in the singularity of individual lives as they knit together relations that have become frayed. Caruth, for example, is forceful in her account of repetition:

In modern trauma theory as well, there is an emphatic tendency to focus on the destructive repetition of the trauma that governs a person's life. As modern neurobiologists point out, the repetition of the traumatic experience in the flashback can itself be retraumatizing; if not life-threatening, it is at least threatening to the chemical structure of the brain and can ultimately lead to its deterioration. And this would also seem to explain the high suicide rate of survivors, for example survivors of Vietnam or of concentration camps, who commit suicide only *after* they have found themselves completely in safety. As a paradigm for the human experience that governs history, then, traumatic disorder is, indeed, the apparent struggle to die. The postulation of a drive to death which Freud ultimately introduces in *Beyond the Pleasure Principle*, would seem only to recognize the reality of the destructive force that the violence of history imposes on the human psyche, the formation of history as the endless repetition of previous violence.[24]

There is a somewhat breathless succession of arguments here from destructive repetition in a person's life to neurobiology to history as an endless repetition of previous violence—each component could do with much more careful thinking. For instance, the nature of the real posited in each case is surely of a different order. At another level, the evidence on suicides that occur after a traumatic event when the person is in a relatively safe environment does not account for the other kind of evidence in which one just gives up the struggle and allows oneself to be killed, as reported in situations during war or for inmates of concentration camps.[25] I would submit that the model of trauma and witnessing that has been bequeathed to us from Holocaust studies cannot be simply transported to other contexts in which violence is embedded into different patterns of social-ity.[26] Further, the relation between the literary and the everyday has to be worked out patiently so that while we remain mindful of the way that lit-erary genres influence narrativization of experience in everyday life, we also recognize that there are other ways in which relatedness is created and sustained in everyday life. The idea of unclaimed experience is, of course, central to any theory of experience, but rooting this notion in everyday life might, I suspect, bear different kinds of fruit.

Sometimes in the course of my fieldwork I would come across situations in which I could not say for sure how I knew, in the sense that I felt that I could not tell *precisely* how I knew. For instance, after I had watched Asha's expressions when she talked about her relations to her first husband's family, it dawned upon me that there was something about the temporal depth in which she was seeing relationships that seemed like fragments of a mythical time to me. It was as if she wanted me to know something of her relationships but not to *tell* me something as if that would mark it as simply offered to satisfy my curiosity. I had the same sense with the women in Sultanpuri whose mode of sitting in stillness among the burned houses in the streets where the scenes of carnage had taken place two days before I went there seemed to me not so much a representation of the wounded worlds but an expression of these, much as Wittgenstein talks of the body as being a picture of the soul, by which I take him to mean that the body is an expression of the soul—not its habitation or its representation.

In his reflections on this region of thought in Wittgenstein, Cavell says that remarks that read the body as giving expression to the soul might be read as myths or fragments of a myth that do not exclude the idea that there might be arguments about it[27]—arguments, for instance, on what it means for me to treat someone as one with a soul or how it is that we begin to read a baby as it begins to smile or to pucker its lips as giving expression to the idea of a soul that the baby is developing. What the notion of a myth or fragment of a myth excludes as experience is the idea that one was present at the point of its origin. This is one kind of absence but a necessary one—for one would stop living a myth if one became too curious about explaining it. Thus when the women in Sultanpuri sat in the posture of stillness, letting their bodies grow dirty and disheveled, refusing to comb their hair, thus defiantly as well as sorrowfully embodying pollution and dirt—the thought occurred to me that this was somewhat like the figure of Draupadi in the Mahabharata proclaiming her violation through public expression of her pollution.[28] But I cannot say that the women devised a strategy or that this was a tactic of everyday life carried into the realm of the political. Instead I have to say that thinking of this as living fragments of a myth makes far better sense to me. It was as if the past had turned this face toward them—not that they had translated this past story into a present tactic of resistance.

What might it mean to think that I am absent from or to my own experience? One picture of unclaimed experience comes from Caruth and other trauma theorists who draw attention to the fact that I am unable to give expression to my injury, and it is through such symptoms as repeated nightmares that my wound finds "voice." I am thinking instead of the picture of absence when a particular aspect of the situation simply fails to dawn on me. Thus, for instance, Cavell draws attention to the famous duck-rabbit picture in which by seeing the duck I fail to see the rabbit. This is not because the rabbit has been hidden by the picture—indeed, the picture from one perspective *is* the picture of the rabbit—but rather because that which is present may still be invisible to me. It is this aspect of blindness that I read as providing one way of thinking of what it might mean to be absent from life.

The second image of such absence is in the way in which we become unhooked from our words. In some ways my attachment to my words is an expression of my attachment to my life. Yet, in the case of rumor, it is precisely the failure of signature that makes the words uttered in secrecy or words emanating from a crowd so utterly lethal. The aspect of rumor that has struck me most is that the words that are uttered do not belong to anyone in particular. In some ways the visage of the other that acquires shape in my mind because I have struggled with the singularity of this particular person as the other, struggled with what it means that he or she has a separate existence—this is what leads me to accept that our togetherness is still made up of things I will never fully understand about this person. In contrast, the kind of sociality brought about by rumor solidifies the otherness in ways so that within certain boundaries drawn around categories of persons, one person is perfectly substitutable by another. Thus, for instance, for the crowds proclaiming a Hindu identity and seeking revenge for the assassination of Mrs. Gandhi, the power of rumor effaced the face of the Sikh as a concrete other. Instead, the logic was that if the bodyguards who killed Indira Gandhi were Sikhs, then any Sikh would do as the substitute victim on whom revenge could be enacted. This at least was the imagination at the level of rumor. Interestingly, in the actual enactment of revenge, even within the frenzy of violence perpetrated by crowds, the histories of ongoing relationships in localities could not be effaced and gave shape to the violence within specific local communities. In chapter 8 I will visit the question of how the violence that was proclaimed as a generalized revenge on the world acquired local meanings. Still, the lethal character of voice in the region of rumor continues to haunt me for its power to undo everyday life. Many years after I had completed much of my writing on the riots of 1984, another political leader, Rajiv Gandhi (the son of Indira Gandhi), was assassinated by a female suicide bomber, widely believed to be a member of the Tamil Tigers. That evening outside the residence of his widow, Sonia Gandhi, one heard the slogans shouted by a crowd that had gathered. One of the slogans was as follows:

Bhaiya ke katil zinda hain
Bhabhi hum sharminda hain

Our brother's killers are alive
Oh, *bhabhi* (brother's wife),[29] we are, indeed, ashamed

It was reported in the press the next morning that Mrs. Sonia Gandhi had sent a polite message to the slogan shouters that she did not wish to be disturbed in her grief.

What kind of statement was the crowd making? Read literally, it seems to be an indicative statement about the present, but to one schooled in the grammar of Indian politics its threat is obvious. First, it creates kinship ties not out of love or fidelity but through the rhetoric of vengeance—brotherhood here is created solely through the obligation to kill. Second, the latter part of the verse (*bhabhi,* we are ashamed) is a statement suspended between the present and the future. Like the statement "the sky looks threatening today," I suggest that it is statement about the future via the present moment—the feeling of shame can only be overcome by setting into motion a circle of revenge, settling the obligation to the dead. In immediately refusing to tolerate these slogans, Sonia Gandhi refused a politics of vengeance. At the time of Indira Gandhi's death, the picture of kinship forged in a similar manner (e.g., the slogan stating that you have killed *our* mother) was not overcome, and the consequences were tragic (which is not to say that rumor caused the events to happen, but it certainly authorized them).

What is it to come out of such hallucinated states of being as crowds possessed by the lethal power of rumor? To Cavell this concern presents itself in the form of a question: What is the body's fate under skepticism? I am not contending that the problem of skepticism under literary or philosophical analysis is the same as under anthropological analysis, but I claim there is a symmetry. On the literary and philosophical issues, I take the liberty of quoting Cavell in some detail here:

> A second, and an extended final illustration I choose, from which to study the body's fate under skepticism, are equally familiar moments and more or less familiar as a pair. I ask how it is that we are to understand, at the height of *The Winter's Tale,* Hermione's reappearance as a statue. Specifically, I ask how it is that we are to understand Leontes' acceptance of the "magic" that returns her to flesh and blood and hence to him. This is a most specific form of resurrection. Accepting it means accepting the idea that she had been turned to stone; that that was the right fate for her disappearance from life. So I am asking for the source of Leontes' conviction in the rightness of that fate. Giving the question that form, the form of my answer is now predictable; for her to return to him is for him to recognize her; and for him to recognize her is for him to recognize his relation to her; in particular to recognize what his

denial of her has done to her, hence to him. So Leontes recognizes the fate of stone to be the consequence of his particular skepticism. One can see this as his own sense of numbness of living death projected on the other.[30]

I shall not carry further Cavell's discussion of how *The Winter's Tale* is paired with *Othello* or how one is a commentary upon the other. What I find profound in Cavell's reading of *The Winter's Tale* is the idea that the man's refusal of knowledge of his other is an imagination of stone. In both cases, the refusal to accept the flesh and bloodedness of the other—hence the fate of oneself as an embodied being—gets enacted in terms of staving off the knowledge one has of the other by putting one's faith instead in the world's capacity for rumor.

This takes me to another story about betrayal and the imagination of the woman as made of stone. This is the story of the abandonment of Sita by Rama in the Sanskrit epic Ramayana. Here too Rama knows her to be chaste, and yet he exiles her on the words of a washerwoman, seeing what Sita's visage would be in the gossip of people rather than seeing her visage in his own heart.[31] In the poet Kalidas's subtle rendering: *Avaimi chenam anagheti kintu lokapvado balvan mato me*—I know her to be without stain, but the gossip (literally, denunciation) of people has strength. After he has exiled Sita, Rama lives with a golden statue made to her likeness, and toward the end of the epic, when he is ready to accept her, Sita asks her mother earth to open up and receive her as the proof of fidelity that Rama demands, for what he offers is no recognition at all. I leave aside for now that this imagination of the other as made of stone is perhaps a peculiarly male doubt—thus skepticism turns out to be not only a dateable event but also a gendered one.

With these thoughts hovering between the two parts of the book, it is time to return to the ethnography of rumor, to the violence it engenders and its intimate connection with the form of the state in India. And then finally I show how women themselves incorporate this imagination of stone as a sitting in stillness, as if they were indeed made of stone as a sign of their absence from life. This absence, though, is enacted to reclaim the dead, as one way to inhabit their devastated worlds again. This too was unclaimed experience—but this time in the service of life, its creativity and its unpredictability. To these new tracks on which the story moves, I now invite you, the reader.

SEVEN

In the Region of Rumor

RUMOR OCCUPIES A REGION OF LANGUAGE with the potential to make us experience events, not simply by pointing to them as to something external, but rather by producing them in the very act of telling. In this chapter I try to show how the processes of translation and rotation that we identified work to actualize certain regions of the past and create a sense of continuity between events that might otherwise seem unconnected. Unlike objects around which we can draw boundaries, it is not easy to say when an event begins and when it ends, or for that matter how events in one space-time configuration mime events in another. We might treat the assassination of Indira Gandhi in October 1984 as either a unique event or one that occurred within a history of political assassinations. Alternately, it may be useful to think of it as unfolding within a series of events that included the Partition of India, the rise of the Sikh militant movement in the Punjab, the corresponding counterinsurgency practices of the state in the 1980s, the military action in the premises of the Golden Temple (better known in Punjabi as the Darbar Sahib), and finally the assassination of Mrs. Gandhi. My emphasis here is not on cause and effect but on the chains of connection through which the processes of translation and rotation, mentioned in the last chapter, actualize certain regions of the past. It leads me to think of the social in terms of unfinished stories.[1]

I begin with outlining the incident and then show how language and event constituted each other, gathering the past and making it present in a contracted form. I am not making the argument that language itself had the power to *make* these grievous events out of nothing, but rather that memories that might have lain inert came to life in the form of rumors. Enmeshed into local histories of conflict, such rumors became part and parcel of scenes of devastating local violence. My claim is that the process of rotation as described in Bergson[2] turns around certain facets of the past, making them come alive in the present. The actual translation of these memories into action, however, depended upon a host of local factors without which the specificity of the violence would be hard to understand. In this and the following chapter, I try to show the twin working out of these two processes.

ASSASSINATION OF A PRIME MINISTER

The prime minister of India, Indira Gandhi, was shot by two or more of her security guards who were Sikhs on October 31, 1984, at about 9 A.M., though the public announcement of her death was not made until late in the evening. An aura of secrecy surrounded the event. Speculation was rife in Delhi, where I observed these happenings, as to whether Mrs. Gandhi was alive, though seriously wounded, or dead. There was no official announcement of the religious identity of the assassins until the next morning. However, rumors about her death and the identity of her killers abounded even before the official announcements. People somehow "knew" that she had been killed by her Sikh bodyguards. There was speculation at that time in Delhi about what caused her bodyguards to shoot her as people wondered what consequences this might have for the safety of Sikhs in the city.

As for the genealogy of events, many people connected this assassination to Operation Blue Star, which had been launched by the Indian army in July 1984, allegedly to flush out the militants from the Golden Temple in Amritsar. The Sikh militant leader Bhindranwale was alleged to have died during this operation. The forced entry of the army in the *gurudwara* (Sikh temple, literally, the doorway to the Guru) was seen in this context as a deliberate desecration—many if not most Sikhs found the event deeply hurtful. We shall see the various constructions and counter-constructions of this event later. At this point let me note only that according to many rumors circulating even before the assassination, it was said that right after

Operation Blue Star some Sikhs had taken oaths in *gurudwaras* to avenge this insult by assassinating Mrs. Gandhi before the end of October. There were also rumors, especially after the assassination, that Mrs. Gandhi had been warned by the personnel of the special police security assigned to her that it would be dangerous for her to have Sikh bodyguards, but she had ignored their advice. There were many debates about the morality of the assassination among Hindus and Sikhs in the print media as well as in casual discussions. Even within the Sikh community, opinion was divided as to whether the two bodyguards were to be regarded as martyrs—risking their lives in penetrating the security system of the formidable Indian state[3]—or whether they were to be labeled cowards who had shot a defenseless woman who had trusted them against the advice of her security personnel. It is interesting to note that the identity of the assassins was assumed purely based on rumors. This sense of an uncanny knowledge, I believe, may be traced to the unfinished character of Operation Blue Star—the sense that the story had not been completed with the death of Bhindranwale during this military operation, and therefore it was bound to have a sequel in the form of a calamitous national event.

My interest in this chapter is to see how this event came to be seen as an authorization of a terrible violence against the Sikhs, as not only a revenge against the perpetrators but also as a way of regaining a lost masculinity on the part of Hindus. At the level of discursive forms that authorized such actions, the analysis of rumors continues the themes of nationalism and of the state as essentially a contract between men as husbands and fathers that we analyzed in chapter 2 in the post-Partition debates about the recovery of women. But I go further here, linking this in the next chapter to the spatialization of violence in one of the low-income neighborhoods located on the periphery of Delhi. Thus, while the circulation of images of masculinity and femininity, self and other, humiliation and revenge created a sense of an emergency, not all Sikhs were equally targeted. So how is it that Sikhs living in some spaces became specific targets of violent action while others were spared?

It is, indeed, a difficult task to hold both kinds of explanations together—one level of analysis anchored to the general sense of panic and the other showing the specific ways in which general images of hatred, imperatives to revenge, and so on were translated into actual acts of violence. I argue that the sense of crisis created by the political event of Mrs. Gandhi's assassination became the ground for conditions under which certain groups of people could designate themselves as "enraged Hindus" enacting violence against Sikhs, supposedly as revenge enacted on behalf of a larger Hindu community. Further, even when many Hindus did not directly inflict violence on Sikhs, they participated in the atmosphere of fear and mutual hatred that pervaded the city. Many Hindus and Sikhs found themselves constructing images of self and other from which the subjectivity of experience had been evacuated through the medium of floating rumors. In this production and circulation of hate, the images of perpetrator and victim were frequently reversed depending upon the perspective from which the memories of traumatic events and of everyday violence were seen and relived. In stunning reversals of what was the experience of violence here and now, panic rumors created a kind of screen in which aggressors came to identify themselves and even experience themselves as victims.

In the previous chapter I discussed the famous duck-rabbit image and the "aspect blindness" that this image creates when one picture or the other disappears from view even though it is not hidden anywhere. What we shall see now is an aspect blindness to the present: for the idea of a past in which one was a victim seems to have completely eclipsed the violence being perpetrated against the so-called aggressors *now*. To explain this intriguing phenomenology of panic rumors, I need to give a brief account of the discourse of militancy to which I have referred and to show how the images of Hindu and Sikh embedded in this discourse traveled to become implanted in public consciousness.

THE DISCOURSE OF MILITANCY

The emergence of a militant movement among both Sikhs in India and emigrant Sikhs was an important phenomenon of the 1980s.[4] It is not my intention to provide a comprehensive account of this complex process here. I will only recapitulate some of the images and stereotypes of Hindus and Sikhs in this literature, showing both how these mirror the anxieties around masculinity and citizenship that we detected in the post-Partition debates on the recovery of abducted women and how they became generative of new anxieties around the place of minorities in the state of India.

In the period between 1981 and the end of 1984, Sikh leaders led a series of mass civil disobedience campaigns against the Indian government for fulfillment of several demands while simultaneously propagating the use of violent means for achieving these ends. In the process of formulating these demands, new stereotypes of the images of Hindus and Sikhs were created within the published militant literature, in posters, and in oral discourses. Simultaneously the growth of an intolerant militancy among Hindu fundamentalist groups mirrored many of these stereotypes, especially with regard to the "weak" and "emasculated" Hindu.[5]

In the organization of images in the Sikh militant discourse, the self of the Sikh was portrayed as that of the martyr whose sacrifices had fed the community with its energy in the past.[6] The Hindus simultaneously were represented as weak and effeminate or cunning and sly who had depended earlier on the protection offered by the Sikhs but who were now ready to betray the same erstwhile protectors. In the written and oral discourses of Sikh militancy, the Hindu "character" was envisaged in terms of dangers that it posed to the masculinity of the Sikhs. There was a further move to establish that the history of Sikhs was inscribed on the body of the martyr and was a reflection of the masculine Sikh character while it was the feminine Hindu character that was imprinted on the history of the Indian nation.[7] Thus, masculinity became the defining feature of the Sikh community, while the Hindu community was characterized by an emasculated femininity that, in turn, slides into the idea of the Indian nation.

COMMUNITY, KIN, AND MASCULINITY

Metaphors of male relatedness were used extensively in the oral discourse of the militants to create a sense of community among the Sikhs. Kinship ties, as already suggested, were used in two different senses—one was the true tie of father-son relations to be acknowledged and celebrated; the second was an earlier relation between Hindus and Sikhs that was also considered to be that of a *parent* religion (Hinduism) and its descendant (Sikhism) but that was now imaged on the metaphor of an implied insult of illegitimacy. For instance, in one of his speeches Bhindranwale, while addressing a congregation, stated, "*Khalsa ji* [you, who are the pure ones], the Sikhs are the son of the true king Guru Gobind Singh *ji*. Now, you know that a son must resemble his father. If the son does not resemble his father, then you know the term used for him [i.e., bastard]. If a son does not *behave* like his father, then people begin to view him with suspicion. They [the Hindus] say the Sikhs are the descendants of Hindus. Are they pointing a finger at our pure ancestry—how can a Sikh bear to be called anyone else's son?"[8]

The concern with establishing "pure ancestry" with the accompanying doubts about illegitimacy and true paternity are *male* doubts. They point to the extent to which the imagined nation, whether Sikh or Hindu, was conceived as a masculine nation and belonging was construed as a matter of genealogical connections between fathers and sons. This imagination of being worthy of having a nation, of being able to lay claims on a homeland, moved on the axis of being deserving sons of a valiant father—a claim that was articulated through the motif of being capable of making the sacrifices, bearing pain and hardship as would a martyr. I need only briefly note here that in the Hindu imagery of the nation, the homeland was a *motherland,* and though the nation was conceived as masculine, it was made up of the sons of a mother. The imagery in the nationalist discourse during the struggle against British colonialism represented the nation as a mother who was shackled by foreign rule and laid claims on her valiant sons to rescue her. Thus, the concern with masculinity marked both the Hindu and Sikh militant discourses—but the differential genealogy (sons of a father, or sons of a mother?) as well as the imagination of how one achieves masculine adulthood shaped the notions of self and other in diverse ways.[9] What complicates the situation still further is that in his nonviolent movement, Gandhi transformed the notions of masculinity and femininity, taking the strategies of resistance such as fasting, of offering the body to receive wounds through passive submission rather than the more masculine strategies of violent resistance.[10]

It is interesting to note therefore that in the written and oral discourse of the Sikh militants, it was repeatedly stated that the Sikhs could not belong to a nation that claimed a feminine figure such as Mahatma Gandhi for its father (*bapu*—the affectionate title given to Gandhi by the general populace). The anxiety about the principle of nonviolence as the defining principle of the Indian nationalist struggle, which was said to be "passive" and "womanly," became palpable in the oral discourse, for it seemed to threaten the inheritance of a manly way of confronting evil, further characterized as the natural inheritance of the Sikh. Thus, the nonviolent movement led by Gandhi, it was said, was appropriate only for the feminized Hindus. In one of his speeches Bhindranwale propounded the idea that it was an insult for the Sikhs to be included in a nation that considered Mahatma Gandhi to be its father, for his techniques of fighting were quintessentially feminine. He (Gandhi) was symbolized by a *charkha,* the spinning wheel, which was a symbol of women. "Can those," asked the militant leader, "who are the sons of the valiant *guru,* whose symbol is the sword, ever accept a woman like Mahatma as their *father?* Those are the techniques of the weak, not of a race that has never bowed its head before any injustice—a race whose history is written in the blood of martyrs."

It should be evident that the construction of the past in terms of a genealogy of father-son relations was also a construction of the self and the other. To be able to claim true descent from the proud Gurus[11] (the ten acknowledged founders of the Sikh religion), it was argued, all corruption that had seeped into the Sikh character because of the closeness to the Hindus was to be exorcised. Through the particular narrative web of Sikh history as a history of martyrdom, Sikh heroic character was created while the negative counter of this was the Hindu feminized character. The dangers of a "Hindu" history, it turned out, were not just that Sikhs were denied their rightful place in history but that the martial Sikhs became converted into a weak race:[12] "The Sikhs have been softened and conditioned during the last fifty years to bear and put up with insults to their religion and all forms of other oppression, patiently and without demur, under the sinister preaching and spell of the narcotic cult of non-violence, much against the clear directive of their Gurus, their Prophets, not to turn the other cheek before a tyrant, not to take lying down any insult to their religion, their self-respect, and their human dignity."[13] The danger as seen in this discourse was not of a heroic confrontation with a masculine other, but that the feminine other would completely dissolve the masculine self of the Sikh. "With such an enemy," said one warning, "even your story will be wiped out from the face of the earth."

In this particular articulation of community as the community of men we detect not the anxiety of the father—is this *my* son?—but rather the anxiety of the son—am *I* truly worthy to claim this man as my father? Further, all signs of the mother have been erased from this ancestry. Thus, it is not surprising that there were direct exhortations in the oral discourse of militancy asking Sikhs to rid themselves of any signs of a feminine self. The most visible sign of the masculinity of the Sikh in this discourse was his sword. In many speeches there was the simple exhortation *Shastradhari howo*—Become the bearer of weapons. In most of his speeches Bhindranwale asked Sikh households to collect weapons, especially Kalashnikov rifles, so that they could protect the honor of the community when the time came.

The sword was seen as the sign of the masculinity of the Sikh that was external and a product of history. The other visible sign of the Sikh's masculinity, it was said, is his beard. Bhindranwale exhorted the Sikhs to let their beards grow: "If you do not want beards then you should urge the women to become men and you should become women. Or else ask nature that it should stop this growth on your faces. Then there will be no need to exhort you to wear long beards. Then there will be no need for me to preach (*prachar karna*), no need to break my head on this affair (*matha khapai karna*)."[14] Another leader, a functionary of the Akali Dal, stated that the flowing beard of the Sikh man was a direct challenge to the authority of the state.[15] The threat to the Sikh community was articulated in terms such as "they" have their eyes on "your" sword, on "your" beard (*ona di nazar twadi kirpan te hai—ona di nazar twadi dadi te hai*). Thus, we see the importance of the theme of the feminine other destroying the community by robbing it of its masculinity and bestowing a feminine character on it. The production of communal hate in this case was not based upon a long history of hostility between Hindus and Sikhs pitted against each other—it was rather the case that hate became a shear with which a shared history and an ecology of connectedness was to be torn asunder.

A narrative of Sikh history in terms of a series of systematic dualisms separating the Sikh self from the Hindu other could not be built without a systematic "forgetting" of the close relations between Hindus and Sikhs in everyday life, especially the bonds of language, common mythology, shared worship, and the community created through exchanges. In fact, even the participation of the Sikhs in the communal riots against the Muslims, testimony of which is not only present in textbooks of history but in the personal lives of the people, was not acknowledged anymore. All the darker aspects of the past were purged by being projected on the Hindus.[16] For instance, these publications discussed incidents of communal tensions from the 1920s primarily in terms of Hindu-Muslim conflicts, as if the Sikhs did not figure in these conflicts at all. Under the subheading "It Happened Before," the white paper prepared by SGPC entitled *They Massacre Sikhs,* to which reference was made earlier, stated the following:

> This phenomenon in which Sikh religious sensibility is calculatedly outraged and their human dignity cruelly injured has its historical antecedents in this part of the world. It was in the late twenties of this century that a cultural ancestor of the present anti-Sikh Hindu urban crust wrote and published a small book, purporting to be a research paper in history under the title of *Rangila Rasul: Mohammad, the Pleasure Loving Prophet.* . . . The entire Muslim world of India writhed in anguish at this gross insult to and attack on the Muslim community, but they were laughed at and chided by the citified Hindu press of Lahore. . . . But the process of events [*sic*] that led to bloody communal riots in various parts of India till the creation of India and Pakistan and

the partition of the country itself, with tragic losses in men, money, and property, is directly and rightly traceable to a section of the majority community exemplified in the matter of *Rangila Rasul*.[17]

The first act of willful forgetting, then, was related to the purging of the community of any evil, now projected onto "the citified Hindu majority." The second act of forgetting was to construe all acts of violence, both those directed within the Sikh community in such institutional practices as feuds and those directed outward in communal violence as the violence of martyrdom. Finally, there was the assumption that the state was an *external institution,* in fact, a Hindu institution, that had been imposed upon the Sikh community rather than one created through the practices prevalent in the region itself. While there is ample evidence of gross violations of human rights in this period by the state in India, the army and the police force were not exclusively Hindu. This construction, however, not only allowed the Sikh community to absolve itself from all blame in relation to the corrupt practices of the institution of the state, which were projected onto the Hindu character, but it also created a discourse of betrayal.

THE BETRAYED LOVER

One of the metaphors that repeatedly occurred in the militant discourse was that of the betrayed lover, with the Sikhs as the betrayed lovers of the Indian state. It was said that though the sacrifices of the Sikhs brought freedom to India, they were denied their rightful place in the new configuration of nations. As an example, Bhindranwale stated in a speech that while Muslims got Pakistan and Hindus became the de facto rulers of a de jure secular India, the *nishan sahib* (i.e., the flag that would be the sign of the Sikh nation) was not allowed to fly over the country. He sometimes liked to tell another story, that an agreement had been reached during the discussions on the national flag in a Congress session, that the saffron color as a symbol of Sikh martyrdom would fly over and above the other two colors—green for the Muslims and white for the Hindus. He attributed this agreement to the "fact" that it was always a Sikh who led the procession of *satyagrahis* (Gandhi's term for the nonviolent protesters, literally signifying the adherence to truth), as Hindus were too cowardly to do so. It is needless to add that this is not how the scheme of colors in the national flag is interpreted in official narratives—but the story has the power of anchoring a floating truth with a stamp of authenticity.

In other examples, he and others compared the character of the Hindu to the character of the snake. One of the posters declared: "A Hindu never kills a snake. He asks the Muslim to kill the snake. If the snake dies the Hindu is happy: if the Muslim dies the Hindu is happy." It concluded: "In confrontation with such a community even your name will be wiped out from the annals of history." The theme of the untrustworthiness of the Hindus found further elaboration through reference to the feminized character of its rulers. Thus, the leader, Indira Gandhi, was said to be a widow, one born in the household of Pandits—the Brahmin caste that in the Sikh rendering was always subservient to the powerful ruler castes.[18] It was implied that only the Hindu could accept being ruled over by a woman. Thus the superimposition of the images of femininity and masculinity over the images of Hindu and Sikh assumed the presence of the state as an overarching presence, providing the context within which these contests were to be framed. One could go further and say that it is in relation to this overarching presence that we can understand how images of Hindus and Sikhs were torn apart from their anchors in everyday life.[19] Propelled into public spaces, these negative and hateful images of self and other slowly seeped into the understandings of many people, forming the unconscious grammar through which the grievous events of Operation Blue Star, the assassination of Indira Gandhi, and the collective violence against the Sikhs in Delhi in 1984 were both produced and interpreted. Thus, while the eventfulness of what followed was not what everyday life was about, these events could only have been grown out of the soil of the everyday.

THE PHENOMENOLOGY OF RUMOR

Let me now turn to the diffused understandings of Sikh and Hindu character that found expression in the phenomenology of rumor in the specific context of the societal crisis constituted by the assassination of Indira Gandhi. The characteristics of this crisis were a mounting panic that signaled the breakdown of social communication, the animation of a societal memory seen as constitutive of incomplete or interrupted social stories, and the appearance of the panic rumor[20] as a voice that was unattributed, unassigned, and yet anchored to the images of self and other that had been circulating in the discourses of militancy. The withdrawal of trust from normally functioning words constituted a special vulnerability to the signifier, leading one to ways of acting over which all control seemed to have been lost.[21] It was in these moments that images generated in the speeches of

Bhindranwale and later mirrored in speeches of Hindu leaders such as Bal Thackerey, Uma Bharati, or Sadhvi Rithambra found a place in the collective repertoire of social groups and displaced the subjectivity of everyday life by a subjectivity more appropriately described as close to a form of death.

The emphasis on the displacement of subjectivity of everyday life in the rumors sees the functioning of rumor in a somewhat different light, as compared to many other formulations. A brief detour to lay out the contour of this difference may be useful, especially to indicate the social contexts in which rumor may sometimes perform a critical function, but at other times may create lethal conditions for circulation of hate. The tempo of panic rumors follows the tempo of skepticism in that both function in such a way that our access to context is removed. At the very least, it shows that a theory of rumor independent of the forms of life (or forms of death) within which it is embedded is not possible.

On the side of our understanding the positive power of rumor to mobilize crowds, we are much indebted to historians of the French Revolution such as George Rudé, whose study of the Revolution remains a classic.[22] Following him, many scholars have seen the power of rumor to mobilize crowds as agents of collective action for redressal of moral wrongs, in a positive light. In Indian historiography, the unique voice of Ranajit Guha secured an analytical place for rumor as a form of transmission in popular peasant uprisings.[23]

In Guha's formulation, rumor is important as a trigger and mobilizer, "a necessary instrument of rebel transmission." Guha further identified the anonymity of the source of rumor, its capacity to build collective solidarity, and the almost uncontrollable impulse to pass it on as important elements on which to build a theory of rumor. He drew repeated attention to rumor as an important means of mobilization of the peasantry, one that was "specific to a pre-literate culture," reflecting "a code of political thinking which was in conformity with the semi-feudal conditions of the peasant's existence." From the official point of view the peasant insurgencies fueled by rumor were instances of peasant irrationality: for the peasant insurgents these were means of spreading the message of revolt.[24]

Homi Bhabha deftly isolated the two aspects of rumor from Guha's analysis that he considers important for building a general theory of rumor. There are, first, the enunciative aspect and, second, the performative aspect. "The indeterminacy of rumor," he says, "constitutes its importance as a social discourse. Its intersubjective, communal adhesiveness lies in its enunciative aspect. Its performative power of circulation results in its contiguous spreading, an almost uncontrollable impulse to pass it on to another person."

He then goes on to conclude that psychic affect and social fantasy are potent forms of potential identification and agency for guerrilla warfare, and hence rumors play a major role in mobilization for such warfare.[25]

Other orientations, especially derived from mass psychology, have emphasized the emotional, capricious, temperamental, and flighty nature of crowds. The French scholar Le Bon had declared that crowds are everywhere distinguished by feminine characteristics. Some of this denigration of crowds may be easy to understand in terms of Guha's formulation of elite prejudice against the subaltern forms of communication, but it is difficult to ignore the fact that the twentieth century has also seen the spectacular politics of crowds in the Nazi regime and nearer home in the communal riots. In these cases too there are certain moral premises (in terms of their own understanding of events) within which crowds act, but the unconscious exchange of images draws upon a repertoire that cannot be schematized within the kinds of subaltern politics that Guha writes on. In his analysis of Nazi crowds Muscovici suggests that crowds come to be spoken of as a woman simply to mask the exchange of homosexual images between an "active" leader and a "feminine" crowd.[26] I have elsewhere suggested that themes of revenge dominate in the imagery in which a crowd is mobilized around the image of a raped woman or a dead child: further, the imagery of a community that has been emasculated and that seeks to recover its masculinity through crowd action plays on the register of gender in various ways.[27] What is common in these various situations in the deployment of rumors is the perlocutionary force of words, their capacity to do something by saying something,[28] through which words come to be transformed from being a medium of communication to becoming bearers of force.

These preliminary remarks, I hope, authorize me to conclude that the essential grammatical feature (in Wittgenstein's sense) of what we call rumor is that it is conceived to *spread.* Thus while images of contagion and infection are used to represent rumor in elite discourse, this is not simply a matter of noncomprehension, on the part of elites, of subaltern forms of communication: it also speaks to the transformation of language, namely, that instead of a medium of communication, language becomes communicable, infectious, causing things to happen almost as if they had happened in nature. I return to the specific connection between the assassination of Mrs. Gandhi and the uncanny sense that people had that it somehow completed the story of Operation Blue Star.

We need to remember that the events of Operation Blue Star had themselves been the subject of contending versions since July 1984. There was an

insistence on the part of the government that the sacred shrine of Amritsar
—the Darbar Sahib (or the Golden Temple, as it is otherwise known)—had
become a sanctuary for militants and terrorists and that illegal weapons had
been stored in the shrine in large quantities, endangering public order and
the sovereignty of the state. The militant literature made the army operation out as a case of flagrant violation of the rights of the Sikhs to their
sacred shrines. They argued that Operation Blue Star was a deliberate insult
to the Sikh religion and the Sikh community and therefore would not go
unavenged. Many civil rights groups also maintained that innocent pilgrims had been shot, among whom were women and children. The army's
contention, on the other hand, was that they had gone into the temple with
their hands tied behind their backs, because the terrorists[29] had used innocent pilgrims as human shields. They claimed that the army losses were far
in excess of what might have been expected in such a confrontation because
the army had to protect ordinary civilians. For each element of the story
there were allegations and counter-allegations. Thus there was an unfinished character to the story—much of the event lived in different versions
in the social memory of different social groups. It was thus that the uncertainty introduced by the assassination of Mrs. Gandhi *in the present* seemed
to many to have a link with the past in the form of the incomplete character of the story of Operation Blue Star—it completed one segment of the
story. It was as if this particular turn in the story was part of the plot that
had been unfolding since Operation Blue Star. And the uncanny knowledge of the identity of the guards embodied in rumors was part of that
experience of the seriality in which events were unfolding themselves. Yet,
despite the uncertainty in which events were shrouded for the first few
hours, when rumors of Mrs. Gandhi's having been shot began to spread
and before their confirmation by the official media, as I said earlier, there
was no sense of panic in the streets of Delhi. It was only later in the evening
that events began to take a different turn.

RUMORS OF CELEBRATION: WAS THE STATE COLLAPSING?

From speculations to judgments about the act of assassination, the stories
that began to circulate toward the evening of October 31st were about the
uncertainty of context within which this event was to be placed. There was
some speculation that this was like the opening of the curtain to announce
the coming of more momentous events. It was said in many parts of the
city that along with this singular act of daring, the Sikhs had started massive

violence against the Hindus in the Punjab. Some people claimed to have heard that trains were arriving from the Punjab loaded with dead bodies. There were rumors that Sikh militants planned to poison Delhi's water supply, that there had been widespread defections from the ranks of the army and the police, and that the collapse of the state in India was imminent. It was said by some that these events had already been announced in the *gurudwaras,* which is why instead of being frightened of reprisals, the Sikhs were celebrating all over the country. Some people expected that the creation of Khalistan would be announced in the wake of the utter chaos that would reign in India, that negotiations had already been held with powerful countries, and hence while the United States itself would not rush to recognize Khalistan, it had persuaded some small countries to give recognition to the new state. Mrs. Gandhi's assassination was then seen as the first act in a massive conspiracy that was to follow. The representation of the crisis drew considerable energy from the exaggerated claims about the vulnerability of the Indian state and the support that militants were expected to receive. As an example, Bhindranwale had reported in one of his speeches that he had been asked by some journalists if the Sikhs would fight on the side of India if India were to be attacked by the Khalistani Liberation Force, situated in the United States, Canada, and the United Kingdom and supported by the American army, and he had replied that not a single Sikh would lift a weapon against such a holy force. It may be interesting to see how these images entered into rumors and the mechanisms by which they made a claim to the real—thus becoming persuasive enough to exercise the perlocutionary force that Austin located in certain kinds of utterances. In the following representation I show how a particular strand in a rumor derives credibility from stories about earlier events, regardless of whether a person had experienced those earlier events or not. Thus a reality effect is created through anchoring a particular strand in denser stories from the past. This mode of laying claims over the real gets its affective force from the sense of uncertainty created through political events that pry open ideas of a settled social life.

Elements of the Rumor vs. Claims over the Real

There was massive violence against the Hindus in Punjab. Trains full of dead bodies were arriving from Punjab.

The credibility of this element of the rumor took the experience of the Partition riots as *proof* that such events did happen. In homes, on street corners, elderly persons would tell younger people, "You are too young to remember this . . . but I with my own eyes . . . " as if "having seen" such things in 1947 showed the veracity of what was heard in 1984.

Sikh militants were planning to poison Delhi's water supply.

This strand of the rumor is evoked in almost every communal riot that I know of. The fear that living in the city means that one has no control over such vital elements of life as water, and thus one is a hostage in the hands of the enemy, shows both a fear of city life and a sense of vulnerability in the hands of unknown enemies. It is, however, not only the city that evokes this fear. Rumors about poisoning of wells and ponds can occur in villages.

There had been widespread defections from the ranks of the army and the police.

People evoked examples from the past. For instance, while declaring the Emergency in 1976, Mrs. Gandhi had quoted the call given by Jai Prakash Narain to army and police officials not to obey orders. Similarly, after Operation Blue Star, a Sikh junior commissioned officer had killed the commander of the Jodhpur regiment. The commander had gone unarmed to this man because he believed that loyalty to the regiment would stand above all other loyalties. This particular strand in the rumor showed that institutions of state began to be seen as fragile in popular constructions as compared to traditional institutions. Yet I should point out that another rumor in the Punjab during Operation Blue Star was that a Sikh army officer had made the pilgrims crawl on their stomachs before him "to teach them a lesson." The fact that both kinds of rumors could be evoked in different times should warn us against giving too much stability to the representations of state and community in popular consciousness.

Sikhs were celebrating everywhere. They were dancing in the streets, distributing sweets. One man related to me that a Sikh colleague in his office had brought a box of sweets and given it to his Hindu colleagues, saying that he was consoling them because their mother was dead.

I believe it was this strand of the rumor that gave credibility to so many others. If Sikhs were celebrating, then they must know of the immediate future in ways that were not evident to others. The image of Sikhs dancing in the streets in England, shown on the BBC World Service, was seen as "evidence of the eyes" that they were celebrating in the towns of India. Others quoted similar events that were only heard about but were taken to be true because the rumors of BBC coverage of the event had spread among even those who did not have access to the BBC. Ironically it was the reputation of the BBC for impartial reporting that was quoted as evidence of the celebrations by the Sikhs.

The assassination of Mrs. Gandhi was just the first act to be followed by creation of chaos and anarchy; it was said that the creation of Khalistan would be announced in the wake of this chaos. Local gurudwaras were said to have made these announcements to the congregations, who were therefore in a celebratory mood.

This rumor was heard in Delhi at the time of Operation Blue Star. Many people had then claimed that the government had been compelled to act because Bhindranwale had amassed missiles in the temple and would announce the creation of Khalistan from the temple precincts. It was the same rumor that was repeated now as evidence of the vulnerability of the Indian state.

We can see that rumor operated here in the twilight of judgment. Carlo Ginzburg has suggested to me that it would be useful to distinguish between those events that did happen (such as trains full of dead bodies traveling from one side of the border to another during the riots in 1947) and those events that were only alleged to have happened (e.g., water being poisoned by the terrorists). The difficulty with drawing a sharp distinction between that which happened (the brute fact) and that which was only alleged to have happened (the imaginary) is that such distinctions can be seen with clarity only after the event. The regions of the imaginary to which the claims of the real were anchored were varied indeed—they ranged from images *seen* on television, *reported* to have been seen on television, as well as stories *heard* about other times. Contrary to the notion that certain classes of people are protected from the mesmerizing effect of rumors (e.g., the educated), I found that many professional bureaucrats, teachers, and medical doctors inhabited for a while that twilight zone in which it was difficult to know whether it was safer if they trusted in rumors or in the official versions of events. (It is interesting to ask how people, e.g., some professionals, members of a Jesuit seminary, and students, who later provided the foundation for organizing relief work in affected areas, were able to resist the force of rumors that they were under threat.) The diffused rumors thus created within the space of twenty-four hours the sense that there was a conspiracy against society that the authorities responsible for the protection of citizens' lives and maintenance of public order would be quite unable to handle. Thus, instead of creating the Sikhs as a group vulnerable to mass violence and hence in need of the protection of law, the rumors now fed on the images of the Hindus as weak and vulnerable and the state as having already collapsed in the light of this massive plot against it. It is not very difficult to see that the frequent claims made in the written and oral discourses of militant leaders about the emasculated character of the Indian state, the exhortation to all Sikhs to carry weapons, the repeated assertions that when the moment of reckoning came every Sikh would be ready to fight on behalf of Khalistan with the Kalashnikov rifles that had been carefully stored in Sikh households—all came to be believed with a vengeance. The assassination of Mrs. Gandhi became some kind of proof of the power of the Sikhs and the vulnerability of the Hindus, and these ideas began to be evoked with greater and greater intensity as many Hindu men and women repeated these rumors to each other with mounting panic. There was a blindness toward the present inasmuch as the Sikhs one encountered were flesh and blood characters and not direct embodiments of the images that had been created about them.

THE VULNERABILITY OF THE SIKHS

While rumors that Hindus were unprepared to meet the challenge of a Sikh attack were being freely discussed and circulated in the street corners and at *paan* shops in Delhi, many Sikh households were fearful of being attacked.[30] On October 31st, the newspapers had reported that hoodlums and thugs had gathered in different railway stations and that in many places Sikhs had been dragged out of trains and beaten up or killed. The absence of the police at these crucial public places and the fact that official pronouncements completely denied any attack on Sikhs convinced many of them that the antisocial elements had the support of the police. For many Sikhs this event was seen in continuity with Operation Blue Star, since both were about teaching Sikhs a lesson. Being able to interpret the rumors correctly became a matter of life and death for many. Let me illustrate with an example.

On the morning of November 1st on the deserted streets in the Civil Lines, my husband and I met a distraught Sikh gentleman waving wildly at us to stop. He was an employee of the National Defense Institute and had been working through the night. He knew nothing of the events following Mrs. Gandhi's assassination, as he had been in his laboratory the previous night, but he could sense that something eerie was happening. There were no buses running, and the usual street sounds were missing. Could we help him and drop him at the nearest bus stop, he asked, so that he could get home. We told him that there were reports of attacks on Sikhs and it might be best to avoid the streets. One of our friends lived nearby, and we suggested that we could take him there and he could telephone his family. We also suggested that he could stay there until things quieted a bit.

As we were talking I had opened the door of the car for him, and he had seated himself in the back muttering words of thanks. Within a moment of his action a group of four or five men materialized from somewhere. They did not have a threatening look, but they spoke in conspiratorial tones. Further ahead, they said there was a mob. If it saw a Sikh in our car, it would not only drag *him* out and beat him or kill him, but it would also attack us. I became visibly angry. The men shook their heads sadly and said they were doing their best—what more could *they do* except warn us of what lay ahead? They suggested that it would be better for the man to hide under the seat and for us to drive the car fast so that he was not visible from outside. They would neither talk directly to the man nor look at him, as if they were discussing a troublesome object rather than a person. At this point the Sikh man visibly panicked. I assured him that our friend's house was a minute's drive and if he wanted he could simply stay there where he would be safe. "No," the man said, "why should you risk your life for me?" He opened the door even as the car had begun to move and stumbled out on the road. "He will not come with us," my husband said. "He probably fears that we may trick him and deliver him to his killers." I shouted to the man that he should not try to negotiate the roads—he should just go back to Metcalfe House where the institute was located and hide there for a few days. I lost sight of him then but many months later saw him in the vicinity of Metcalfe House—he obviously survived.

Although many Sikhs were persuaded to take shelter in the houses of Hindu or Muslim friends, it was with fragmented pieces of information that Sikhs were making their choices—the full impact of the violence had not hit home. There was horrendous violence that had begun on the evening of October 31st against the Sikhs in resettlement colonies in Delhi, in which more than three thousand Sikhs died, but the full horror of this came to be known only on November 1st and was not officially acknowledged until much later.[31]

A NEW TURN

As the facts about the extent and brutality of attacks against Sikhs came to be known through reports in newspapers and through the work of several voluntary agencies the rumors began to take a new turn. Now it was whispered that news had come in from several places that Sikhs who had been given shelter by Hindus had actually killed their hosts, stolen their goods, or raped their women before running away in the middle of the night. Names of several residential colonies were evoked where people said they knew someone who had seen it or heard it or had known the family. This rumor was stitched onto the assassination of Mrs. Gandhi by her security guards. If her security guards, whom she trusted enough to ignore the advice of her security personnel, could betray her trust and kill her because they had been sworn to exact vengeance, then what further evidence was needed, people said, to convince one that Sikhs did not have any loyalty above that to their religion? The Sikh character was compared to that of snakes who turn around and bite the very hands that feed them milk. This analogy to the snake was to recur. For instance, one man I knew who was helping in the running of a relief camp went to buy milk for the children from a *gwala* (milk vendor). "Why do you need so much milk?" asked the *gwala*. "Do you have a wedding in the family?" The man replied that he was getting milk for the children of Sikhs in the Ludlow Castle camp. "You want to feed the snake's child with milk—but when he grows up, he will grow up to be a snake, not a man. *Astin ke samp—mauka pate hi das lenge*—snakes nourished in your shirt sleeves[32]—they will bite you as soon as they get a chance."

The second strand of this complex of rumors was to attribute the very facts of flight on the part of scared Sikhs to the preparations they were making for revenge. In the earlier complex of rumors that I identified, the theme of the collapse of the state and the simultaneous passage of power into the hands of the Sikh militants was prominent. By the second day after the assassination, it was clear that this was not about to happen. The new prime minister had been installed. Reports of sporadic attacks on the Sikhs were trickling in, and many people were scared to go out on the roads for fear that the mobs described persistently in newspapers as "antisocial elements" would take the opportunity to harm not only the Sikhs but others too. Yet the rumors continued to construct the Sikhs as aggressive, angry, and waiting to strike. When large numbers of Sikhs took shelter in *gurudwaras,* people said that they had amassed a vast number of weapons and would launch an attack from there. Several middle-class localities organized neighborhood watches at night so that they would not be caught unawares when attacked by Sikhs.

In one incident, a group of frightened Sikh taxi drivers who normally slept in makeshift shelters on the taxi stand itself had, to avoid identification, shaved off their beards and cut their hair on the evening of October 31st when they heard about the attacks on Sikhs in the city. They were hiding in the dark shadows of the towering walls of a women's college when they were spotted. The rumor immediately went around that they had assembled there to attack the college and rape the women. On receiving calls from the college, the police went there and took the frightened men away to a relief camp that had been set up nearby. So, for many, the Sikhs remained the aggressors until the very end. This particular angle through which events were seen—which turned the vulnerable victims into aggressors, simultaneously creating a sense of panic among those who (if one were granted a god's eye view)[33] were under no special threat—is extremely important in my perception. I shall try to draw out the implications of this at a later stage.

The other strand in the rumors through which Sikh character was constructed needs mentioning. This was the theme of the fanaticism of the Sikhs approximating the model of "madness." The emphasis could shift in the narratives, but a slippage from courage to fanaticism to madness occurred in the distribution of stories. Take, first, a relatively benign construction. During one of the first visits we made to Sultanpuri, the resettlement colony where I was engaged in the work of relief and rehabilitation, we were taken to a street where not much physical damage seemed to have occurred. But a group of men and women were vociferous in trying to claim *victim* status. One woman said, "We were all attacked— our men were killed in large numbers, but we say that they were not murdered—they were martyred."[34] A young Punjabi boy who was in the team of students helping me said, "Sikhs have such an urge to claim martyrdom"; then with a change of voice mimicking a supposed Sikh, he said, "We want to be martyrs—just give us any place and date for our action" (*asi tan ji shahid hona hai—jagah te tarikh tusi pa lao*). He then described stories he had heard about Sikhs refusing to be moved to the safety of refugee camps and trying to challenge fully armed mobs with the few weapons they had and dying in the end. I too had heard these stories, but my interpretation was not that they were seeking martyrdom but that it was difficult in those conditions to know whether they were being taken to a refugee camp or being entrapped in an unknown situation where death and degradation awaited them. I have already referred to the social memory of the Partition riots in which people were lured to their deaths in a similar manner, which may have given this direction to their thought.

Let me now come to the second theme—that of fanaticism turning into madness. In an effort to organize medical help for the victims during the work of relief and rehabilitation, I was talking to a group of physicians about fifteen days after the riots. My major contact in this group was a socially conscientious physician (a member of the Arya Samaj) who had read an account of our work in a newspaper. He said that he wanted to organize his colleagues to help but found them to be so prejudiced against the Sikhs that it was impossible to get their cooperation. "Please don't think that they [the physicians] are bad people," he said. "One of them worked day and night in a government hospital on a voluntary basis when a tornado hit the city in 1978 and hospitals were finding themselves very short of staff. But somehow even he cannot be persuaded to work with the Sikhs." I decided that by talking directly to this group and telling them of the suffering of the victims in Sultanpuri, I might be able to get their help.

In the course of my descriptions of what I had seen, I met with sullen resistance—what I construed as a refusal to listen. In retrospect this may have been because my tone against the Hindu community was accusatory, and they may have felt unfairly accused. Then a woman doctor said that in her opinion the Sikhs had brought all this upon themselves because they were like mad people. To substantiate her point she told me that she had heard that in the tire market near Bada Hindu Rao where many shops were owned by Sikhs an angry mob had put burning tires around the necks of the owners, locked them inside their shops, and let them burn to death. Normal people, she said, would have shouted and asked for mercy or forgiveness, but one Sikh was seen gesticulating threateningly from the windows with his fists closed toward the mob, which had laughed hysterically at this sight. Another person said laughingly that the weight of their long hair piled on their heads perhaps made them mad.

The creation of these images did not seem to have anything to do with the experience of these physicians. They had not themselves gone around burning people or looting shops—yet there was a voyeuristic pleasure in these rumors of madness and extraordinary behavior of the Sikhs. As the discussion gathered momentum, others began to offer diverse kinds of evidence. One claimed that in the Sikh tradition one who died for the cause of the Gurus did not feel any pain even under torture. This is why, he said, they behaved like fanatics in taking questions of life and death so lightly and why there had always been so much violence in the Punjab. Someone offered another example. Sikhs in the Punjab, one member of the group said, had proudly proclaimed the story that when the Indian army had rounded up a number of Sikh boys who were caught in the Golden Temple during Operation Blue Star, they had been asked to shout *Bharat mata ki Jai*—Victory to Mother India, but they had shouted in unison *Jo bole so nihal—bolo sri sat sriyakal,* the ritual proclamation of Sikh faith, and the Indian army officer had allegedly killed these young boys.[35] How could one explain such madness, he asked, which did not value the life of the young? He seemed completely unaware of the irony that we were discussing precisely the brutal killing of the Sikhs when he evoked *their* lack of respect for life as evidence of their madness and hence an exoneration of the violence against them. I could give many more examples of this overlaying of the four strands to create the Sikh as aggressive, vengeful, incapable of loyalty, and mad—and correspondingly the Hindu as vulnerable, frightened, and acting out of self-defense against a powerful enemy. But I shall conclude this part of the description with an example that gives a slightly different angle to this theme.

A Hindu priest told me that a meeting was held on October 31st in a recently built temple just on the outskirts of Delhi, known for its lavish interiors and its patronage by politicians and powerful members of the underworld. Here there had been a major discussion on whether Sikhs were part of the Hindu community and therefore whether the assassination of Mrs. Gandhi should be treated as an individual aberration/crime or whether the whole community was to be implicated. It was agreed that for the last several years the Sikh militants and terrorists had killed, terrorized, and looted Hindus in the Punjab.[36] Therefore, he continued, the Sikhs were now like a god who begins to behave like a demon.[37] Such gods, he said, do not learn through reasoned conversations—they have to be kicked to rid them of the evil. The phrase he used in Hindi was *laton ke devata baton se nahin mante* (the gods who need kicks cannot be pacified with words). The common saying is *laton ke bhut baton se nahin mante.* The word *devata* means god while *bhut* is demon. He had substituted the symbolism of demons with the symbolism of gods (though the term *devata* is used for lesser gods). Thus the language of exorcism and possession here becomes a political language through which the violence links the aggressors and the victims on the model of the exorcist and his patient.[38] At the risk of some schematization that I shall modify later, it may be useful at this stage to present the unfinished events of Operation Blue Star, as they appear in an ideal typical form in the Hindu construction and the Sikh construction, and then to see how these were fed into a Hindu imagination of society in siege after the assassination of Mrs. Gandhi. Let me hasten to add that this does not mean that all Hindus believed in one kind of construction and all Sikhs in its binary opposite. Indeed, the very examples I have given of solidarities created in these periods of crisis across communities are evidence of the fact that such totalization is resisted.[39]

There were, however, two important consequences of the rumors—first, that they built a structure of thought within which Sikh character was placed and that had characteristics similar to that of paranoia; and second, that the rumors stabilized a reality that intruded upon the lives of the residents of resettlement colonies like Sultanpuri who had to live through this brutal violence. Thus the movement of images that built the stereotypes of Sikh and Hindu character in the militant discourse traveled to the Hindu constructions in giving form to rumors that in turn made brutal violence against the Sikhs a "thinkable" response even for those who did not directly participate in the violence. In the following representation, we can see that the same event, the death of pilgrims during Operation Blue Star, found life in different versions in popular Hindu and Sikh discourses.

Hindu and Sikh Versions of Operation Blue Star

Hindu: Bhindranwale was about to announce the formation of Khalistan from the precincts of the Golden Temple when the Indian army stormed the temple and foiled the plot. Mytheme A

Sikh: Operation Blue Star was meant to teach Sikhs a lesson. Mytheme a

Hindu: Terrorists used pilgrims as human shields, leading to greater civilian and army casualties than would have been the case if normal rules of warfare had been observed. Mytheme B

Sikh: Indian army officials shot at innocent pilgrims. Mytheme b

Hindu: Even young children were compelled by militants to act as human shields so that they could be claimed as martyrs for the cause. Mytheme C

Sikh: Children were lined up and shot in the Golden Temple by army officials when they refused to obey their command to shout nationalist slogans. Mytheme c

Hindu: Bhindranwale's death during Operation Blue Star will surely convince Sikhs that he was not a saint. He died like a coward. Mytheme D

Sikh: Bhindranwale did not die during the army operation. He is like a sleeping bull who will rise to lead the Sikhs against the Indian state. Mytheme d

The manner in which the Hindu reading of Operation Blue Star and their perception of Sikh interpretations fed into the imagined sequel of Mrs. Gandhi's assassination in a Hindu imaginary may be schematically presented as follows.

Mrs. Gandhi's assassination was obviously part of a bigger plot since the militants had already once achieved near success in declaring the formation of Khalistan.

This was validated both by the Hindu version in which Operation Blue Star had been necessitated with great urgency because of the success the militants had achieved in reaching so close to their goal, and by the Sikh version, which proclaimed that Operation Blue Star had not succeeded in eliminating Bhindranwale, who was still alive and waiting to lead the Sikhs against the Indian state. [Mytheme A and Mytheme d]

The Sikhs would easily overcome the Hindus in any fights because they had martial traditions whereas Hindus were weak and effeminate. Sikhs were fanatic enough to even sacrifice their children.

Much of the militant literature had emphasized the martial character of Sikh religion and the weak and effeminate character of Hindus. The rumors of how the militants and the pilgrims had courted death, of which Mytheme c is only one example, built up this idea of an inherently "heroic" or "fanatic" character of the Sikhs. The television news after Operation Blue Star in July had shown clippings of terrorists surrendering before the army, but it became clear that the vision of Sikhs in the first two days of the riots was of people who would defy death by coming and attacking Hindus in suicidal attacks. [Mytheme B/Mytheme b/Mytheme c]

For the Sikhs, the situation took a parallel but not strictly symmetrical development. This was because of a deep ambivalence toward the assassins of Mrs. Gandhi. None of the militant groups were willing to condemn the assassins in unambiguous terms. Sometimes public statements were claimed to have been made condemning the assassination from Sikh religious organizations that were later withdrawn. For many Sikhs who were not necessarily sympathetic to the militant cause, Operation Blue Star was seen as an insult to the whole religious community. Hence they saw the aftermath of the assassination as a further step in the politics of teaching Sikhs a lesson. Many were rightly offended that instead of being treated as an individual crime the assassination was being seen as an event that had cast the whole Sikh community as culprits. Hence, instead of being treated as individual citizens who had nothing to do with the alleged crime, they were being targeted as people to whom a lesson had to be taught. It would be a grave error to assume a homogeneity of opinion and a consequent totalization of affect among the Sikhs: opinions varied from the celebration of the act in the tradition of martyrs as in the militant literature to the distancing of the self from the assassins to outright condemnation of their act.

This variation was, however, given no recognition in the stabilization of the attributes of "Sikh character"—although the individuality of different kinds of persons who make up a community was clearly articulated in social practices. Such acts of totalization seem to be a normal characteristic of times of collective violence, as well as in the processes of ethnic and religious mobilization in the service of violence. What I would like to emphasize here, though, is the manner in which the categories of aggressor and victim were reversed through the application of these notions for many Hindus. Table 1 shows how the different strands in the creation of the Sikh character were anchored upon the different kinds of rumors that were floating about in the general population.

The purpose of presenting this schematic representation is to explicate the participation of many Hindus in the collective violence even though they may not have themselves engaged in any killing or looting. The form of language—its force, its lack of signature, its appeals to the uncanny— gave it the perlocutionary force that brought a new form—not a form of *life* but a form of death—into existence. Indeed, in some ways the past was present here, all at once, but it did not produce a flowering of more pluralist and accepting ways in the problematic of self and other—rather, it revealed the darkest of possibilities that a negation of life could hold.

Different strands of rumor combined here to (a) create a sense of vulnerability among the Hindus through the creation of an imaginary world in which the whole social order was seen as if it was about to collapse through a massive conspiracy on the part of the Sikhs, even though it was the Sikhs on whom the violence was being unleashed, and (b) vacate the imagined Sikh of all human subjectivity, endowing him with traits of madness and demonic possession, hence the assumption that he was not worthy of being treated as *an other with a face.* The peculiar nature of rumor—its lack of signature, the impossibility of its being tethered to an individual agent—gave it the stamp of an "endangered collectivity." It led to the world being transformed into a "fantasmagoria of shadows, of fleeting, improvised men."[40]

TABLE I
Creation of the Sikh Character

| Character Traits | Strands of Rumor | | |
	Betrayal	Aggressiveness	Fanaticism/Madness
A Sikh does not believe in any loyalty except that to his religion. He can betray the closest trust.	Mrs. Gandhi's security guards had betrayed her despite the close trust she had placed in them.	Sikhs had gathered in *gurudwaras* to attack Hindus in large numbers and to declare the formation of Khalistan.	Sikhs believe that one who dies in the cause of his religion does not suffer pain even if he is being tortured.
A Sikh is like a snake. He will bite the very hands that feed him.	Sikhs who had been given shelter in Hindu homes had stolen goods from those houses, killed their hosts, and raped their women.		
Sikhs are naturally aggressive and attracted to violence. They are not capable of observing normal social constraints.	Sikhs were caught trying to poison the water supply.	Sikhs had gathered near a girls' college because they wanted to use the opportunity created by the riots to rape the girls.	
There is a fanaticism bordering on madness in the Sikh character.			Even when being burned alive, a Sikh had been seen to gesticulate in anger rather than plead for mercy. Sikhs were proud of children who had courted death in the cause of the Sikh religion. The Sikhs could be compared to those who were subjected to demonic possession.

I want to conclude by suggesting that what I have described is the way in which the event grows out of everyday life but the world as it was known in everyday life is obliterated: instead what comes into being is a world that bears resemblance to the structure of paranoia. *My fear of the other* is transformed into the notion that *the other is fearsome.* I have tried to show further that such transformations are bound to the conception of important past events as "unfinished" and capable of molding the present in new and unexpected ways. It is not only the past then that may have an indeterminate character—the present too may suddenly become the site in which the elements of the past that were rejected, in the sense that they were not integrated into a stable understanding of the past, can suddenly press upon the world with the same insistence and obstinacy with which the real creates holes in the symbolic. It is in this manner that rumor's adequacy to a reality that has become suddenly unrecognizable makes it the privileged mode of communication and constructs panic as its corresponding affect in this altered world. Doubts and uncertainties exist in everyday life, but the worst is not what one expects to happen every time.

In contrast, the zones of emergency are marked by diffuse images of the unfinished past, voiding the other of all subjectivity, and the peopling of the world with a phantasmagoria of shadows. The perlocutionary force of rumor shows how fragile may be the social world that we inhabit. The virtual is always more encompassing than the actual: here it showed that images of distrust that might have been experienced only at the register of the virtual may take a volatile form when the social order is threatened by a critical event and so transform the world that the worst becomes not only possible but also probable. In the next chapter I try to show the precise local conditions under which violence was actualized in the resettlement colony of Sultanpuri. I show how events are grown out of the everyday, but although in the case of the survivors of the Partition such as Asha and Manjit the return to the everyday provided some acceptance that community is rebuilt through the very bits and rubble of what was left, in the case of Sultanpuri I am not able to comprehend even now, after all those years, what it meant to be able to reinhabit the ordinary again.

EIGHT

The Force of the Local

I WANT TO BEGIN THIS CHAPTER with a meditation from Deleuze on the nature of the event:

> How different this "they" is from that which we encounter in everyday banality. It is the "they" of impersonal and pre-individual singularities, the "they" of the pure event wherein *it* dies in the same way that *it* rains. This is why there are no private or collective events, no more than there are individuals and universals, particularities and generalities. Everything is singular and thus both collective and private, particular and general, neither individual nor universal. Which war, for example, is not a private affair? Conversely, which wound is not inflicted by war and derived from society as a whole?[1]

I want to pursue the idea of an event being simultaneously collective and individual as a problem of ethnographic description. For me "society as a whole" is too large and abstract a concept to be of use *here,* though I do not say that it might not be useful elsewhere. In chapter 1 I alluded to Marilyn Strathern's idea that in anthropology we learn about abstract relations by following concrete relations.[2] In a similar vein, I want to see the relation between an event and the everyday by locating or localizing it in spatiotemporal terms.[3] I ask how it is that an event that might have remained distant for inhabitants of Sultanpuri—perhaps seen on television or heard as news from those who traveled often to the center of the city—acquired an immediacy affecting them directly.

How did the assassination of Mrs. Gandhi become an event of specific local importance in Sultanpuri, folding in it so many lives from peripheral colonies in the city? I want to argue that to understand the subjectivity of the crowds we have to read how institutions of the state and the local networks of political allegiances and hostilities left their tracks in the acts of violence. These crowds enacted vengeance on behalf of a supposed Hindu collectivity that we saw posted in rumors, but what did these crowds have to do with the affects that were generated in the rumors discussed earlier?

The quotation from Deleuze with which we began this chapter suggests an intriguing relation between the third-person "they" and the fourth-person "it" in the grammar of the event.[4] If the "it" is the way events just happen as in nature so that it is not possible to read any signature in an event, then how does the event become located, embodied, or actualized? My burden in this (and the next) chapter is to show that acts that might appear as fruits of absolute contingency can be shown to bear the tracks of histories, of institutional failures, and of the routine violence of everyday life in the low-income urban neighborhoods in Delhi where I worked. In that sense the everyday grows the event; violence, even if it appears shocking, shares in the heterogeneity of everyday life.

THE FIRST REPORTS

Let us go back to the moment when Indira Gandhi was shot and the subsequent unfolding of violence in Delhi. I construct my account from various newspapers, which allows me to show how this event might have lived in our memory as mediated knowledge available only through newspaper records and official pronouncements if specific local knowledge was not available to correct those. Let us recall that after her security guards shot her on the morning of October 31, 1984, Mrs. Gandhi was rushed to the All India Institute of Medical Sciences (hereafter AIIMS) for urgent medical attention.[5] Although rumors of her death started immediately, it was only at 2 P.M. that the spot news of different newspapers announced her death. Meanwhile, a large crowd had gathered outside AIIMS. The first incidents of violence started about 4 P.M. outside this institute. People who were present gave different accounts of these incidents. Some described the violence as a spontaneous reaction of an enraged crowd. Others present, including the veteran journalist Dev Dutt, stated that they saw a

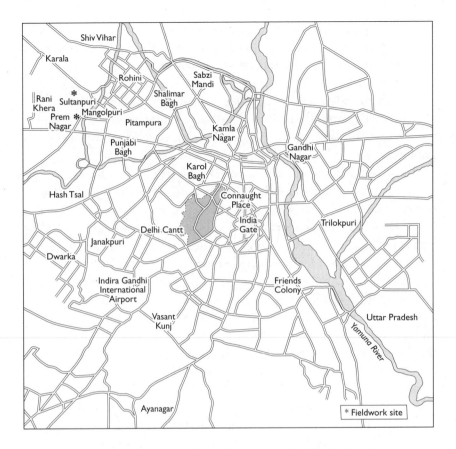

1. Fieldwork sites and areas most affected by violence in West Delhi. Other areas where terrible violence took place were in East Delhi, across the Yamuna River.

crowd of thirty or forty young men slowly separate themselves from the crowd and then began to shout slogans, disrupt traffic, and attack many Sikhs who were gathered outside AIIMS. The All India Radio announced the death of Mrs. Gandhi at 6 P.M. At the same time, it announced that her son, Rajiv Gandhi, who was a member of Parliament, had been sworn in as prime minister.

On the following day (November 1st), the newspapers reported that following the death of Mrs. Gandhi, widespread violence had taken place. Large numbers of scooters, cars, and trucks owned or driven by Sikhs were burned while their occupants were badly beaten up. Shops were burned in many parts of Delhi including Karol Bagh, Connaught Place, South Extension, Sabzi Mandi, and Azad Market (see map 1). Newspaper reports on November 1st described these acts in such terms as "irate public was venting its venom," "youths wielding *lathis,* iron rods, and other weapons were attacking Sikhs." The reports attributed this crowd violence to the fact that the police had been heavily outnumbered and were powerless to cope with the situation. The police denied any casualties, but under mounting criticism of inaction, a curfew was announced for the night, though there is evidence that it was not seriously enforced to control the spiraling violence.

Mrs. Gandhi's body was moved to Teen Murti House, which had been the official residence of Jawaharlal Nehru, her late father and the first prime minister of India, where it was laid in state so that mourners could pay homage. The newspapers described hundreds of thousands (*lakhs*) as having gathered there with a combined affect of sorrow and anger. Meanwhile it was assumed by most people that random acts of violence being reported were due to "mob frenzy" and were isolated in incidence. Rajiv Gandhi's speech on taking over as prime minister confirmed this interpretation when he stated, "The foremost need now is to maintain our balance. We should not let our emotions get the better of us because passions would shroud our judgment." Several editorials and appeals issued by prominent citizens appealed to people to stop the madness and to rise above communal frenzy.

Headlines on November 2nd announced that Delhi burned as mobs ruled the streets. It was reported that several trains coming from outside Delhi had been attacked, and Sikh passengers had been dragged out and beaten or killed.[6] Rioting was reported from areas in central and south Delhi while a passing mention was made of trans-Yamuna colonies. The prime minister was reported to have sternly told his officials to check violence at all costs. According to reported news, three hundred persons injured in "mob violence" were brought to the Lohia hospital, and fourteen persons in critical condition were admitted at AIIMS. Crack troops were told to take up positions.

Despite the assurances given by government on November 2nd that the violence would be controlled, ghastly murders committed in Block 32 of Trilokpuri, a trans-Yamuna area away from the center of the city, became known on November 3rd. The newspapers reported that on November 2nd, a crowd had surrounded Block 32 in this area and killed one hundred persons by burning them alive. Some residents of this area, accompanied by journalists, went to the local precinct headquarters to report the carnage even as crowds were killing people and burning houses and shops, but police made no attempt to control the violence. Later investigations by members of human rights groups showed that two journalists had come to the area when they had received information of violence being committed and had tried to enter Block 32, but were turned away by hostile crowds. They had immediately reported to a senior police official that they feared gruesome acts of violence were taking place in Block 32 and made an urgent request for him to take preventive action, but police did not take any steps to prevent or control the situation. Later (on November 5th) one of these journalists, Rahul Kuldip Bedi, filed a criminal complaint against these officials for dereliction of duty. Because of the outrage expressed by several civil rights groups on the complicity of the police in the violence, lower police officials—namely, Inspector Sukhbir Singh and Duty Officer Justi Ram of the Kalyanpuri Police Station—were arrested, but there was no further information provided about any concerted steps by the police to punish negligent officers.

Although by this time the army had been given orders to bring the situation under control, army jeeps that went around the colony that day did not have information about the precise locations in which the worst violence was taking place. The description of the crowds in the newspapers continued to deploy the same language, casting them as "street urchins," "antisocial elements," "thugs," and "lumpen elements." Alternately they were described as "irate mobs" or a "bloodthirsty mob of youths who came in waves."

While the carnage at Trilokpuri finally brought home the extent of the brutality and the terror to a reading public and information about it seeped into various circuits of talk, it is clear that many peripheral areas in which violence was taking place remained hidden from view. Mangolpuri, a colony adjoining Sultanpuri, was mentioned in the newspapers for the first time on November 4th. A report prepared by four university professors (including myself) published in the *Indian Express* on November 11th gave the first full account of violence that had continued in peripheral places like Sultanpuri until November 3rd and showed that there was a strong element of organization and of involvement of prominent Congress politicians in the riots. Simultaneously, inquiries by journalists and civil rights activists provided decisive information on these issues.

Mrs. Gandhi's body was cremated on November 4th. On the same day the police commissioner of Delhi, Mr. Tandon, made the statement that only forty deaths had occurred in Delhi but admitted that the situation in peripheral areas was bad. The same day corpses loaded onto four trucks were recovered in Block 32. The lieutenant governor of Delhi, Mr. Gavai, who had refused to admit the seriousness of the situation, was removed from office, and the then Home Secretary, Mr. Wali, took over as lieutenant governor.

On November 5th, Mr. Wali gave a press conference in which he stated that 450 deaths had occurred and twenty thousand people had been given shelter in relief camps. He said that five relief camps had been established and that with the arrest of 1,809 antisocial elements the situation was expected to quickly return to normal. He gave a clean chit to the Delhi police and said that they had done an excellent job in curbing the violence. He attributed the violence to antisocial elements and ruled out the possibility that any residents of the riot-torn areas had been involved.

Relief efforts had meanwhile started primarily with the help of voluntary organizations. Many Sikhs had taken shelter in *gurudwaras*. On November 4th an ad hoc organization (Nagric Ekta Manch) formed by concerned citizens in their haste to meet the contingencies of the situation set up relief camps in several public buildings such as schools and colleges. These were run primarily by voluntary efforts and, while heroic under the circumstances, were obviously inadequate to meet the needs of the affected populations. Some prominent citizens of Delhi, including former bureaucrats and servicemen, retired judges, teachers, and some politicians, were putting pressure on the Home Ministry to deploy the army to deal with the violence and to give some sense of security to the frightened Sikhs who were given shelter in relief camps, but they uniformly reported a lack of serious response. Meanwhile the number of people given shelter in these camps rose to fifty thousand. There were twenty-eight relief centers set up by November 5th, and conditions were understandably chaotic. Only on that date did the administration recognize ten of these camps, and on November 6th bureaucrats of the rank of joint secretaries were put in charge of the camps. The Citizens' Commission set up by prominent citizens of Delhi in January to enquire into the riots commented upon the lack of interest on the part of the administration in providing relief to the affected population. Its report contained a stricture: "In the event, it was left almost entirely to non-official agencies to provide cooked food, medical relief, clothing, shelter and most importantly, psychological reassurance to the ever increasing number of victims."[7]

The initial understanding of the situation in media reports attributed the violence entirely to unruly crowds and depicted them as irate, mad, bloodthirsty, and composed primarily of antisocial elements. The power of the model that depicts crowds in terms of madness and its metaphors was obvious. Initially it was assumed that, crazed by grief, people had lost control, but this description was soon replaced by the notion that it was street urchins, thugs, and antisocial elements who had taken advantage of the temporary collapse of state order and gone about looting property and killing people. Newspaper reports assumed that the police force was outnumbered, thus explaining their inability to restore order.[8] I shall treat this particular account as the official narrative of the riot. As the description culled from the newspapers makes clear, representatives of all major political parties as well as concerned officials reiterated its essential elements, constructing agency in terms of madness. Settling for this particular representation of the crowds would have exonerated the authorities from fixing responsibility since madness is said to be its own explanation.

It was only later when results of the detailed investigations by voluntary organizations began to be reported that a different story emerged, challenging this view of the violence.

THE SECOND NARRATIVE

In direct contrast to the account given above, a second story emerged through the investigative labors of voluntary groups that proposed an explanation of the violence that implicated various state functionaries in collaboration with some prominent politicians of the Congress Party in having planned the riots to teach Sikhs a lesson and to mobilize support from the Hindus. The strongest formulation of this was found in a report by Citizens for Democracy. The authors of this report stated, "We have shown in this report that several meetings were held all over Delhi—central, outer, and trans-Yamuna areas in the late hours of 31st October to give final touches, as it were, to the plan already prepared with meticulous care, with an eye to every minute detail that nothing was left out to successfully exterminate the Sikhs."[9] As evidence, they presented the following facts.

After interviewing hundreds of victims they had found that "not a single Sikh was killed on 31st October." Second, they gathered from these interviews that on the night of the 31st, meetings of Congress functionaries were held in different parts of Delhi in which every act was planned in meticulous detail. The authors inferred that this is when it was decided that on the morning of November 1st between 9 and 11 A.M., attacks would be launched on Sikhs simultaneously in various parts of the city. The attacks, they state, came in four phases: first, *gurudwaras* were attacked;

then Sikh houses were looted and set ablaze; next, men were humiliated by shearing their hair and shaving off their beards, and then they were killed; finally, women were molested and raped, and some were killed. The purpose of this carnage, according to the report, was to get the sympathy vote of Hindus to win upcoming elections.

Other reports were more measured in their claims, but all of them found evidence of some previous organization and the involvement of local leaders of several lower castes and some Congress (I) leaders. The police invariably were found to be partisan or passive.[10] With this description I now turn to a detailed mapping of the unfolding of the violence in one locality situated in West Delhi on the border of Uttar Pradesh and Delhi.

LOCALIZING THE NARRATIVE

As I mentioned in the introductory chapter of this book, my involvement in Sultanpuri was not brought about by a conventional idea of fieldwork. I felt enraged in the days following Mrs. Gandhi's assassination at the brutal violence against Sikhs and became part of the collective effort to gather data for relief and rehabilitation but also to contest the claims of the state. By sheer coincidence, I came across some survivors from Sultanpuri in a relief camp where I was volunteering and learned they feared that other residents of the colony who had failed to make it to the camp faced greater danger because the killers were at large there and still threatening the residents with further violence. With the help of Jesuit priests from a seminary (Vidya Jyoti), we managed to go to Sultanpuri as a group on November 5th. Later I became completely involved in this locality and especially in one of the blocks.

I was extremely fortunate in securing help from the Indian Express Relief Committee that allowed me to remain engaged in the work of attending to the needs of the survivors, especially in A4 Block of Sultanpuri.[11] I was, however, always conscious of the fact that there we were in an adversarial relation to the state, so that for each claim on behalf of survivors, we had to produce what would count as evidence.[12] This is what accounts for the fact that, even in the middle of devastating violence, it became necessary for us to devise questionnaires to get the names of the people who were dead or injured and to record the extent of damage to houses. It was remarkable that even in this atmosphere of fear and uncertainty, a team of fellow teachers and students came together to gather these data. Even after the immediate sense of urgency had passed I continued to visit the

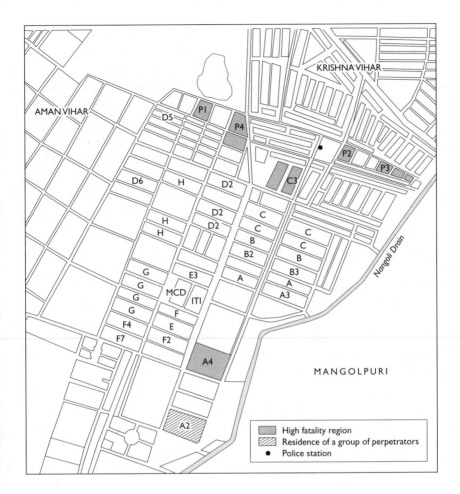

Map labels:
KRISHNA VIHAR
AMAN VIHAR
P1
D5
P4
P2
P3
D6
H
D2
C3
D2
D2
C
H
H
C
B
C
B2
C
B
G
E3
B3
G
A
A
G
MCD
ITI
B3
A3
G
F
F4
E
F7
F2
A4
A2
Nangoli Drain
MANGOLPURI

High fatality region
Residence of a group of perpetrators
• Police station

2. Sultanpuri.

locality every day for over a year. I introduce all these factors because I think they account for the particular modality of the fieldwork that I did with its emphasis on muscular "facts"—those that could stand up, in my mind at least, to the toughest interrogations of the bureaucrats and the courts. The first part of this work was the surveys that we conducted, based on which I am able to give this account of the unfolding of the violence in this locality and to show how it was mapped on the earlier distribution of conflicts with local salience.

Our team surveyed affected 523 households in thirteen blocks in Sultanpuri.[13] Each block was spread over several adjoining streets (see map 2).

Since only the Sikh households could be surveyed,[14] I do not have information about the total number of households in these blocks, but the largest concentrations of Sikhs of different castes were in Blocks A4, B2, C3, D2, D6, E3, F2, and F4.[15] There were several *jhuggis* (shanties) in F7 in which Sikhs resided. However, the point to remember is that the Sikhs were not a homogeneous group—they differed by caste, sectarian allegiance, and place of origin, and these differences could be mapped on the spatial organization of the resettlement colony. The first survey of these households was conducted between November 18th and 28th. A second survey became necessary in January 1985 to assess the nature and amount of relief that had reached the victims and to identify individuals who had not received compensation or any other kind of help. Subsequently we conducted some smaller surveys to assess specific needs.

It must be remembered that the surveys were conducted, not for any disinterested social science enquiry, but because we were engaged in the urgent task of collecting information that we hoped would help to identify the guilty and that would help us to organize the relief work in a systematic way. Until late in the night of November 3rd, the lieutenant governor of Delhi had categorically stated to various teams of volunteers that there were not more than four widows as a result of riots in the city of Delhi. The army was called out in the city on November 2nd but was not visible in the affected colonies until the evening of the 4th, while complete devastation and destruction had stalked the streets of resettlement colonies in the west and east of Delhi.

So it was that when we were conducting our first survey there was very little material help and we could not assure the victims that, apart from the daily struggle of providing them food and making sure that they would not be attacked again, we could promise anything. Ultimately these surveys helped enormously in distributing relief gathered with the help of voluntary organizations (especially the Indian Express Relief Committee) and for identification of widows or other heirs of the dead who, after much pressure from civil rights groups, were granted compensation of Rs. 10,000 for each deceased by the central government. Although we made extensive use of these surveys for bureaucratic purposes, my initial writings on the subject were on the experiences of the survivors. It took me ten years to look at the dry record of facts in a systematic way—who was killed in each family, at what time did the killers come, what was the mode of killing, who were the people in the crowd, who were the other relatives of the survivors who could be contacted, what goods were looted by the rioters—as explicating something important about the riots themselves in addition to being instruments for organizing the work of relief and rehabilitation.[16]

As stated earlier, there was sporadic violence in the streets on October 31st, but from all available evidence this was anonymous violence. One family was killed on that evening in Sultanpuri (the importance of this event will appear later), but the maximum number of people killed in an organized manner was on November 1st and 2nd with some sporadic killing on the 3rd. In one of the blocks, though, a cluster of *jhuggis* made up of new migrants, the violence took place on the evening of the 3rd.

The following gives an idea of the nature of the community inhabiting each of these blocks and the kind of violence that they were subjected to:

Block A2. There were five households of Siglikar Sikhs on the edge of the street and one mud structure on the corner. The people described their work as that of *pheri,* that is, the supply of small iron and metal clippings for construction work and repairing iron tools. They were migrants from Alwar and nearby villages in Rajasthan but did not have other relatives staying in Delhi. Three men were killed, and some household goods were looted. One person who was reported missing was found later. The rest of this ward was inhabited by members of a scheduled caste. Sometimes they were referred to as Chamars from the neighboring state of Uttar Pradesh and other times as Bhangis. Some of them told me that they had migrated from Baraut and Baghpat near Meerut in Uttar Pradesh.

Block A3. There were only three households of Siglikar Sikhs. The houses were mud structures with asbestos roofs. No killing or looting was reported from these households. The block had a mixed membership consisting of some Muslim families, some lower-caste families, and some migrants from Nepal.

Block A4. There were 190 households that we could survey, of which 125 were of Siglikar Sikhs from Alwar and neighboring villages. Twenty more households were of Sikhs from other parts who resided as tenants in the houses of the Siglikar Sikhs. Each house was on a twenty-five-yard plot. The Siglikar households were on two adjoining streets in A4. The total number of houses was 350, and in addition there were plots marked up to number 500. Our work was confined to the two streets in which the Siglikar Sikhs lived.

The houses of the Siglikars in this block were *pucca* (concrete) structures. The Siglikar families in this block constituted a single kinship network with a bilateral kindred structure, that is, with relatives tracing connections through both male and female sides. There were other relatives of these families living in Blocks D2 and D6 and in some cases in Mangolpuri and Trilokpuri. Of all the surveyed households the highest concentration of households with men working in countries in the Middle East was from A4. There were forty-two men who had been or were currently in one of these countries. The highest number of killings was recorded from A4: seventy-seven men and two women were killed by being either burned alive or beaten and burned, and in one case shot. Everything was looted, and most households reported losses of gold and silver ranging from 2 to 10 tolas,[17] large amounts of cash, imported clothes, watches, and electronic goods. The houses were all burned, and windows and doors were systematically broken.

B2, B3. We surveyed only forty houses in this block since it seemed completely unaffected. The inhabitants were a caste of bangle makers and bangle sellers. The houses were mud structures with very little signs of affluence. The killers did not come into this block—not a single death was reported.

D2, D6. The members residing in the streets of D Block were part of the kinship network of the Siglikar Sikhs in Block A4. This block also showed affluence in the form of *pucca* houses, double-storied structures, and household *karkhanas* (workshops). One death was reported of a person who ran a *jhatka* meat shop in the area.[18] There were no reports of arson and looting from this block, although some residents tried to register cases of looting when the relief process started.

E3. This block had scattered Sikh households from the Lohar (iron monger) caste, migrants from Lahore who came to Delhi in 1947. There were three households of auto-rickshaw drivers. No deaths were reported from this block. On the edge of an adjoining street, there was a single household of a *granthi* (Sikh functionary charged with reading the scripture in the *gurudwara*) who was caught in a nearby unbuilt-on plot grown up with grass and weeds and burned alive. His wife was from Mathura in the state of Uttar Pradesh, and they had no kinship connections in the colony at all. In table 2 I show this death in E3 for convenience.

F2, F4. These were two adjoining streets that again showed a certain cohesiveness since the households were all from the Lohar castes. Only five households reported male members to be working as masons in the countries of the Middle East. Our records showed a total of 120 households in these two blocks with some low-caste Hindu families living as tenants in F2. In all, twelve deaths were reported from these two blocks, but unlike A4 Block, the streets and houses did not bear the same visible signs of arson and destruction.

F7. The Sikhs living here were living in *jhuggis*. Unlike the blocks in which houses had *pucca* structures, here the men worked as day laborers in construction work, and the women were employed as part-time workers in the households of various adjoining colonies. Some of the *jhuggis* belonged to members of the Hijra (transgendered or third-sex) community, who lived with either a single male or shared the household with his family. There were four deaths reported from Sikh households in the *jhuggis*. The caste background could not be ascertained in these cases. Two persons who were killed were scooter drivers and had been caught on the morning of November 2nd when they had gone to defecate in the fields. Their scooters had been burned. Two others had been dragged out from the *jhuggis* in which they were hiding and burned alive. No looting was reported from here, but then there was nothing to loot in the *jhuggis*.

P Block. Although our initial survey did not include the *jhuggis* in the P block, which were on the other end of the colony from A4, subsequently we did work among the survivors here. In the absence of the survey, exact numbers of Sikh households or numbers of deaths could not be ascertained, but at least twenty households reported the death of male members on November 3rd. The *jhuggis* were of a mixed composition. The area had more than two hundred *jhuggis* and included a larger number of Muslims than any other block. According to our estimates the Muslim households numbered between forty and fifty. The inhabitants of the *jhuggi jhopdi* colony in Mangolpuri that was adjacent to the sewage canal that divided the two colonies were subjected to similar violence. According to the PUCL-PUDR report, murder and arson took place on November 1st in the Mangolpuri *jhuggis*, and the bodies were dumped in the sewage canal.[19] Later the canal was dredged during a departmental inquiry initiated by the police commissioner, Mr. Ved Marwah, who had replaced the earlier commissioner, Mr. Tandon. The information on how many bodies were recovered was not made public.

Table 2 summarizes the information given above.

TABLE 2
Distribution of Sikh Households and Number
of Persons Killed, by Block

Block	Sikh Households	Persons Killed
A2	5	3
A3	3	0
A4	145	79
B(2, 3)	40	0
D(2, 6)	180	0
E3	30	1
F(2, 4)	120	12
F7	Uncounted	4
P1	Uncounted	20
Total	523	119

THE LOCAL AS LOCUTIONAL

It would be evident from the brief description of the blocks and the differentiated picture of the violence that the general theories of riots and crowd behavior would be unable to account for this differentiated picture. If crowds were like rational agents and were acting here to right a moral wrong, then how did the Siglikar households in A4 become the primary target of their attack? Suppose it were true for the moment that Hindu groups reacted with anger and acted to "punish" the Sikhs who were held to be collectively responsible for the assassination of Mrs. Gandhi—then how did they differentiate between the bangle-maker caste of B Block and the particular kinship network of the Siglikars who resided in A4? Conversely, if the riots were simply an expression of a blind rage in which all normal taboos had been suspended, how did the crowds act to differentiate the different kinds of persons against whom violence was unleashed? Finally, if it is sufficient to explain the riots as "state sponsored" or a result of a well-planned Congress conspiracy as many activist groups and scholars argued, then how do we account for the particularity of the choices that seem to have been made?

Let me respond to the pressure of these questions with the following observations:[20]

a. The violence in Sultanpuri shows that while Hindus and Sikhs would
   be thought of as totalities in terms of discursive communities, this

formulation eclipses the actualization of the violence, which shows how sectarian affiliations were broken by caste differences and divided into fractions of "working classes." These account for the shape of the conflict in the locality, though outside of local memory the representation of the riots continues to treat this as "communal" conflict between two sectarian groups. This does not mean that the discursive forms were false, but rather that introduction of perspective or point of view pluralizes the narrative task.

b. The extreme violence we saw was continuous with everyday violence that implicated both the state and the community and demonstrated clearly that violence was not set apart from sociality: rather, the agency of the violence rendered the social as an entity to be "made" rather than that which was given. Again, to say that the extreme violence was continuous with everyday life is not to say that it was the same, but rather that the everyday provided the grounds from which the event could be grown. However, without being anchored to the national event of Mrs. Gandhi's assassination and its own genealogy we would not be able to account for the newness of the event.

c. The violence had the nature of being both clandestine and public— clearly the public here was constructed through the acts of violence staged as display as well as by the use of slogans and publicly uttered formulations that placed what was happening in Sultanpuri as if it was continuous with the assassination of Mrs. Gandhi. The capacity of stitching together an emergent national event with the fabric of the social at the local level converted these local spaces into a stage for a national drama—yet the publics that produced this violence were made out of the local in significant ways.

d. Violence produced the categories of perpetrator and victim, but these were not expressions of already existing structural inequalities that could be simply mapped onto these categories—the form of sociality engendered in these peripheral urban localities is much better portrayed in terms of the ubiquity of violence produced by state practices that make everyday life full of perils that became visible in the riots.

THE RIOTS IN SULTANPURI

Although news of Mrs. Gandhi's death and the sporadic violence in central and south Delhi became known in Sultanpuri immediately because of television sets and information carried by those who work in those parts of the city, the Sikh families in Sultanpuri did not fear any reprisal for the assassination. As several of them told me, what did they have to do with the assassination? They had been much more worried about an altercation that had happened between two local leaders that carried immediate consequences for them, at least as they understood what was at stake for them.

Some days previous to the assassination, a fight had broken out between the Pradhan (headman) of the Siglikars in the A4 community and the Pradhan of the Chamar (untouchable) community in A2 Block. These two persons had often been in quarrels. Each had ambitions to displace the other as the major local link connecting political practices in the locality to that of a powerful leader of the Congress Party in this locality. Let us call this leader X. There were different kinds of advantages to be had from this patronage. First, the legal status of the plots allotted to people in this locality was never clear. They had been *jhuggi* dwellers who had occupied land near the embankment of the Yamuna River until 1977, when the beautification drive of Sanjay Gandhi during the Emergency led to their forcible relocation in this area.[21] As many of them told us, their *jhuggis* were destroyed by the demolition squads, and they were bodily displaced to this place, which was nothing but open ground then. "We had nothing but the sky above our heads. We were given Rs. 50 each and were told that these plots of land had been allotted to us. Nearby were the villagers whose common lands had been forcibly acquired, and they were hostile. It was by sheer hard work that we built *pucca* houses here." X, who had risen due to the patronage of Sanjay Gandhi during the Emergency, was seen by them as a patron, and they believed that it was on his mercy that their entitlement to the plots of land depended. Although they said that they had been given legal documents proving the allotment of land, they were not able to produce these. In the case of the households in A4, the subsequent arson and looting did not leave anything in the houses intact, but even in other blocks, legal documents were not available from the people. I suspect that a lot of encroachment had taken place.

Over the past seven years this community had become affluent partly because of the spurt in the construction industry in Delhi and partly because opportunities had opened up for semiskilled labor in the Middle East. The patronage of X was important, though, for them to get employment contracts, visas, and other necessary papers to go there, for which they apparently had to pay substantial sums of money.

The affluence gained in the Gulf was visible in the form of consumption items for "display." The women had clothes imported from these countries.

Every house had a television; some had tape recorders, and many kept gold and silver smuggled from these countries. The community had also gathered in strength by inviting relatives from Alwar and adjoining villages to Delhi. In contrast to the visible affluence of the residents of these two streets in A4, the street where the Chamars lived had only some mud walls to mark the boundaries of individual plots and almost no consumption items displayed in the manner of the Siglikar houses. Various kinds of conflicts had surfaced between the inhabitants of these two streets in the last two years, in which the Pradhans of the two communities played an important role.

When I asked people what the employment of the Pradhan of A2 Block was, they said, *vaise to uski Corporation mein naukri hai par vo goonde palta hai,* which would roughly mean that though he had a job in the Municipal Corporation, his main job was to oversee hoodlums and secure their services. (One would normally use the verbal phrase *palta hai* for domesticated animals. It was also a contemptuous reference to the fact that many households in A2 reared pigs.) People said that his power came from the fact that he could provide the manpower for any activity—for murder, for theft, for breaking strikes, for intimidating people. He was an important source for keeping the colony under control for the Congress leader and for collecting crowds for political demonstrations or rallies. Although his control over violence was acknowledged by all, he was not by any means the most influential person in the locality. He was in turn controlled by certain Jat leaders who were from the nearby village, by two Muslim big men, and by a Bania trader in the locality. In turn this network was linked to X, who was the major user of their services. The Station House Officer (SHO) of the local *thana* (police station) also owed allegiance to X.

In the last two years fights had erupted because the Siglikar community had occupied some land in the plot between A2 and A4 and built a small *gurudwara* there. The Pradhan of the Chamar caste of A2 felt this to be a direct challenge to his power since control over all persons in that locality and command over common resources were markers of the power of X and his lieutenant, and the Chamar Pradhan's own power was derived from his connections with them. One important way that power of a local big man was articulated here was in the control that he exercised over the common spaces and resources—parks, streets, and water pumps to which residents were assumed to have access due to his patronage. This power could be translated into money, but that was not necessary. For the Pradhan it was sufficient that people acknowledged his "territory." This was what the affluent A4 residents seemed to be challenging.

Other squabbles had broken out, the Siglikars said, because their afflu-ence was offensive to the Chamars (*hum se jalte the*—they were envious of us). Finally, some women among the Siglikars flouted their comparatively higher-caste status by taunting the Chamar women that Chamars had tra-ditionally survived by eating the leftovers of others (*dusron ki juth pe palte the*).[22] All these factors came be articulated in the "speech" of the perpe-trators as the following incident will show.

When we went into this locality initially on November 5th, we were sit-ting in a nearby *dhaba* (roadside tea stall) having tea when a group of young men strutted in aggressively. They were in fits of laughter recalling the three previous days of the carnivalesque violence. Snatches of conver-sation that I overheard were "So I said, what happened to your swagger—do you feel light in the head?" Later we learned that they were referring to the fact that men who were spared their lives had to agree to have their hair shorn publicly to the accompanying jeers of the crowd. "And how the women had to grovel (*gidgidana pada*)—where was all that arrogance (*ainth*) of foreign-made clothes?" Later we shall see how the commodities that seemed to have defined the bodies of the Siglikar women and were the cause of pride for their men "spoke" through other bodies. This and other such evidence we gathered pointed to the regular sources of tension between the two streets. But as many families in this and other blocks told us, there were tense exchanges and occasional fights, which had reached the maximum pitch of *pathrav*—fighting by pelting stones at each other. While there had been cases of street quarrels and even physical violence, such brutal violence as in the aftermath of the assassination had not been seen at the collective level before.

On October 31st, fights began to erupt between the Siglikars of A4 and the Chamars of A2 Block. There was some stone throwing and exchange of abuses. According to many residents, both Sikhs and others, the situa-tion would not have deteriorated so much if the two Pradhans had not been completely inebriated. The rumors that some Sikhs had celebrated the assassination of Mrs. Gandhi had filtered in. The Pradhan of the Chamars had begun shouting that the Sikhs must apologize, and the Prad-han from A4 had laughed and taunted him that he (a Chamar) was a person of no worth (*do kauri ka admi*—a "two-penny-worth person"). Some elders had tried to restrain the Pradhan from exchanging insults and abuses with the Chamars. But he told them that they had no reason to fear. Instead of restraining himself, he had begun to taunt the Chamars with such remarks as *are Chamar logon ke hath mein kabhi bnaduk ayee hai—pakadna bhi ata hai bunduk ko*—Has a gun ever reached the hands of a Chamar—would you even know how to hold one? This was in response to jeers from the other side that the guards of Mrs. Gandhi had been cowards, killing a defenseless woman.

It appears that there was a lull in the fighting that evening. But the entire locality—including the other blocks—was now alive with rumors that Sikhs were being killed in the city. Some people wanted to negotiate, but the Pradhan was adamant that no one had the guts to touch them. According to many people they heard later that there were negotiations and plans made between the Pradhan of the Chamar colony, two local Muslims, the ration shop owner, and X. According to them X's car was seen in the vicinity several times that night. On the night of the 31st when people were in their homes, a crowd came at about 10 P.M., led by the Pradhan of A2 Block. They were accompanied by the local SHO and some police constables. People in A4 Block said it was not a large crowd—probably only thirty to forty persons—most of them neighbors whom they recognized, some Jats from nearby villages such as Sultanpur and Pooth, and some persons whom they had seen earlier but could not identify. They were firm that although they had later told several journalists (*akhbar wale*) that they were attacked by outsiders, this was only because they were too scared to name their neighbors.

The crowd came and stood outside the house of the A4 Block Pradhan and challenged him to come out.[23] The Pradhan owned a revolver (the term used was *bandook*) and came out with it. He was ordered by the SHO to go and leave the revolver in the house. Some others hearing the noises gathered near. All the Siglikars were told that they should go into their houses—otherwise they would be hauled off to the police station. Frightened and somewhat confused, they went back to their homes.

When the Pradhan came out without his revolver, accompanied by his two sons, the crowd started hurling abuses at him. I am not very clear as to what was said at this time, but it seems that the abuses and insults were a mixture of fragments from different kinds of discourses. There was the continuing anger at the Siglikars' having made good and the admonishment that now they could pay the price for having been so arrogant about their wealth. But other abuses were also hurled. One frequent challenge (*lalkar*) was *khun ka badla khun* and *tumne hamari ma ko mara hai*—Blood must be avenged with blood, and You have killed our mother. These slogans had been occasionally shouted by the crowds that had gathered outside the hospital and were to gain in intensity for the next few days until the funeral. It appears that at the moment of violence, a certain "nationalist" discourse, picked up from the images on television, began to speak through the body. The Pradhan was badly beaten, the crowd asking him repeatedly to seek forgiveness, to apologize. "Apologize for what?" he asked repeatedly. For having arrogated privileges beyond the status of the Siglikars, for having killed "our mother." The more he tried to fight, the more he was beaten with *lathis* (sticks). His sons tried to come to his aid and were beaten. Finally the leaders assisted by the constables poured kerosene over his beaten and bruised body and set fire to him. The same fate was handed out to his two sons. His wife, who was inside hiding, could not contain herself when she heard her sons calling out to her—she was threatened, but she insisted on coming to her sons and was similarly killed. All the while the bodies were burning and the dying persons were calling out for water, the SHO was shouting that if anyone dared to come out and interfere with the law (*kanoon ke khilaf kisi ne hath uthauya*), he would be shot dead.

The crowd dispersed—no one could tell us when—but the SHO announced that all the Siglikars were to stay inside their houses if life was dear to them. People said that, at first, they were stunned. Was this a legal operation? The SHO had evoked the authority of the law. Suppose the crowd came back the next day? Should they try to escape under cover of darkness? But escape where? When some people tried to sneak out to the neighboring houses to consult with their neighbors (and here we have to remember that many of the neighbors were close kin), they discovered that a watch was being kept from the terraces of two houses, and they were warned that if they did not return immediately, they would be shot dead. From the voices and from their personal knowledge of past histories, they all identified the two voices as one belonging to a local Muslim and one to a Jat from the Pooth village. Nevertheless some persons did try to sneak out. From the records I have, there is definitive evidence that early in the morning at about 4 A.M., three young men sneaked out dressed as women. They were initially reported missing but found their way back in a fortnight's time. They told me that they had hidden in some relatives' houses in Blocks D2 and D6.

The crowd returned at 7 A.M. the next morning and then started a carnage of pulling men out from the houses, dousing them with kerosene obtained from the ration shop, and burning them alive. Most of the seventy-six men who died in this block were hit by *lathi* blows, followed by dousing with kerosene and being set afire. One man was thrown down from the first floor (the second floor, in American usage). The men who escaped were the tenants in this block, although their houses were also looted. The crowd went around setting fire to every house, breaking doors and windows, looting and carrying away cash, gold, silver, electronic equipment, stainless steel vessels, and whatever they could lay their hands on. This carnage went on for two days. On November 1st, the crowds came at approximately 7 A.M. and then again around 11 A.M., 3 P.M., and 7 P.M. They were accompanied by the SHO and some constables. On the second day, they were accompanied by more men including a dreaded henchman of X's and the assistant of a local don well known for his underworld activities. Apparently these two men made the killings more technical by using what people called a "white kind of chemical" that burned very quickly. In between, watch was kept by two gun-wielding men from the terraces of adjoining blocks as well as two constables who were posted on "duty" at the entrance and the exit of the block. At least two men who tried to escape when they thought there was a lull in the intensity of the killing were shot dead. The marks left by the bullets, the blood splattered on the walls, and the heaps of ashes and the burned-out houses that we found when we went to the block on November 5th bore evidence to the truth of these horrific accounts.

After the first night it seems that leadership of the crowd shifted to hands other than those of the Pradhan of A2, who now had to undertake the job of removing and disposing of the bodies. X is said to have arranged for *tempos* (small trucks) in which half-burned bodies were dumped and carted under cover of darkness to the cremation grounds near the Yamuna River. Subsequently I was tipped off that two prominent persons from the Dom and Panda communities who lived near the cremation *ghats* arranged to have the bodies cremated en masse.

On the morning of November 3rd three terrified Sikhs who had houses in A2 Block tried to escape and were caught and beaten to death. On the morning of the 4th when the army moved in, there were no bodies to be found—but the evidence described earlier of destroyed houses, bullet holes, burned doors, and small heaps of ashes, as well as the devastated human survivors was very much there.

As news of the carnage in A4 began to spread in the other blocks of the colony, several blocks acted in different kinds of ways to protect themselves. In A3 Block all families attested to the fact that they were helped to hide by their Hindu neighbors. One man and his wife were hidden in a nearby mosque by a Muslim neighbor. In B Block, the bangle sellers did not apprehend any danger to themselves. They were assured by their neighbors that what was happening in A4 was a tale of vengeance between the Chamars and the Siglikar Sikhs. Though frightened, they said they thought they were too poor for the crowds to be attracted by the prospect of looting them.

The cases of D2 and D6 Blocks was entirely different. The inhabitants of D2 were part of the same kinship network as A4. They were also affluent, with *pucca* structures and many of the goods that had aroused envy against the Siglikar Sikhs of A4. As news of the carnage in A4 began to come in, and especially the complicity of the police in the carnage, their leaders decided that they could not expect any help from anyone. So they collected together all the able-bodied men, collected whatever weapons they could lay their hands on, and worked through the night to erect barricades at the entrance and the exit of the block. The few Hindu households in this block cooperated with them completely and acted as spies to bring news of what was happening in the other blocks.

We had asked families in A4 Block if anyone had come to their aid during the killing and looting, and the invariable answer recorded in our survey is that neighbors did not help, for they were themselves the killers. Their relatives in D Block were aware that they had left their kin such as married daughters or close cousins to the mercy of the killers. But as the D Block residents explained, "What could we do? We did not have the weapons to fight with the police. But we were determined that we were not going to go like the sacrificial goat (*bali ka bakra*), we would fight and injure them if they came near us." It seems the crowd did come several times but apparently decided not to fight with the people in this block. The lone death was of a meat shop owner who was caught unawares when he went out to defecate.

In Blocks F2 and F4, there were similar deaths of people who were caught outside their houses. There were two cases of scooter drivers who were outside the colony and were caught and killed by anonymous crowds. Two others were caught in the fields where they had gone to defecate while some members of a crowd were returning on the night of November 2nd. The bodies of the two scooter drivers were never found, but some people reported that they had been killed quite close to the colony.

In the F7 *jhuggis* the story was different. Here the police had been locked in a earlier conflict with the *jhuggi* dwellers when a person (a balloon seller by the name of Wilson) was arrested on suspicion of theft, had been taken to the police station, and had died under torture. A group of Jesuit social workers had filed a criminal complaint against the SHO with support from the *jhuggi* dwellers. Two Sikhs who had been active in their support of the social worker had been dragged out and burned alive by the police constable and some persons accompanying him.[24]

There were numerous killings in C and P Blocks that we could not investigate. As I said earlier, we did get involved with the rehabilitation of the *jhuggi* dwellers in P1, but we had not initially surveyed the households. P1 Block was a cluster of *jhuggis* at the edge of the colony with a park and a broad street dividing the *pucca* dwellings from the *jhuggis*. At a little distance from the other side was a sewage canal, the Nangloi drain, that divided Sultanpuri from a *jhuggi jhopdi* colony in Mangolpuri. The *jhuggi* dwellers of P1 Block, both Hindus and Muslims, had assured the Sikhs living with them that they would be protected at all costs. On November 1st and 2nd when aggressive crowds sometimes accompanied by policemen had roamed around the colony, the Sikhs in this block had hidden in their neighbor's *jhuggis*. On the night of the 3rd a police jeep had gone around announcing a curfew and threatening the *jhuggi* dwellers that if they continued to keep the Sikhs hidden, their whole cluster would be set on fire, as it was illegal to hide the Sikhs. Frightened by these threats to their neighbors and feeling themselves under a moral obligation not to endanger the lives of their neighbors, the Sikhs decided to run toward the sewage canal that divided the colony from Mangolpuri. Some hoped to hide in the fields, but the police followed them and shot at them. It was later stated by the SHO that these were trouble makers who had tried to defy the curfew. Although precise estimates are not possible, at least twenty persons died in this carnage.

There were also sporadic killings. For example, one man from a *pucca* house in P Block who was a scooter driver had hidden in an abandoned house along with his three sons. A crowd, among whom the widow and his daughters had recognized some of their immediate neighbors, had doused the house with kerosene and set it ablaze, after challenging him to come out.[25] We could not discover any history of previous quarrels. This and similar deaths that did not fall in any clear pattern happened toward the end, that is, November 3rd. The only interpretation I can offer is that previous enmities were woven into the event. Breaks in normal constraints pried open the social context and allowed people to act in ways that were not otherwise feasible. It was as if violence offered the possibility of acting on long-standing problems and resolving them at one stroke.

I found three other cases of this kind of settling of individual scores, of which I relate only one story. I was repeatedly begged by a woman to go and visit her in the *jhuggi* where her brother lived, which was in an extremely crowded settlement near a drain, about two miles away from her conjugal home. This woman's husband had been reported missing. For a long time I was hesitant to go there because she insisted that I had to come alone, and I was scared that this might be a trick to ambush me and hurt or even kill me.[26] But one day I simply gave in and went to this *jhuggi,* where she told me that her husband was not killed or missing but was in hiding. She said that she had a clandestine relationship with another man, and they had had many quarrels over this. Seeing that so many Sikhs were being killed during the riots, her husband had probably taken the opportunity to kill her lover and had then run away to avoid suspicion. She was scared to report this to the police because then her lover's family would be unable to claim compensation and would turn against her, and her husband's family would also "finish her off." She wanted my advice—I could not give any.

VIOLENCE AND THE LOCAL SUBJECT

Some influential work on the patterns and processes of riots looks at the local as an *example* of wider processes. Stanley Tambiah in his work on crowds takes ethnic riots in various places (Karachi, Delhi, Colombo) and in different periods to arrive at a general theory of collective violence. Thus an incidence of an ethnic or sectarian riot serves for Tambiah as an example of these wider processes that he names *focalization and transvaluation* to explain the trajectory of riots from the local to the national, on the one hand, and *nationalization and parochialization,* on the other, to explain the opposite processes through which "nationally mounted issues at focal centres have their dispersed and fragmented manifestation in local places in terms of local cleavages." This attempt at generalization is, in many ways, part of a language through which ideas of scale are sought to be understood, in which the local stands for something smaller and the nation for something larger. Similar concepts have been used to understand the relation between so-called little traditions and great traditions, as, for instance, in the terms *universalization* and *parochialization.* Thus, for instance, Tambiah talks of how local conflicts build up into an avalanche labeled "ethnic riots."[27] My own view of the local is much closer to Appadurai's idea of the local as a structure of affect rather than something contained within the national in a container-contained relation.[28] The processes identified by Tambiah that see trajectory in terms of movements of scale—as smaller to larger and larger to smaller—fail to capture the specific affect of *violence*. It seems to me that we have to pay close attention to the specific ways in which language as bearing a perlocutionary force transforms everyday concepts into lethal weapons.

Let us return once more to the registers of speech[29] as the crowd publicly enacted the scenes of violence in the streets of Sultanpuri.

First, there was the register of caste, as in the snide references made by the Siglikars to the status of Chamars as receivers of leftover, polluting food or in the Pradhan's proud boast that the Chamars would not even know how to wield a gun. Though it might appear as if this register indicates actual caste relations in everyday life—a part of the *habitus,* so to say—it would be hazardous to rely on these discursive forms alone. In everyday life, Siglikars did not occupy upper-caste patron positions that would have put the Chamars in a client relation to them, nor were the relations in this urban neighborhood generally structured through a traditional *jajmani* type of relations. Thus the caste slurs here enacted ideas about caste status in the abstract rather than in relation to lived exchanges of commensality or occupational specializations.

Second, there were the references to the commodities acquired in the Gulf that signified the wealth of the Siglikars. These had been displayed as imported clothes, television sets, and tape recorders. The riots and the looting created a capability, acquired through violence, to make other bodies speak through these commodities. Thus, in the first month of my fieldwork, I would sometimes encounter groups of young men from the Chamar street who seemed to be in fits of laughter at the sight of clothes or jewelry they had looted from the Siglikar houses and that were now defiantly worn by their women. They would mock the Siglikar men— Where is the *ainth* (pride, arrogance) of your women now? One might think of this as the revenge enacted by the poor not upon the rich, but upon the distortions in everyday relations made possible by the processes of transnational migration.

The third register was enacted by the crowds in slogans such as "You have killed our mother," referring to Mrs. Gandhi as mother, thereby constructing themselves as the true sons of the nation. That the poorest and the most oppressed sections of urban society enacted violence to claim intimacy with the highest echelons of national polity shows the way discursive forms can expand community, but this is not over the homogenous empty time of the nation as in Anderson's notion of the nation as an imagined community.[30]

All three registers of speech lead me to believe that the subjectivity of the crowd can be understood only as a flight from the ordinary made concrete through an imaginary in which the crowds were simultaneously constructing themselves as upper caste, participants in a global economy, and intimately related to the highest echelons of national politics. I would like to think of this as a "brokered" subjectivity in which the publics created in the streets of Sultanpuri somehow transcended the local for those few days that they completely ruled the streets. What we see then is the subversion of the subject rather than his[31] realization that was finally and tragically brought home later to the perpetrators and participants in this carnival-like violence. I offer an example of this from a conversation I had with some of the residents of A2 Block. The changing context of this conversation was as follows.

As the work of voluntary organizations became more systematic in Delhi, there were repeated demands made on the government to bring the culprits to task. This demand became more pronounced as many officials were transferred and new officeholders were charged with the task of restoring calm in the city. It is part of the bureaucratic culture in India (and not only there) that culpability is frequently assigned to those who are lowest in the power hierarchy of the organization.[32] In the case of Sultanpuri, pressure came to be put on the local police, who then rounded up the local participants in the riots, raided their houses, and "recovered" looted property. A number of women from the block of the Chamar households who had looted the property with impunity said to me angrily one day, "It is because of you people that the same police who had said that we could go ahead and take the things from the Siglikar households because they were to be punished for the killing of Indira Gandhi have now turned around and are beating our men and arresting them for having looted these things."

After six months of these events, another young man from the same block one day stopped me and said, "Sister, you are doing so much to help the Siglikars—why don't you do something for us—we are also poor people. The government is now giving jobs and compensation to the Siglikars, but we came out of this empty handed."

Both conversations showed me that the theatrical performances of violence created a subjectivity that could not be carried forward in time. This invites us to rethink the way that we posit anthropological subjects, for we cannot often assume that subjects are in possession of the knowledge that they are enacting. In the famous formulation of Lévi-Strauss the logic of myth inscribed itself in the speaking subject, but how it did so was difficult to pose in his structuralist models of either myth or kinship.[33] It is well known that when asked to explain why they are doing what they are in ritual performances, informants might end up by concocting a rationalization or taking recourse to time-honored tradition as if that constituted an answer.

Are the subjects created in low-income neighborhoods whose bodies bear the marks of the operations of the state similarly to be conceptualized as acting without knowing? Indeed, many anthropological concepts such as that of *habitus* work with the notion of concealment: the conditions under which the *habitus* was produced are said to be concealed from its subjects almost as a condition for practices to be actualized.[34]

Indeed, if we persist in defining the subject primarily through her relation to knowledge, then we would have to move in the direction of showing how the subject is *only* constituted through loss. In the literary rendering of the Partition, as we saw in chapter 3, this loss was seen as the inability of the women to find a way of telling their story as part of the story of the nation—but in their small communities defined by everyday relations, women were able to redefine themselves through the work of repair that they performed. So one has to understand not only the themes of loss and concealment and the almost hallucinatory quality of the speech generated in the riots but also the themes of how one might shift one's gaze to the inhabitation that comes not from the knowing subject but from the subject as engaged in the work of stitching, quilting, and putting together relationships in everyday life. At the very beginning of this book, I addressed the question of the state and how the inaugural movement of independence was imagined as one in which men emerged as husbands and fathers and women as those who had to be restored to their respective communities. That picture of the state referred to the founding violence; in the present chapter we saw the maintaining violence of the state. The picture of law now turns on the question of how it represents the state as both a distant power and one that has burrowed itself into the nooks and crannies of everyday life. In some sense, the state of emergency at the time of the Partition was dramatically visible. In the case of the violence against Sikhs, the state of exception was much more embedded into the everyday life of the peripheral colonies in Delhi. It is to the theoretical and ethnographic task of making visible the working of the state in the zone of indeterminacy that I turn in the next chapter.

NINE

The Signature of the State
The Paradox of Illegibility

RECENT FORMULATIONS ON THE GENEALOGIES of the state have taken inspiration from Benjamin's discussion on the oscillation between the founding and maintaining violence of law and especially his insight into the ways that the legal form detaches itself from what it is supposed to "represent."[1] While this approach has been extremely productive in showing the importance of states of exception as lying both inside and outside the law, it also has tended to render sovereignty as if it were best analyzed as a spectral relic of a past political theology. I want to argue, instead, that if we see how authority of the state is literalized and embodied in the contexts of violence in the Sultanpuri low-income neighborhoods I describe, we come to see the state as neither a purely rational-bureaucratic organization nor simply a fetish, but as a form of regulation that oscillates between a rational mode and a magical mode of being. As a rational entity, the state is present in the structure of rules and regulations embodied in the law as well as in the institutions for its implementation. From the perspective of the people with whom I worked, the law is the sign of a distant but overwhelming power that is brought into the framework of everyday life by the representation and performance of its rules in modes of rumor, gossip, mockery, and mimetic representation. But this is not the end of the story, for the survivors of the riots also looked to the law as a resource for seeking justice, although they knew that its use is fraught with uncertainty and danger. As I shall argue, the state acquires a presence in the life of communities through these local practices that I call magical. I deploy the notion of magic here not to suggest that the state tricks the audience, a notion used by Fernando Coronil with great effect in his recent study of the state in Venezuela.[2] Instead, I wish to make four specific claims in this regard.

First, magic has consequences that are real—hence I prefer to speak of the magic of the state rather than the fictions of the state.[3] Second, the forces that are mobilized for performance of magic are not transparent. Third, magical practices are closely aligned to forces of danger because of the combination of obscurity and power. Finally, to engage in magic is to place oneself in a position of vulnerability. While I hope to show the modalities by which the state in India is suspended between a rational and a magical presence, the ethnography, even at its dramatic moments, rests on everyday practices. This is why instead of counting on theatrical performance of state rituals, the theater of kitsch, or the grotesque parodies of the double funeral as described by Taussig,[4] I look at the spectacular as nevertheless grounded in the routines of everyday life. And it is here that I find myself proposing that the idea of signature, tied as it is to the writing technologies of the state, may be useful in capturing this double aspect of the state.

WRITING AND SIGNATURE

We owe to Jacques Derrida the idea of writing as occurring in a context that is never fully saturated.[5] Derrida has argued forcefully that in understanding writing, we need to go beyond the usual understanding of writing as an extension of oral communication. Writing, for him, is not only a means of communication with absent persons, but more importantly, it questions the very model of language as a system (or only as a system) of communication. Derrida's critiques of intentionality, which tie intent to the presence of the person in speech acts and to the appending of a signature in writing, point to the force of breaking that is inherent in the act of writing itself.[6]

Thus if the written sign breaks from the context because of the contradictory aspects of its legibility and its iterability, it would mean that once the state institutes forms of governance through technologies of writing, it simultaneously institutes the possibility of forgery, imitation, and the mimetic performances of its power. This, in turn, brings the whole domain of infelicities and excuses on the part of the state into the realm of the public. One of the methodological observations that follows from this is that to study the state we need to shift our gaze from the obvious places in which power is expected to reside to the margins and recesses of everyday life in which such infelicities become observable. There is, of course, a paradox here, for it is in the realm of illegibility, infelicity, and excuses that one reads how the state is reincarnated in new forms. While Taussig talks of the spasmodic recharge, the circulation of power between the dead and the living, the state and the people,[7] I would like to start with certain inscriptions.

TWO EXAMPLES

Let me first describe the two different kinds of documents that I encountered during my work among the survivors in Sultanpuri after the assassination of Mrs. Gandhi. I found these documents intriguing. The first was a typical form of the First Information Report (FIR) that many survivors filed at the police stations after the riots had been brought under control in Mangolpuri and Sultanpuri. The second was the divorce agreement drawn up by the caste *panchayat*[8] in these localities to formalize "divorce" between a widow and her dead husband—duly executed on stamped court paper. Let me revisit the scene of the riots in these two places after the assassination of Mrs. Gandhi and the way I came across these documents. Since I described the chronology of the riots in the previous chapter, I take the reader to certain scenes that exemplify the way that survivors tried to make claims on the state for justice and also the picture of law as it was actualized in the activities of policemen of the local precinct.

After three days of killing and looting, the riots had been brought under partial control, and some of the survivors in Mangolpuri and Sultanpuri who had been moved to relief camps in the city gathered enough courage to go to the police station to register criminal cases against those who had looted their property or killed someone in their family. This was more to obtain official proof that these grievous events had, indeed, occurred and that they had been affected by these events than in any hope that the perpetrators would be caught or punished, because the survivors were well aware of the complicity of the police in the riots. The policeman on duty at the police station insisted on dictating the framing sentences of the FIR.[9] Hence the standard framing sentences of the FIR written in Hindi ran as follows:[10]

Dinank 31.10.84 ko Bharat sarkar ke pradhanmantri Shrimati Indira Gandhi ki unke do suraksha karmachariyon dwara nirmam hatya karne ke karan Bharat ki rajdhani Dilli mein janta mein bhari rosh hone ki vajah se

*kai sthanon par janta nein majma khilafe kanoon banakar agjani, lootmar
va katle aam kiya, vibhinn Gurudwaron Sikh gharon va unki dookanon ko
loot liya.*

On date 31.10.1984, due to the fact that the prime minister of India,
Mrs. Indira Gandhi, was cruelly murdered by her two security guards,
the people in Delhi, the capital of India, being enraged, engaged in
illegal activities of arson, looting, and mass killing. Several *gurudwaras,*
Sikh families, and their shops were looted.

The FIR then became specific in enumerating the names of members of
the family who were killed or maimed, and the property that was looted or
destroyed.

How is it, then, that the framing sentences of the FIR used language that
attributed a certain subjectivity to the crowds claiming that *they had been so
maddened by anger* that they attacked people and property? After all, the
victims were well aware of the fact that the crowds had been led or orches-
trated by local politicians and were under the command of the local Station
House Officer. First, when someone went to the police station to register a
complaint, one did so because one had been told by local power brokers
(*dalals,* as they were known in the locality) that it would be difficult for
them to claim any compensation for their losses without legal proof. In the
police station the first part of the FIR was dictated to them. They were told
that a complaint would not be registered without such a formal statement.
Such formulaic modes of recording complaints are routine in police stations and are often oriented to the imagination of how the case would be
presented in a court of law. In this case, though, a term such as *katle aam*
(mass killing) suggests the evocation of a historical imagery of chaos in
which invading armies killed local populations en masse. What is haunting
in this case is that these very FIRs, which encoded what one might call the
lie of the state, were also required by other organizations engaged in relief
work as proof of the victim status of the claimants. For instance, even the
gurudwara committees, which offered pensions to widows of the riot victims, demanded FIRs as proof that a woman's husband had died in the
riots. Thus, ironically, those who were locked in a combative relation with
the state and who had direct evidence of the criminality of the state[11] nevertheless ended up being pulled into the gravitational force of the state
through the circulation of documents produced by its functionaries.

The second example I want to take is from the documents known in the
community as *talaqnamas* (deeds of divorce). These were executed by the

caste *panchayat* of the Siglikars on stamped court paper. These recorded the agreement between the natal family of a man who had died in the riots and his widow to the effect that they would divide the compensation received from the government equally. Under this agreement, the parents of the dead man agreed to give a "divorce" to his widow. As we shall see in the next chapter, because of the custom of leviratic marriage in this community, there was a strong pressure on the young widow to marry a brother of the dead man if one was available. The government decision to award compensation for the dead man to his widow meant that many young women could get independent access to cash incomes. In addition, the *gurudwara* committees instituted a "pension" for the widows analogous to what a widow receives from the government if her husband dies in the line of duty, as in war, or in an accident. From the perspective of the community the rightful heir of a dead man was his coparcener—that is, either a father or a brother. Even a man's mother was said to have a stronger moral claim on the money awarded in compensation for his death than his widow did. Hence, there was considerable tension in the community over the conflict between norms deriving from their conception of inheritance and state norms. A resolution was sought in the nature of a compromise so that if a widow refused to marry her deceased husband's brother or another suitable kinsman, she was given a "divorce" after the division of the compensation between her husband's father and herself, so that mutual claims between her affinal kin and herself came to an end. I was not able to attend any of the *panchayat* meetings because these were held at night and there was an air of a clandestine operation around these meetings. In addition, because of various threats I had received from those engaged in the violence, it would have been foolhardy for me to risk going to the area at night when the meetings were held. So I was even more interested to learn that even in arriving at a community consensus that violated state injunctions, they should have evoked the authority of the state. Equally stunning is the fact that they tried to make their decisions "legal" by evoking the authority of the very state that had been the perpetrator of terror.

I hope these examples show the mode in which the state is present in the life of the community—its suspension between a rational-bureaucratic entity and a magical entity. As a rational entity it is present in the structure of rules and regulations: community customs are made to appear valid in the shadow of these rules and regulations. But its magical qualities are apparent in the uncanny presence it achieves in the life of the community even at the moments of the community's defiance of the state—it is as if the community derives its own existence from a particular reading of the state.

I realize that the term *community* here may give the impression that I am setting up a binary opposition between state and community. I hope it is sufficiently clear from my descriptions that the life of the community was completely entangled with the forms of governmentality that were set in motion after the riots. However, it is important to keep in mind that the forms of governmentality are themselves instituted through sporadic, intermittent contact rather than an effective panoptic system of surveillance. Nor is the state dealing with isolated individuals. Urban neighborhoods, especially in the fringes of the city, are made up of migrants with strong kinship and caste networks so that a set of related kin come to occupy contiguous housing set up on land that has been either allocated under different governmental schemes or simply occupied by them. These material conditions allow certain forms of community to be re-created[12] but can be maintained only by entering into various kinds of negotiations with the agents of the state, such as policemen or state inspectors. The ability of communities living in these neighborhoods to protect their houses from demolition or harassment, even those houses that have been constructed illegally, depends upon their negotiations with these agents of the state— a point I elaborate in the later parts of this chapter.

I shall now go on to suggest that what allows the double existence of the state between a rational mode and a magical mode to be sustained is its illegibility.

READING THE LAW

Allow me to loop back to the devastation of the riots in one of the streets in Sultanpuri. As I argued in the last chapter, the variations in the spatial pattern of riots are best understood in terms of the anchoring of local hostilities to national events, but what interests me here is how the perpetrators evoked the image of law. The interpretation of events as they were unfolding in their streets was not easy for the victims to decipher, for the distinction between the legal and the illegal was so blurred in their everyday lives that they could not quite read what was happening. The accounts given by the survivors of the violence of the crowds who had been gathering and were accompanied by a policeman, the Station House Officer (SHO), are frozen in my memory. As I stated earlier, the altercation between the two Pradhans was described by many as the turning point, when violence moved from verbal abuse and pelting of stones to killing.

One form of utterance is worth recalling here. When the crowd had set fire to the Pradhan and his sons and the dying persons were calling out for water, the SHO was shouting that if anyone dared to come out and interfere with the law (*kanoon ke khilaf kisi ne hath uthaya*—literally, raise their hand against the law) he would be shot dead. Let me also recall the case of the *jhuggi* dwellers in another street, P1, which was at the edge of the colony, with a park and a broad street dividing the *pucca* dwellings of P Block from the *jhuggis*. On November 1st and 2nd when aggressive crowds sometimes accompanied by policemen had roamed around the colony, the Sikhs in this block had hid in their neighbors' *jhuggis*. On the night of the 3rd a police jeep had gone around announcing a curfew and threatening the *jhuggi* dwellers that if they continued to keep any Sikhs hidden, their whole cluster would be set on fire, as it was *illegal* to hide the Sikhs.

The examples show how the documentary practices of the state, on the one hand, and the utterances that embody it, on the other, acquire a life in the practices of the community. It is the iterability of writing, the citability of its utterances that allows a whole realm of social practices to emerge that, even in resisting the state, reproduces it in new modes. The circulation of words like "law" during the riots and the fact that crowds were led in several instances by a policeman showed the blurred lines between law and its violation. In recalling the events of November 1st, people repeatedly stated that it was not clear to them whether the Sikhs were going to be punished for the crime committed on behalf of the community. Although many protested that they had nothing to do with the crime, their legal responsibility for the act was never very clear to them. Thus, even the question of which community they belonged to was tied to their reading of the law. Were they part of the local Siglikar community, which had no connections to the militant movement, or were they now to consider themselves as part of the larger Sikh community, which they believed was, in some ways, responsible for the assassination? The presence of the SHO in uniform, the evocation of "law" (if anyone dares to lift his hand against the law) made the state present precisely where its absence as a rule-governed entity was most evident. The voice of the policeman evoking the authority of the law when the law was clearly dead was what announced the spectral presence of the state. It is this *illegibility* of the state, the unreadability of its rules and regulations, as well as the location of the legitimacy of customary institutions such as the caste *panchayat* in their ability to replicate the documentary practices of the state that makes it possible for the oscillation between the rational and the magical to become the defining feature of the state in such margins.

THE LIFE OF THE STATE

The examples I have given might suggest that I am making a sharp distinction between the functionaries of the state and the members of a community to whom the state is illegible. In fact, it is my argument that many of the functionaries of the state themselves find the practices of the state to be illegible. I was not able to interview the SHO about his own role in the carnage, so I turn to other scenes.[13]

I conducted interviews with other policemen about their role in the counterinsurgency operations in the Punjab, and I found their way of talking about their role in the maintenance of law to be shot through with ambivalence. Rather than talking as those who are engaged in implementing rules and regulations, there were occasions when they talked as if they directly embodied the law. I suggest that it is a complicated entanglement of state and community that makes them act as if they are direct embodiments of the state, especially in relation to harnessing the energies of the dead. Here are excerpts from an interview with a senior police officer, Mr. Tej Singh,[14] who was directly involved in anti-insurgency operations in the Punjab. The same policeman was later shot dead by one of his own junior officials—I will give a brief account of the retelling of that event by another police officer later. I have to be somewhat circumspect in giving precise dates and locations because of the conditions of anonymity under which such information was offered.

Tej Singh was stationed in Amritsar, one of the centers of the militant movement. During Operation Blue Star he was part of the team that had surrounded the temple and was charged with giving cover to the army personnel as they moved in. The army and the police had sustained heavy losses in this operation, yet he bore little resentment about the risks he had been made to take. In fact, he deflected any discussion about the actual operation by describing, instead, a small local event in the police station about one week prior to Operation Blue Star. He spoke in Punjabi laced with occasional English phrases. Here he is describing the atmosphere in the police station in those tense days and the visit of an astrologer who would regularly offer informal advice:

The Pandit[15] came to the police station—he used to come to collect some money, and we would ask him to predict the future. So I said "Pandta, look at my hand and tell me what will happen." He studied my palm and shook his head, putting his hands on his ears and said "*parlay, parlay*" [referring to the flood mentioned in Hindu sacred texts that brings an era in the cycle of time to an end]. I said, "Stop this *bakbak* (nonsense)—tell me what you see." He said, "*Sahib, duniya khatam ho jayegi par tu bachuga*" (Sahib, the world will come to an end, but you will survive). When I was standing on the terrace of a house in the street giving cover and bullets were coming from all directions, one grazed my headgear and I thought of the Pandit.

This vignette shows in a small way how police officers may be charged with implementing the rules and regulations of the state, but they do not cease being members of local worlds with their own customs and habits. The astrologer's weekly visit to the police station when they were in the middle of extremely risky operations is described with a sense of the absurd—but it points to these kinds of connections. The next example, however, shows how the local imperatives within which the rationality of the state is embedded led Tej Singh to experience himself as the direct embodiment of these contradictory discourses, which included reference to locality and caste. In this interview, he was reflecting on the militant movement and on his own sense as a police officer belonging to a previously "untouchable" caste:[16]

We know these boys—we know that there are some to whom Khalistan means something and others for whom it is an occasion to indulge in liquor, drugs—we also know who are the big men who are using the young men to carry out their own ambitions. The genuine leaders of the movement trust me although we are on the opposite sides, but these other kind—they really fear me. So they have been after my blood. [This phrase was in English.] So one day as my driver and I are going down a high road at night, this truck bears down on us at high speed. The truck driver fled after hitting us; my driver was in a coma. I know who those buggers—excuse my language—were. My driver was in the hospital for two months, but he recovered. By some miracle, I escaped. Then three months later, I was sleeping on the lawn of my house. My subordinate officer came over and whispered to me that the man who had arranged for my "accident" was caught in an encounter. Now, I know that the correct thing is to hand him over to the law, but I also know these buggers—*they have bought the law* [said with emphasis].

I told my subordinate not to wait till morning but to bring him in the dark to this large public park.[17] I then took a bath, put on a white *kurta pajama*, drank a whole bottle of whiskey, and then went to the park. There I kicked this man till he was begging for mercy. He was a Jat [high caste, landowner]—I am a Chamar, and I remember him boasting once that when have the Chamars wielded a gun independently?[18] So when I kicked him to death I showed him that he can buy up the upper castes in the police and the courts, but he cannot buy me, this low-caste Chamar.

I must confess that I was chilled by this story—not because I did not know that such framed encounters were indeed common, but because this police officer had the reputation of impeccable integrity, even among the militants. Having risen from the lowly caste of untouchables, he was widely respected in his village across the different caste groups for his charisma. A few months after these interviews took place, he was killed, and I was told that the militants announced an informal cessation of hostilities for two days after his death so that the funeral could be conducted without any mishap. Ironically, he died not as he had anticipated—at the hands of a militant or on the orders of the mafia—but by a bullet mistakenly fired by his own subordinate officer.

The story that another policeman told me later was that a trusted constable, Sukkha Singh, was assigned to penetrate one of the militant organizations. Sukkha became very involved in their affairs and began to receive drugs and illicit money. He became a party to these transactions either because he did not want to blow his cover or because he became greedy and began to accept money for himself. As the policeman explained to me, one could never say with certainty what kind of transactions these were, for the boundaries between the licit and the illicit are so thin. In any case, Sukkha Singh received a notice to face an inquiry. Since he was very close to Tej Singh, the latter told him that he would be there during the inquiry and that he had nothing to fear. In fact, I was told that the previous evening Tej had himself dictated a written response to the charges that the policeman was to face. On the day of the inquiry, one of the senior police officers in charge of the inquiry asked Sukkha to hand over his service revolver. It is purely routine to require an accused policeman to hand over his weapon, and the revolver would have been restored to him after he was cleared of any charges. However, for some inexplicable reason Sukkha completely lost his cool. He responded angrily, "No one asks

Sukkha Singh to hand over his weapon," and he pulled the trigger, first killing Tej Singh and then himself. Those present were certain that the shot was not intended for Tej, his own senior officer and his friend, but Tej got in the way and was accidentally shot dead. Tej's last words were "*Sukkha tu?*"—Sukkha—even you? So there was confusion, the police officer told me sadly: perhaps Tej Singh died with the thought that Sukkha Singh had been bought by the militants after all.

The version of the story I relate here was not what appeared in the newspapers or in the official versions. The police officer who told me this story did not treat it as exceptional. He insisted that this kind of misreading happened more often than could be admitted. Thus, the illegibility of the rules and also the human actions that embody these rules appear to be part of the way that rules are implemented. It is not that the mode of sociality to be found in the institutions of the state is based on clarity of rules and regulations and that these become illegible to the poor or the illiterate, but that the very persons charged with implementing rules might also have to struggle as to how to read them.

In the next section I address the problem of the relation between law and regulation in the context of the illegibility of the state, drawing from some work on the Emergency in India in 1975 when draconian measures were taken to both reduce the population and clean up cities by removing slum dwellers to the periphery. It is these processes that brought the Siglikars into Sultanpuri. I follow that with examples of how similar processes are operative in other low-income neighborhoods in a variety of contexts, even when the political situation seems "normal." While this might seem like a digression, I want to suggest that riots do not bring something entirely new into existence. The peripheral colonies, in which the poor have come to be "resettled," are scenes of the arbitrary nature of state regulations so that the everyday experience of the state is marked by all kinds of negotiations between the local functionaries and the residents. The policies on housing and sterilization came to be linked, of course, because of the special dispensation of the Emergency and were applied with special rigor in Delhi in 1975. They constitute an earlier link in the lives of the urban poor in their relation to the state, and though these policies are not linked anymore, one can see certain continuities in the mode of surveillance that I explore later. In the popular imagination, the Emergency was known as the time of *nasbandi* (sterilization). This period shows with stark clarity how the politics of the body lies at the intersection between law and regulation.

Emma Tarlo offers an excellent analysis of the manner in which two administrative schemes—the Resettlement Scheme and the Family Planning Scheme—that were part of the state's normal housing policies and family planning services for the poor came to be implemented during the national Emergency.[19] The center of gravity in her analysis is the everyday ecology of fear and greed through which the poor ended up as partners in the coercive programs of the state.

The Emergency was a period when all fundamental rights were suspended on the grounds that the country was in danger of falling into anarchy. It was also a period when there was pressure generated to obtain results in the family-planning program—the targets of which were primarily the urban poor. Though targets had always been part of the implementation of family-planning policies in India, the Emergency was widely regarded as a period of crisis in which the government was able to exercise unbridled control over the implementation of these targets.[20] As with most coercive and ill-planned programs, this generated pressure at every level of the bureaucratic hierarchy to produce results, but it was the lower echelons of the bureaucracy who bore the brunt of this pressure to meet targets and produce results. The authoritarianism of Mrs. Gandhi's rule in this period and the destruction of institutions made it imperative for the bureaucracy to implement the policies of the government, not in accordance with rules and regulations, but in accordance with their reading of the wishes of their superiors. The state was literally seen to be embodied in the person of Mrs. Gandhi and her younger son, Sanjay Gandhi, who became, as was widely acknowledged, the extra-constitutional center of power.[21] It was common knowledge that instead of written orders, the bureaucrats received oral orders to implement policies.[22] Rumors about the fate of those who had defied these orders or implemented them in half-hearted ways made lower-level officials extremely anxious about their jobs. So on the one hand, normal bureaucratic procedures were suspended, and, on the other, it was widely acknowledged that Sanjay Gandhi was emerging as an important center of power and that the beautification of Delhi and control of population growth were his favorite programs. While all this is generally known, Tarlo provides a meticulous examination of the files in the slum development department of one of the localities in Delhi in which these schemes were implemented. She shows how the poor were first forcibly removed from their habitations in the city and, second, that their claims to housing in the peripheries of the city were made dependent upon the production of sterilization certificates. While none of this was strictly legal, the paraphernalia of recording claims, examining certificates for their authenticity, and the like gave it the aura of a legal operation. In other words, the life of documents continued as if everything were business as usual.

The government's unacknowledged ways of linking claims to housing with sterilization were translated at local levels into a structure of co-victimhood—people searched for poorer relatives or neighbors who could be induced to undergo sterilization for money. An informal market in certificates developed in which the poor migrants, beggars, or other homeless persons could be induced to undergo sterilization, and the certificates were sold to those who needed them to show that they had motivated others to become sterilized, so they could keep their jobs or their houses. By portraying the poor as active participants in the state policies of repression, rather than as passive victims or noble resistors, Tarlo is able to show how the political regime of the national Emergency was able to draw different sections of the people through fear and greed into its implementation. The point is that neither the lower-level bureaucrats nor those who were relocated on production of sterilization certificates could draw a line between the legal and the illegal. The certificates, once they became a part of the normal bureaucratic operations of recording, became proof of the "legality" of the operations. In the local-level offices in which housing was allocated, the processes of recording the certificates and enumerating claims sanctioned on the basis of them gave the whole operation an air of business as usual.

Although Tarlo states that there are lines of continuity between the state's normal practices and forms of governance during the Emergency, she does not provide us with any ethnography of the continuity of these practices at the time of her fieldwork in the urban neighborhood she studied. I take this opportunity to provide a brief description of the functioning of the state in everyday life and especially of how forms of governance and modes of surveillance are put in operation in the offices of petty bureaucrats or on street corners where the police constables patrol neighborhoods. It is at these sites that bribes for illegally running *karkhanas* (small industrial workshops) in people's homes are negotiated, or new migrants who often occupy state-owned land learn how to avoid eviction, or stealing of water or electricity is condoned in exchange for bribes, votes, or other services that are linked to the underlife of politics. My intention is not to romanticize these practices—for very similar processes operate in upper-income neighborhoods in which bribes are offered for stealing of electricity or running of factories in residential colonies—but under the conditions in which residents of *jhuggi jhopdi* colonies live, such negotiations become necessary to ensure economic survival. These sites then are particularly important for understanding how states manage the populations at the margins, but also how those living in these margins navigate the gaps between laws and their implementation.

Let me take two examples of these processes in everyday life from a low-income neighborhood in Delhi, not very far from the resettlement colony that Tarlo studied. When I initiated my present study in health practices and local ecologies in 1999, I was given directions to the house of the local Pradhan, Nathu Singh (a fictitious name). I went to meet him and to explain my study to him. Within a couple of days, another man confronted me and said that *he* was the leader of the locality and warned me against those who had misled me into thinking that Nathu Singh was the Pradhan. Over a period of time, I was able to work out the contours of the complicated relations between these two men. It appears that the second person had been the caste leader but had been displaced from his position through a series of contests with Nathu over who could offer better services to the local community by negotiating with the forces of the state. In brief, Nathu had proved to be more adept in dealing with the "outside world." As he told me how he secured leadership of the local community, Nathu attributed his ability to deal with the new kinds of problems that the community was facing to the experience he had gained as a "room boy" in a prominent hotel, which had propelled him outside the neighborhood into new kinds of experiences. Although he had spent his childhood in the village from which many members of the community who lived in this neighborhood had migrated, he had studied until eighth grade in the village school. His father had migrated to Delhi sometime in the early 1950s, so it was easy for him to leave the village and join his father in 1970. He then got a job in the hotel, and, as he said, he learned how to talk to people and how to hold his own in conversations with educated people and how, as he put it, to hold his head high. Further, he was able to put aside money from the tips he received from the guests at the hotel. Then in 1982, a number of people from the village put up *jhuggis* on the land that they were now occupying. This led to serious disputes with the earlier settlers in neighboring areas. The members of the Gujjar community who were living in the nearby areas were angry with this group—especially because of caste rivalries and the feelings of the Gujjars that they did not want to live in the proximity of "untouchables." Then one night several men from that community came to attack the residents. Nathu was able to gather enough men to fight and chase away the aggressors. This gave him prestige in the eyes of the local residents.

However, Nathu was worried about the security of their claims over the land that they had occupied. So he negotiated with a policeman who was responsible for patrolling the area to provide them with security in exchange for a *hafta* agreement (an agreed-upon weekly bribe with almost the force of custom). He asked every household for two rupees (about four cents) a month as a voluntary contribution to deal with various kinds of state officials, and though he claimed that the contributions were not steady, it gradually became clear to everyone that he was a more effective leader for the community than the caste Pradhan. Similar to the mediators described by Anna Tsing in her ethnography of Indonesian big men,[23] Nathu Singh displaced the traditional leader to become an effective negotiator with the new forces of the state. I give one example of the modality of state presence and the kind of negotiations that have to be effected.

Since this colony is an unauthorized colony, there are no electric connections in the houses—however, every household has drawn lines from the electric pole in the street to its dwelling. Some years ago it was rumored that if a dwelling unit were to have an electric meter installed, then that would eventually become proof of occupation so that the government could not evict such households and reoccupy their land. In law, the land on which people have made their *jhuggis* is owned by the state, but the legal position is complicated. This is because some years ago Nathu Singh had managed to get a stay order from the High Court that restrained the government against evicting residents from their land unless alternate housing was provide to them. Nathu had employed the help of a lawyer to register the residents as an official Society of Harijans (scheduled castes, who enjoy certain benefits under the constitution because of their depressed position in society)—thus securing some kind of legal status for themselves. The judge used this provision to grant the stay order to the registered society. Now it appeared that while the households could not be evicted from their dwelling units, there was still the problem that those who installed meters but never paid the electricity bills suddenly found that subsequent to the recent privatization of electric supply in Delhi, they were faced with huge bills. They simply did not have the resources to pay these bills. This created a precarious situation for them.

On a visit to the locality in December 2002, I found the whole place plunged in darkness. When I made inquiries, Nathu Singh told me that he had heard rumors that there would be a raid on the locality by government officials and that they might demolish those houses that had not paid their electricity bills. But this would put all the houses into jeopardy because they were all engaged in one illegal activity or the other, and one thing could lead to another. While under the earlier arrangements the local government officials understood this and condoned the infringements (helped by the weekly bribes), a new set of officials might put the whole arrangement at risk. To avoid this, all households had decided to cut off their electric supply so as to not give any official a pretext to visit the area. I asked how they were going to deal with this problem since they could not live without electricity forever. I then learned that several Pradhans from adjoining localities were going to hold meetings and they were planning to go on a *dharna* (sit-in) in front of the High Court. They were all hopeful that since there was a general election scheduled in 2004, and they constituted important vote banks, they would be able to have their colony authorized. It will be recalled that during the national Emergency it was by obtaining sterilization certificates that people were able to gain legal claims over their houses. Now it seemed that the struggle was to put pressure on the local government to grant a legal status to the colony and thus titles to the land that was occupied so that they could get electricity, water, and installation of a sewage system. I hope that these examples make it clear that the Emergency brought out the practices of governance in sharp relief, but for the poor such practices were not exceptional. The intermittent nature of government control, the illegibility of the law, and the negotiations around the thin lines between the legal and the illegal are part of the everyday life of these neighborhoods. The state is present in the form of rumor—its signature is read everywhere. It may be worth remembering Benjamin here, who stated that the tradition of the oppressed teaches us that the state of emergency in which we live is not the exception but the rule.[24] The precarious nature of the everyday in the neighborhoods I have described gives us the grounds to believe that this is not a metaphysical statement, but one located in the conditions of life and labor in these areas.

LEGITIMACY AND THE QUESTION OF SIGNATURE

I hope the iterability of utterances and actions in which the signature of the state can detach itself from its origin and be grafted onto other structures and other chains of signification is clear. How does the state then claim legitimacy in the face of obvious forgeries, corruption within its own procedures, and the mimesis of its structures? To understand this I turn to the realm of excuses—a classical subject in Austin's analysis of language but not often used in understanding the realm of politics.[25]

In Austin's understanding, excuses point to the realm of infelicities when performative utterances fail. Utterances with illocutionary force are felicitous when the context is in place and our trust in conventions is secure. It is then that we can say that accuracy and morality are on the side of saying "my word is my bond." However, my claim in this paper is that fragility of context is built into the situation in which a signature cannot be tied to what one might think of as the notion of utterances and actions of the state. It is this fragility that accounts for the oscillation of the state between the rational and the magical modes. Excuses then provide us entry into a region of language in which we confront the vulnerability of human actions as well as the vulnerability of human utterances. My *actions* are vulnerable because of the limitations of the human body, and my *utterances* become vulnerable because my words may be transfigured elsewhere.[26] In ordinary life, this is the region of human vulnerability—I may be quoted out of context, my words can be reproduced in a mood of irony, or they may be infused with another affect. In the life of the state, that very iterability becomes a sign not of vulnerability, but a mode of circulation through which power is produced.

The examples of FIRs, *talaqnamas,* sterilization certificates, ration cards, and hundreds of other such documents show how the state comes to be present in the everyday life of its subjects. Because it can be multiplied and literalized through documents such as court papers, certificates, and ration cards that can be genuine, forged, or even mimicked, it can enter the life of the community, but because the authenticity of these documents can always be put into question, the subject's identity can never be fully assumed in an encounter with the state.[27] Documents can be forged or used out of context, and because the bureaucratic-legal processes are not legible even to those responsible for implementing them, the state can penetrate the life of the community and yet remain distant and elusive.

In its turn the bureaucratic rationality of the state can always evoke the very facts of its illegibility to the poor as the major form of its defense. Consider, for instance, that bureaucrats withhold information in any crisis on the grounds that since people are illiterate or ill-informed they have a tendency to panic. Thus information can be withheld on grounds of public order. Elsewhere I have analyzed the way that this excuse is routinely evoked in the management of epidemics.[28] Bureaucratic logic displaces notions of irrationality and panic onto a credulous public and thus constructs itself as "rational" in its deliberate absence of transparency.

The stability of the representations of the public as credulous and the state as rational became evident to me in 1984 when I was part of a delegation in Delhi petitioning the lieutenant governor to publicly acknowledge the number of Sikh men who had died in the riots. We were told that to publicize these facts would lead to a flaring of public passion that could lead to more deaths. I can offer other examples in which the government explains away its lack of transparency as a necessary compromise for the preservation of public order. In the first chapter when we looked at the Constituent Assembly debates as marking the inaugural moment of the state in India, we saw that men could be seen as capable of entering into a social contract only if their positions as husbands and fathers were secure so that the social contract and the sexual contract were part of the same inaugural moment. Now, what we have seen is not the founding violence of the state but its maintaining violence. It is important to note that it is in relation to this maintaining violence that the realm of excuses as marking the limits of the civil comes into being. How shall we interpret these different moments to shed some light on what it means to construct oneself as a subject of the state as well as a citizen? I offer some tentative steps in thinking out this problem by engaging with some of the recent contributions on the state in India.

TOWARD CONCLUSIONS

We have seen earlier that the inaugural moment of the state brought out the close relation between the social contract and the sexual contract under the specific new imaginaries of Hindu-Muslim relations. As I argued, the entire effort on the part of the state to "recover" Hindu women from Muslim homes and "return" Muslim women who had been abducted to Pakistan was premised on the notion that it was only when men had established the correctness of the sexual order that they could be considered as legitimate initiators of the social contract that inaugurated the independent state. As we saw earlier, an influential strand of thinking about these issues among Indian scholars is to argue that the alien character of the colonial state led to a kind of defense mechanism in which the distinctions between the home or the sphere of the domestic and the wider outside ensured that an interior domain represented by the former would be protected from the colonial state. However, as the practices I describe in this chapter show, one can speak of the community and the state as representing different forms of sociality at some ideal typical level, but in everyday life community, domesticity, and the sphere of the personal bear the tracks of how the state is re-created *within* and not only outside such forms of sociality.

Could one argue that just as there is a difference between the founding violence and the maintaining violence of the state, so the processes of establishing legitimacy differ between the inaugural moment, which is, in some ways, extraordinary and the time of continuity when the state is experienced in the everyday life of the community? From this perspective riots would move the state to try and reestablish its legitimacy. This seems to be the analytical frame in which Thomas Blom Hansen analyzes the state in his important study of violence in "postcolonial" Bombay, although he attributes a certain bad faith to the state in that this is done more to preserve its myth of rationality and neutrality and less to offer justice.[29] Working with Lefort's[30] extension of Ernst Kantorowicz's[31] theory of medieval kingship to the modern state, Hansen states his theoretical position as follows:

> The union of the [king's] two bodies was later reconfigured as the nation, the people and the leader took the place of the sublime-abstract body and made governance of the empirical and profane people possible in the name of this higher principle. Lefort argues that with the advent of democracy this mythical and original source of power became radically empty, since it can only be temporarily occupied by representatives of the people, of the nation, and so on. These representatives stand for the people by occupying exactly that which seems more permanent and enduring: the central legislative institutions of the state.[32]

It is interesting to see the evidence Hansen produces for assuming that it is the scepter of medieval theories of kingship that can best provide the clue for understanding how the state functions in contemporary India.[33] First, he argues that the legitimacy of the state is primarily secured in public in performative dimensions of governance. Hence what remain critical to the construction of "stateness" for him are "spectacles, political rhetoric as well as the pertinence of the 'Law,' of public legal processes, and so on."[34] Thus, Hansen enacts a Durkheimian move in suggesting a deep split in the sacred aspect of the state—its sublime dimension and its profane aspects. But while for Durkheim the profane was realized in the everyday, of which the paradigmatic example was economic activity in

which the presence of society became weak in the individual consciousness, for Hansen the profane is marked by "the incoherence, brutality, par-
tiality, and banality of the technical side of governance as well as the rough
and tumble of negotiation, compromise, and naked self-interest displayed
in local politics."

I ask myself how it is that where Hansen sees only naked interest in
negotiation and compromise I see hope; or how it is that incoherence and
brutality belong to the same chain of adjectives for Hansen, while for me
it is precisely in those gaps that seem incoherent that people find the
resources to see the state as both "threat and guarantee."[35] I think one difference might lie in the nature of the fieldwork, especially in relation to
riots. Hansen, like many others, has had to rely on newspaper reports or
accounts generated by civil or human rights groups for the actual mapping
of the riots.[36] Thus, the local in his account is "Bombay"—but there is no
mapping of the violence within the city.[37] And although he talks of an
anti-Muslim "pogrom involving thousands of people all over the city but
most cruelly displayed in the city's widespread slums and displacement
areas," there is no clear understanding of the fine networks and the cleavages within which violence comes to be located. In many ways the categories he deploys such as "thousands of people" and the affects he assigns
to actors (e.g., "driven by guilt and fear") end up replicating the structure
of rumor in that they are utterances untethered from context and without
signature.[38] Further, we often meet people in Hansen's account to whom
utterances are attributed, but the people who utter them are not placed in
any context. There are examples of a civil servant whom Hansen meets in
a subway train or a Muslim graduate student, and we learn their opinions
and even their fears and disappointments. However, such free-floating
opinions offered in a transitory context are quite different from the stories
collected either through immersion in the everyday life of the people or in
the context of actually negotiating institutions with them.

Hansen's presumption that the sublime aspects of the state are located in
public performances such as the highly publicized public hearings conducted by the Sri Krishna Commission, which was charged with an
inquiry into the Bombay riots, could also bear further scrutiny. I concede
that the government's reasons for appointing commissions of inquiry are
often an effort, as Hansen says, to preserve the myth of the rationality of
the state. However, that is not the end of the story, for commissions of
inquiry are also set up in response to the pressure generated by civil rights
groups who have learned to demand accountability.[39] This is not the place

to go into a genealogy of commissions of inquiry. I simply note that such commissions usually occupy an ambiguous position with respect to the law and signal extraordinary events. This is why they do not have the powers of courts of law—yet by appointing retired judges to these commissions, the government tries to show that the state is willing to admit wrongdoing on its part. Of course, the findings of the commissions of inquiry often end up absolving the government, or the reports are tabled in Parliament but not accepted by the legislative body, or in many cases the findings are never made public. Nevertheless, I suggest that justice is not a matter of all or nothing. The very fact of the possibility that the commission might fault the state becomes a public resource for struggle and for shaming the government in power by publicizing its results in national and international fora. In fact, the Sri Krishna report itself was circulated by citizen groups long before it was released by the government. In the case of the 1984 violence, citizen groups set up an inquiry commission consisting of retired civil servants precisely because the government had consistently refused to set up such a commission. It seems to me, therefore, that it is far too simple an argument to suggest that the performative aspect of these commissions is all that there is to their function or that the state simply uses these performances to legitimize itself. Such an argument also fails to distinguish between different commissions. In the case of the 1984 riots, the Jain Aggarwal Committee conducted an inquiry regarding nonregistration of cases and defective investigations and recommended registration of fresh cases. On its recommendation the Delhi Riot Cell registered and reinvestigated 316 cases. Out of these cases, it is true that 151 were closed as untraceable, but that the committee found evidence of defective investigations and made this public is not to be scoffed at. These are precious resources for a democracy if it is to function, so that a critical apparatus might do better by carefully distinguishing what is achieved by the commissions that do an honest job of investigations and how these processes are to be strengthened rather than simply repeating the binary division between law and justice.

Finally, it is odd that Hansen reads the sublime dimension, not in the sensory quality of state spectacles, but in the appeal they have for establishing the state as a repository of universal reason. Let me dwell on this point a little further.

There has, indeed, been a considerable rethinking of the category of the sublime in relation to the question of political catastrophes. Whereas it was the reading of the Lisbon earthquake that led Kant to formulate the category of the sublime in relation to terrors of nature, Adorno called for a transformation of Western categories of aesthetics to consider the import of the demonstrated human capacity for unlimited violence (particularly after Auschwitz).[40] As Jean-François Lyotard stated this issue, "as for the politics of the sublime, there is no such thing. It would only be terror. But there is an aesthetic of the sublime in politics."[41] This has led to questions such as whether the figuration of the fearful as the sublime would depend upon censorship. We might recall here that Edmund Burke in his essay on the sublime started his reflections on this with a description of the spectacle of state terror.[42] It is therefore difficult for me to imagine how the initiation of such processes as the setting up of commissions of inquiry or the now widespread use of truth commissions, however inadequate they may turn out to be for the task at hand, can be regarded as displaying the sublime aspects of the state unless one could further argue that the stories, pictures, or other evidence publicly displayed are further aestheticized in public circulations. I think this is entirely possible, as the photographs of torture at Abu Ghraib prison seem to indicate. However, Hansen does not provide any such evidence with regard to the Sri Krishna Commission on the aesthetic of the sublime.

As distinct from the sublime, then, the magical aspect of the state, I suggest, arises precisely because the state can be mimicked, literalized, and embodied in ways that break open the limits within which theory expects it to function. Because the state project is always an unfinished project, it is best observed at the margins, but these margins are not simply peripheral places—they run into the body of the polity as rivers run through a territory. Yet it is dangerous to assume that people on these peripheries are somehow passive objects of state manipulation. I hope to have shown that even when projects of seeking justice do not achieve the results that a rational and fair legal process would have yielded, the struggle for such justice shapes the state processes in some ways. This is perhaps what Arjun Appadurai finds in the work of the NGOs that leads him to speak of deep democracy or what Roma Chatterjee finds in the streets of Dharavi, when in the same streets that had been split apart by riots, people begin to organize themselves across sectarian divides to get housing rights.[43] In Sultanpuri, I could not follow the families for more than a year, especially after they were moved to Tilak Vihar, but even in that one year I found enough stories of a kind of street courage that make it difficult for me to think that I can render their lives purely in terms of loss. To these stories we turn in the next chapter.

TEN

Three Portraits of Grief and Mourning

> *I want sukha (peace)—Won't you give me sukha?*
> —SHANTI

I remember these as almost the first words that Shanti said when I met her in her house in Sultanpuri. She was sitting on a bed in a dark room with no windows. Covered with quilts, she seemed to shrink into the smallest space her body could occupy. On one side of the bed was her mother, who had come from Alwar (a nearby town) to look after her. Her unmarried younger sister sat on the floor. An old neighbor, known as the old *amma* (mother, old lady), was standing by the door, half in, half out. "What do you mean?" I asked Shanti, unsure how to react. She looked expectantly at the others. It was my initiation into her mode of speech. She would speak in fragments, condensing in them a whole range of past events, known and shared by many others. Some woman or another would step in to elaborate. "She is asking to be given medicine—so she can die," explained her mother. "I tell her again and again—daughter, do not talk so. But does she listen? Does she care?" Almost on cue, Shanti responded: "What is there to listen to and what is there to care about? If at least my baby had been spared, I would have hugged him to my bosom and somehow I would have gone on living."

I was to learn slowly that her husband and three sons had been killed in the riots. Her husband had hidden with their sons in a nearby abandoned house hoping to evade the crowd, since the violence had come to this street almost at the end of the upheavals. She and her two young daughters, along with other women, were huddled together on the terrace of a house. In the course of our conversations, I learned that she had become suspicious that her mother's brother (*mama*) had revealed her husband's and sons' hiding place to the crowd, buying his family's safety by becoming an informer. "Not even a spoon was looted from their house," she told me.

Once when I was visiting her, I witnessed how angry she got with her elder daughter, who was about ten, telling her that she was cursed since she had failed to save her father and brothers. It seems that the crowd, when it learned that her husband and sons were hiding in the other house, had stood outside and repeatedly shouted taunts: "Why are you such cowards? Why can't you come out and face us?" As Shanti had watched in petrified horror from the terrace of the house where she was hiding with other women, the crowd poured kerosene on the house to set it on fire. In a panic, she had sent Babli, the elder daughter, into the crowd. Babli had tugged at one of the men she recognized and said, "Uncle *ji*, uncle *ji*, my baby brother is there with my father."[1] The man had turned angrily to her and said, "Why did you not tell us earlier? Do you think we are killers of *children?*" By that time the fire had already begun to engulf the house.

On that first day we met, Shanti did not "narrate" any of this—all she kept saying was, "If only my baby had lived, I would have somehow gathered courage, learned patience." At one point the elderly Hindu neighbor, who was standing by the door, interjected. "She carries on as if she were the only one to suffer a loss. Look at the world. Everyone was affected. A storm came upon us, and it destroyed everything in its way. Can we save anyone from such a storm?"

On another occasion when my friend Mita[2] and I were sitting there, Shanti said, "For as long as I thought everyone had been affected I remained in control of myself. But when I went to the camp and found that other women had been able to save their children, my heart burned out. My mother took me to Alwar, but I got worse. I could see all around me—there were children, laughing and playing. My nephews—I felt terrible . . . Why were they alive and my children dead?"

One of the repeated themes in Shanti's memories was the unbearable fact that her children had died, whereas other children had lived. She refused to acknowledge her daughters as her children, as if the death of her sons had annihilated motherhood itself. She took a stoic attitude to the death of her husband. "Well, the Sardars did it to Indira Gandhi. So the fruits of those evil actions (*karma*) would have to be borne, wouldn't they?" But what she could not understand was how all other women had, as she put it, "managed to save their children" while she had failed to do so. It was her failure as a mother, but primarily as a mother of sons, that she found most difficult to bear. She alternately held her husband, her eldest son, her eldest daughter, the community, and herself responsible for the deaths, especially of her youngest child: "I had sent my daughter to my husband, where he was hiding, begging him to give the baby to me. But he just said, 'Your mother is feeble-minded, she will not be able to protect my son.' Had he shown more trust in me, the baby would have lived."

At other times she would begin to beat her daughter, saying she should have persuaded her father to give her the baby, or she should have shouted more loudly when she was in the crowd and they were burning down the house—someone might have heard and then the child might have been spared. One time she put the blame on her husband and older son: "Why did they not open the room and come out and give themselves up to the crowd? The crowd was not out to kill young children. My little baby would have been saved if they had shown the courage to give themselves up."[3] "How were they to know?" I asked. "How could they be sure that the crowd would spare the child?" To this question she responded that one of the neighbors had done exactly that when the crowd went to his house, and his son had lived—the crowd having felt honor-bound to let the child go free. I cannot say if the story was true, but I do know that the idea that there was a code of honor for the crowd would surface in other conversations. Again, sometimes Shanti would say that the community was to blame for her plight: "If the women knew that the crowd was not killing the children, why did they not tell me? They only told me that women were not being touched."

Although Shanti did talk about the responsibility of others in the death of her child, it was around herself that she gathered the final blame and guilt: "It is true, what my husband said. I am feeble-minded. I am half-witted. I am mad. That is why I could not understand what the crowd wanted. They wanted vengeance taken on adult men. They did not want the blood of children."

How did Shanti crystallize all the floating guilt around her and attach it upon her own self? How did the community around her collaborate in this fixing of guilt on her? I don't want to give solidity to the notion of community here, for there seemed to have been a struggle between what was natal and what was conjugal in the defining of the situation—a struggle between what it is to be the daughter of a mother and thus to receive mothering and what it is to be a mother of a son (and simultaneously not the mother of daughters)—and thus to affirm motherhood only by negation. It is a story of the decreation of a woman in which it was not only that individual men were destroying her capacity to remember other ways of being a mother than that sanctioned by the social, but also that the world of men as a whole seemed to be conspiring to do that. She paid with her life, annihilating the possibility for her daughters to have a future with her.

Shanti's mother tried to create circumstances that would allow Shanti to retreat into a kind of childhood. She washed her, fed her, followed her around everywhere to see that she did no harm to herself. All Sikhs, Shanti's mother said, had suffered, and so she tried to tell Shanti she was not alone in her sorrow. A subtle shift in the narrative related to what was going on around her happened when Shanti's husband's father came from Alwar to set up house with them, saying that it was his responsibility to provide what succor he could, now that she was left without any male protection. On the surface, this eighty-year-old man had come to provide support and comfort to his widowed daughter-in-law and orphaned grandchildren, but this was transformed into a situation where Shanti was forced back into an adult world that she felt she had failed to master.

There was no question that the death of his son and grandsons had affected the old man deeply. *Hum to ghar se beghar ho gaye*—From being people with homes, we have been made homeless. He would describe his plight in these simple words. For a time I was blind to the power struggle that was taking place in the house. On reflection, it seems to me that the man spoke with two voices. Sometimes he would implore Shanti to try to recover from her state of paralyzing sorrow, to throw away all thoughts of suicide. Once when I was there he even bent down and touched her feet, begging her to think about her two daughters. These dramatic gestures were, however, accompanied by another message, which was that a wife as devoted as Shanti could not possibly recover from such a trauma. The message would be delivered to the ever-present audience of neighbors. He would sigh and say, "We try our best—but how can she possibly recover? It is the dead who call her." "Poor woman—she has gone mad. She was feeble-minded, but my son always protected her. Alas, that is why Tehal [the son] could not trust her with the baby in those last hours." To help her recovery and to bring peace to his dead son and grandsons, he arranged for an elaborate prayer ceremony, but, as we shall see, it was also to deprive Shanti of whatever sources of strength that remained in her.

Shanti had received Rs. 10,000 for each of the dead kin as compensation from the government. As the days passed, a struggle for control over the money began to take place. Shanti had not been able to refuse money for the elaborate ritual that the old man had demanded from her, for that would have been impious. But despite her anger at her daughters, she was unhappy at the extravagant religious ceremonies conducted for the peace of the dead when the future of her daughters, she felt, had become so uncertain. I find here the essence of tragedy, because even a fleeting concern for her daughters—barely given voice by Shanti—could be constructed by her husband's father as a betrayal of the male line. There were other indications of struggle. The old man insisted that he would manage the household expenditures. He maintained that Shanti was feeble-minded and incapable of handling the money she had received. He also hinted that as the oldest surviving male of the family, it was he who should have received the compensatory sum from the government. Shanti was mute in the face of such allusions woven into the web of everyday interactions. Outwardly deferential, she seemed to be struggling with her anger and yet imbibing his judgment of her as the bringer of this unprecedented misfortune on the family.

The struggle between Shanti and her husband's father appears at one level as the attempt by him to gain control over Shanti. At another level, however, it is possible to see it as a struggle to decreate the female connections through which natality was being offered as nurture by Shanti's mother in opposition to male connections created through ties of conjugality. The money that Shanti had received was in compensation for the death of her male kinsmen. Her husband's father tried to establish the legitimacy of his own claims over this money on the basis of his membership within the male line. Shanti's resistance, however muted, was an attempt to secure the survival of the female line—to place herself, however hesitatingly, in the world of women. Hence, while the old man wanted to spend the money on rituals for the propitiation of his son and grandsons, Shanti wished to conserve the money for securing the future of her daughters. It was a struggle over her own annihilation. Similarly, her appeals to other women, including her mother and Mita, to take care of her daughters seemed a feeble way to activate the potential that was inherent in the female connections but was subverted by superior male controls.

This struggle between the female connectedness and the exercise of authority to break those connections and appropriate each woman *individually* into the male line soon manifested itself in Shanti's mother's decision to leave her daughter's house. The kinship norms in north India allow only short visits to a married daughter's conjugal home. The insinuations by Shanti's father-in-law that she was staying on with her daughter to gain control over her money became impossible for the mother to bear, and she departed for Alwar. The departure of her mother was like the final admission that the land of her childhood, the world of women defined through natality, was disappearing. Although Shanti's younger sister stayed on to look after her, the accusations against Shanti increased. When women around her spoke, they now spoke with a patriarchal voice. Once I heard a woman saying to Shanti, "If you were really so grief-stricken, why did you not kill yourself the day your sons died?"

Thus, Shanti's life had become a statement against the dominant norms that would allow a woman life only as a mother of sons. This is not merely a question of power, nor is it a question of female autonomy versus male dominance. Much more is at stake—the point really is that a life built around female connections was not seen as a life worth living. It is when women themselves occupied a patriarchal discourse and took that voice as their own (as in the woman's question to Shanti—"Why did you not kill yourself the day your sons died?") that the community of women, some relatives, some neighbors, that was forming around her failed her. And finally, just as Shanti was most wounded by such women, so she herself, in her refusal to acknowledge herself as the mother of daughters, ended up by wounding her shattered daughters: "How can I live? You tell me to look to my daughters—to be comforted by them. But they are not my children. They are counterfeit (*nakli*) children. I cannot bear them around me. If my little son had lived, I would have somehow clasped him to my bosom and lived. But I was cheated."

Toward her elder daughter, Babli, Shanti was positively hostile and constantly collated her own failure with her daughter's failure to have wrested her baby brother from the burning house. Neighbors would report that she would slap the daughter whenever the child tried to touch her, blaming her for the loss of her baby brother. She showed some compassion toward the younger daughter but was unable to show her any love. If the girl came near her mother and tried to touch her or hug her, she would push her away, but not with the same hostility as the elder daughter. Sometimes the old lady who was their neighbor would push the younger girl toward Shanti, exhorting her to hug her mother in the hope that the physical contact would awaken the dormant and now suppressed motherhood in Shanti. But Shanti would not allow herself to be touched. "Take her away," she would say. "This is not my child—she is counterfeit, a fraud—my child died." "Look at her," the neighbors would say. "Was this not a girl born of your own womb like the others? Why is she not your child?" "Oh she is a girl. Just send her away—take her away, I cannot look after her."

Shanti's daughters understood the rejection but still tried to comfort her, until the last day. One day Shanti told me that the younger daughter had tried to persuade her that she could be like a son. "I will not marry. I will become a doctor and look after you." Shanti was touched by this and even told me how the little girl had been a great favorite of her father. "When her father used to tease her, whom she wanted to marry, she would say—the same kind of man that my mother married." For a fleeting moment, mother and daughter had smiled together, almost as if the negation of the daughter's female identity implied in her saying that she would not marry could restore the relation to the mother. Soon she relapsed into the theme of daughters being counterfeit children because they could not continue the line—their father would be without ancestral oblations.[4] In effect she was saying that even if the daughters could provide for her in the secular world, they could not replace sons in the cosmic scale of time. In that sense the greatest gift a woman could give to her husband's line within this patriarchal world—that of descendants who could rescue their ancestors from hell by giving them ancestral oblations—had been lost by the death of her sons. On the cosmic scale she and her family had been erased and obliterated. Or so she felt, as if no other possibility of remaking life existed for her.

DEATH WITHOUT HEROISM

> *Were the bodies of my sons and husband only there for pigs and dogs to feed upon?*
> —SHANTI

The survivors were haunted by the absence of dead bodies. Shanti would often get up in the middle of the night and wander to the park opposite their house, where she would gather sticks and make them into little piles, which she would proceed to burn. She was unable to explain what she was doing, but some neighbors believed that she was trying to cremate the bodies of the dead. They said, "They burned them alive, but the dead bodies were not cremated. They must wander around as ghosts and spirits. What peace will they get? What peace will we get?"[5] This was always asked, although the ceremony of *antim ardas* for the placation of the dead was held and the *prasad* for peace was taken by a pious congregation. Shanti felt that they were deceiving themselves with these rituals. As long as the dead bodies had not been properly cremated, the souls of the dead could not be appeased.

According to some neighbors, Shanti had gone to the park[6] one morning to relieve herself when she found some pigs burrowing in a hole and pulling out human bones. Shanti was convinced that these were the bones of her husband. She was unable to look at this decayed body that she thought was the body of her husband. Although there are many Indian legends about mutilated bodies of warriors lying on battlegrounds among which women wander in search of their dead husbands and sons, the mutilated bodies in these legends are symbolic of the heroism of men. The deaths in the riots were not seen as "heroic." In certain kinds of public discourse, for example, in the preaching of some *gurudwaras,* the dead men were treated as martyrs who had died for a noble cause. But for the victims, as well as for the survivors, there was no heroism in these deaths. The cause of Sikh separatism had never been their own. As Shanti repeatedly said, "All we wanted to do was to lead a quiet and peaceful life. We did not want to die for other people's ideas." Hence the bones she took to be the mutilated body of her husband could not signify any heroism to her. It was symbolic of an utterly futile and meaningless death.

Finally, one day, unable to bear this reminder of how their lives had ended, Shanti soon found an opportunity "to do her work." This, at least, is how her elder daughter described what happened. Shanti's father-in-law had gone to the ration office. Her sister had gone to the "fields" (a euphemism for going into the park to defecate), and her daughters were away at school. Her sister came back to find the door shut but not locked. When she opened the door, Shanti's body was hanging from the ceiling. The police were called, and a case was filed. After the formalities were completed, she was taken to the cremation ground and given the funeral that she had so craved for her husband.

Shanti's suicide raised devastating questions to which I am not sure we had the answers. Since she had so often indicated her desire to find peace in death, we repeatedly asked ourselves how we could have prevented her death. Ashok Nagpal, a psychology professor who was part of the relief team, had advised her relatives several times to get her admitted to the psychiatric hospital in Shahadra. Once we had even gone prepared to take her with us, but her father-in-law and the neighbors protested vociferously against it. We were ourselves unsure about conditions in state hospitals for mental patients, for in the 1980s practices such as tying up patients and beating them into submission were still common. Further, Shanti was also receiving advice and some medication from a doctor who, we heard, used to visit the locality, though we did not see him ourselves. Any aggressive action on our part to insist that she be hospitalized could have jeopardized our position in the community, especially if she had died in the hospital.

These dilemmas were faced anew when we tried to arrange for the adoption of her two daughters. Both girls pleaded that they wanted to live with Mita and me. They were permitted by their grandfather to come and stay with us for a few weeks. However, the grandfather felt that he would lose an important source of income if he left the girls with foster parents. Many Sikh families offered to adopt them but did not want to cope with threats from the grandfather or other relatives. The only person who had supported our plans for their adoption was Shanti's mother, who came for the customary condolences at the death of her daughter. In the end, we could not persuade their paternal relatives to allow us either to adopt them or to have them adopted by a Sikh family, or even to arrange for their education in a boarding school. The community itself became hostile at the thought that the two girls might receive more care than other people. We could not press our claims or take recourse to a court, as both these actions would have made us stand in a hostile relation to the community and obstruct any long-term measures that we wanted to plan for work among the children. But even twenty years after the events I cannot figure out questions of responsibility.

A final comment. Why was Shanti unable to find her future in the lives of her daughters? Of course, the social scripts of patriarchy give us different evaluations of sons and daughters, but Indian society, like many other patriarchal societies, provides for mechanisms by which families may find continuity in daughters in the absence of sons. Yet Shanti's time had become frozen on the day of the riots. Her entire present was now nothing more than a slow unfolding and mental replaying of the decisions and events of the riots. Unlike Freud's analogy of the recall of the past as the "looking" at a passing landscape from a moving train, Shanti had no means by which she could distance herself enough from the past so that the present could be made "present" in her consciousness. The traveler in the train, looking at his past as a passing landscape, can describe it from a vantage point of distance.[7] Shanti, on the other hand, could not move from that particular day. Her laments were all about her, or about other people's, failure to read correctly the signs by which her son could have been saved.[8]

One of Shanti's laments was that she alone had been unable to save her child. As we have seen, this fact weighed more heavily upon her than anything else she had experienced. Other women tried to read their suffering as part of the fate that had befallen the whole community. Their suffering was framed in relation to something that transcended the individual circumstance, whether this be the operation of a malignant fate, an incomprehensible god, or past *karmas*—these are all means by which the malignancy and contingency of evil could be comprehended and made somehow more than the personal. It is as if the contingency of suffering provided a guarantee that it was not the *particular* failing of the victim but an impersonal force, such as a storm or lightning, that had brought about the disaster. Such a neutral force was seen as indifferent to whom it hits and whom it spares. The fact that other women had been able to save their children while Shanti had failed became a powerful symbol for her of her particular failure as a mother to save her sons.

Then there was the final question: What was her responsibility toward the dead? Any death raises the question of the obligations of the living toward the dead. We saw how the work of mourning was performed in the case of women such as Asha and Manjit. Resuming the business of life was not to forget the dead but to absorb the poisons, to attend to the repair of relationships. Shanti could frame her obligations to the dead only in terms of her responding to their call. She was the only survivor who committed suicide in the colony. In her willingness, even compulsion, to talk about dying Shanti often presented the taking of her own life as the only proof she could offer herself that her guilt could be assuaged by joining her dead husband and sons in their destiny. She was not able to take the risks of a reengagement with life, including the possibility that she might in time be able to "forget" what had happened to her dead. The forgetting would have included a forgetting of the dominant definition of a woman as integrated individually into the lines of men and a reformulation of life in terms of female connections. Death and masculinity finally broke the hold of life and femininity.

THE COLLECTIVE MOURNING OF WOMEN

I have described in earlier chapters the conditions under which we happened to find ourselves in A4 Block. In this section I hope to show how the gendered division of labor in the work of mourning through which private grief and public lamentations were conjoined opened up a space for political action. It is not so much the words that the women spoke but the pitch and the gesture that marked an insistence on making violence and loss visible. The street here became the stage on which a counterstory to the official denial of any wrongdoing could be publicly performed, just as it was in the streets of these very peripheral areas that violence had been enacted and bodies that were deemed killable were made publicly present. On our first visit to the area we were taken around by a self-styled social worker who attached himself to us and who we later learned was assigned by the local big men to shadow all strangers and keep them informed of events in the colony.[9] We had been able to shake this man off on one pretext or other and had then been shown around by Vakil Singh, who had lost two sons in the carnage. We saw blood splattered on the walls, bullet holes, heaps of ashes in which one could still find bits of hair or skull and bone. But what we encountered in the women was mainly fear. Their men had been killed before their eyes. Their children had been spared but had been threatened with dire consequences if they spoke about the murderers. Yet a sullen resistance formed of anger, fear, and grief was beginning to take shape. They felt surrounded by the murderers, who had established a "camp" in the colony and were ostensibly doing "relief work" to impress the press and social organizations that had come to report the carnage. As one woman said:

> They have asked us to clean up our houses and to go in and settle down.
> How can we settle down here? Do you see the heaps of ashes? Do you
> see the blood? Here, put your hand inside this heap and you will see the
> melted skulls. They would not even let us have the dead bodies. We
> begged them: you have killed our men. Let us have their bodies at
> least—let us mourn them properly. The whole night we hear the voices
> of our dead. I hear my husband asking for water. The killers would not
> even let us give water to our dying. My son cried, mother, mother—as
> he used to when he was little, but I could not go to him. This street is
> now a cremation ground for us. The living have become silent shades,
> while the cries of the dead float up to the sky and fall on us like weights.

More powerful than even the words, though, was the way that the women sat in silence outside their houses refusing to bring mourning to an end. As the civil rights groups and journalists began to visit the area to collect stories, the women were often scared to speak out, but their gestures of mourning that went on and on and on showed the deeply altered meaning of death. Even as the local politicians and big men put pressure upon them to clean up their houses, to wash themselves, and to appear "decent" for the sake of the many important functionaries who were visiting the colony, the women defiantly hung on to their filth and their pollution. They would not go into the houses, they would not light the cooking hearths, and they would not change their clothes. The small heaps of ashes, the abandoned houses, the blood-splattered walls created a funereal landscape, and the sight of the women with their unwashed bodies and unbraided hair was a potent sign that mourning and protest were part of the same event. I think they took it as part of their obligation to the dead to make the violence visible. The prolonged period in which symbols of dirt and pollution dominated the area—for women did not move into their houses until these had been completely repaired and cleaned by relief workers (a task that took three months to complete)—was one in which no visitor to the area could ignore the plight of these families.

As time passed, new questions arose about the obligations to the dead, but the question was always there, surrounding us almost like an atmosphere. It would suddenly make an appearance within all kinds of conversations, admonishments, quarrels. Time does some very corrosive work, so that the unity that women had displayed in the first three months began to break apart as conflicts broke out over who was entitled to compensation received from the government. They asked whether a woman was to remain faithful to the memory of her deceased husband, or should she try to carve out a new life for herself? And what did it mean to be faithful? The questions were particularly poignant for younger widows.

The Siglikar Sikhs have traditionally practiced levirate and leviratic marriage so that there is an expectation that a younger brother or another agnate similarly placed will marry his brother's widow.[10] The particular mode of death of the men, however, created new and complex conditions. First, there were many families who lost more than one adult male member. Thus, other men in the right affinal category were simply not available for leviratic marriages to take place. This meant that the widow would have to be married to a man outside the conjugal family. Second, in the modern judicial and administrative structures in India the widow is considered the legal heir, and so compensation was awarded to the widows of the men who had been killed. This is not a matter of legal technicalities alone, for there is a wider structure of sentiment in which the plight of the widow in India elicits sympathy as a figure of general suffering, as Dipesh Chakrabarty has argued.[11] While Chakrabarty's account is of great relevance for explaining how the figure of the widow circulates within the political and bureaucratic imagination, the residents of colonies such as Sultanpuri inhabit a totally different region of modernity. For most members of the Siglikar community it was not the widow but the parents of the dead, and especially the mother, who inherited the grief and the burden of memory of such gruesome deaths and therefore should have been the rightful recipient of the money.[12] There were many fights between the natal and conjugal families of young widows, each accusing the other of being money grabbers who wanted to profit by the death of a close relation. Many women reported how they were beaten up by the husband's father or his brother so that they would give up their legitimate inheritance.

After many months of these fights and squabbles, the caste *panchayat* (group of elders) met, and a compromise was reached. It was decided that a widow would be given permission to remarry only if she agreed to equally share the money with the father of her dead husband. In every case where a widow was under the age of twenty-five or so, I found that this agreement was adhered to. *Talaknamah,* or documents of divorce, were drawn up in court papers in which the father of the widow and the father of the dead man signed an agreement to the effect that the widow would give 50 percent of the money she had received in compensation for her husband's death to her husband's father, and the latter would agree that all relations with the widow were henceforth severed. I have discussed the implications of this for our understanding of the state in the previous chapter.[13]

One day as I was talking to a young widow, she said bitterly to me, "You do not know how it is with this community. Just as a donkey is tied to a new owner the moment his old owner dies, so a girl is married to a new husband the moment her husband dies. Here a cremation is taking place, and there are the preparations for a wedding" (literally, here the preparations to go to the Yamuna and there a preparation for the bridegroom's procession—*yahan jamuna ji ki taiyyari wahan barat ki taiyyari).*[14] I was constantly struck by the fact that questions about the obligations to the dead could be posed within the kinds of terms described by this young woman and attested to the break between a personal time of mourning and the forcible resumption of the "normal"—so that the same women who had formed the community of mourners sitting in the street and defiantly refusing the demands of the local big men to resume normality could be so deaf to the voices of the younger widows in relation to demands of the "traditional" practices of the Siglikars. I don't quite know how to render this except to say that being subjected to violence does not somehow purify us. Even as the women became involved in some political processes, there were other institutions that continued to shape their subjectivities in directions where their voices were abrogated into the ongoing patriarchal projects. Not all such projects, however, ended up by closing political spaces. I was fascinated by the manner in which newness could arise at the intersection of the patriarchal project of the state and the overlapping patriarchal formulations of the community—both realized at the level of the local.

An example of this newness was how receiving money for the dead as compensation from the state was then translated by women into an obligation to speak up, to recount events, and to engage the governmental agencies and processes of law into seeking justice within the modern democratic process. Recall that many women were scared to give evidence to civil right groups because they feared reprisals against their children. Yet, when reprimanded by others—"You have eaten the money of the dead. . . . Now do what you can for them"—some women had come forward to name the killers who had led the crowds. They gave witness before civil rights groups, journalists, the Ved Marwah Commission (i.e., the Police Commission of Inquiry), and in some cases women signed affidavits for criminal cases to be instituted against the killers.[15] Under pressure from these organizations some of the local criminals were arrested for a short while but were released on bail. My diary from the day on which the local killers were released reads as follows:

A meeting was being held in the street on which the *chamars* lived. Tempers were running high, and we could hear sounds of loud arguments. We could feel the tension in the streets ourselves. There was gloom in the streets where the Sikhs lived. Several people told me in whispers that the killers were at large—they were going to wreak vengeance on them for having given evidence against the killers. As I was going from one house to another, a group of women took me aside. Other women were told to go around normally so that no one would suspect anything. They told me that they needed to send a petition to the "highest official of Delhi" because they knew that their lives were in danger. I said I would try to contact whomever I could so that their fears were communicated to the authorities who were responsible for their protection. But they urged me to take action immediately, for there was no time for delay. "You write out in English what we say and then fix up something for us so that we can meet the highest official immediately." I said I was a rather inconsequential teacher at the university and that I would be turned out unceremoniously if I tried to reach the "highest official." They dismissed all my pleas.[16]

The outcome of this was that I wrote out the petition on a dirty piece of paper that was torn out of an exercise book, and they put their thumb prints upon it. We agreed that they would meet me the next day at a specified spot and would take care that no one in the colony learned they were going to present a petition. I decided to put my faith in the women's belief that I would be able to find my way. I rang up the Chief Secretary's office. My experience on an earlier occasion when I had tried to present a petition to the Deputy Chief Secretary on the difficulties survivors were facing in getting access to printed forms for claiming compensation had been most unfortunate. I had been politely but firmly accompanied out of his office by a policeman and had the impression that the Deputy Secretary expected me to pull out a gun or something like that.[17] This time I was received with great courtesy. The change in attitude was rather mysterious. The Chief Secretary agreed to see the women and consider their petition.

The next morning I found that eight women had come as representatives of the colony. We held a meeting on the lawn of the Chief Secretary's office. I pleaded with them to put forward their case in a cogent way, to speak one at a time, and to avoid getting into quarrels regarding the distribution of relief and mutual accusations about failure to save someone or another.[18] They, in turn, wanted to know the polite expression for such words as "defecation" and "widow," which they needed to use without shocking the sensibility of the Chief Secretary by their rude speech.[19] The Chief Secretary received them with courtesy. The women made three points. First, with the release of the leaders of the rioters, their lives were not safe. Even if there was a police presence in their street, the police could not be expected to go everywhere with them. For example, when they went to the toilets, which were out on the streets, they could be accosted by the murderers and raped or killed. Hence it was imperative that they be provided housing in other areas. Second, the government had plans for rehabilitating them by teaching them such skills as knitting and sewing, but they were ironsmiths and knew how to forge most things if they could only set up *bhattis* (anvils) outside their houses. Therefore, they did not want apartments in multistoreyed buildings, where they knew that widows from other areas were being accommodated; they wanted open plots of land where they could live in shanties and begin to produce goods for sale. Third, any policy that separated the widows from the rest of the community would not only create problems of security but also jeopardize their economic life, for they were dependent upon the men to go and sell the products they made. Their petition was accepted, and the Chief Secretary promised to do whatever he could to alleviate their suffering. On the way out one of the women suddenly started to cry in the traditional manner and to beat her forehead repeatedly, saying, the *sarkar* (government) is said to be our mother and father—so why did you all fail to protect us? She was gently pushed outside by the other women. Although their demands were not eventually met,[20] the women had established their capacity to reorient themselves to their reality in terms of the external world, a world of which they had been relatively ignorant just a few months back.

THE CHILD

In the streets of Sultanpuri one was always surrounded by groups of adults and children. In the stories told by mothers and aunts, children figured as characters—relating how crowds were shouting or the dying asking for water, women would point to a child standing nearby and say, "He was so frightened." Yet children who listened to these stories clinging to a mother's or elder sister's *dupatta* did not seem to me to register the horror. For instance, a child might smile at me shyly, peeking out from the mother's *dupatta* behind which she had hidden, while her mother told me how the child's father had been dragged out and killed. Once I heard a small group of children having a heated argument among themselves about whether the murderers had come to this house first or that house first—*wo hamare ghar pahle aaye the—ja ja, jhoot mat bol woh to hamare yhan pahle aaye the, phir tumhare yahan gaye the*—they came to our house first—go on, don't tell lies, they first came to our place and then went to yours. My own observations on this were then very sparse. I wrote in my diary that they seemed to be talking as if it had happened to someone else; their stories had a third-person quality.

Now, the figure of the child is what I sense haunting Wittgenstein's *Philosophical Investigations*. It is not so much a matter of initiating the child into the world as sensing that children go about stealing bits of language that they try to fit with bits of the world. So in what way were they putting the world together when they played killers and victims? I offer the following words of Stanley Cavell as a meditation on the child:

And we can also say: When you say "I love you my love": the child learns the meaning of the word "love" and what love is. *That* (*what you do*) will be love in the child's world; and if it is mixed with resentment and intimidation, then love is a mixture of resentment and intimidation, and when love is sought *that* will be sought. When you say "I'll take you tomorrow, I promise," the child begins to learn what temporal durations are, and what *trust* is, and what you do will show what trust is worth. When you say, "Put on your sweater," the child learns what commands are and what *authority* is, and if giving orders is something that creates anxiety for you, then authorities are anxious, authority itself uncertain.[21]

And again:

> To summarize what has been said about this: In "learning language" you learn not merely what the names of things are, but what a name is; not merely what the form of expression is for expressing a wish but what expressing a wish is; not merely what the word for "father" is, but what a father is; not merely what the word for "love" is, but what love is. In learning language, you do not merely learn the pronunciation of sounds, and their grammatical orders, but the "form of life" which makes those sounds the words they are, do what they do—e.g. name, call, point, express a wish or affection, indicate a choice or an aversion, etc. And Wittgenstein sees the relation among these forms as "grammatical" also.[22]

Cavell's description of the scene of instruction in relation to the child is quotidian—with the gentle rhythms of putting on sweaters, stroking the kitty, and feeding the meter—yet within that is built the possibility that love could be anxious and authority uncertain and trust betrayed. If this is the language of initiation, then it is initiation into a form of life and not simply into learning which objects which words point to—but it was precisely the figure of life that was put into question for the children in Sultanpuri. So how is one to relate the eventfulness of their everyday life after they had watched from one place or another the killings of their fathers, brothers, neighbors?

With the help of several friends such as Mita and the teachers from an experimental nursery school (Shiv Niketan), I was able to organize a summer camp in my old college (Indraprastha College) at the University of Delhi. There was no great ambition behind this project—we thought that that the children might escape the relentless retelling of the violence for a few hours each day. There were about forty children who partici- pated. I used to go every morning in a van to pick them up from their homes and to return them in the evening.

I soon realized that in our one-hour commute children were beginning to offer comments or little bits of information about the riots. Often the memory was provoked either by the sudden recognition of a space where a parent had been killed, or by watching someone perform an activity in which a member of the family had once been engaged. The children who had seemed dumb within the colony suddenly found language pouring out of their mouths. It is possible that groups of children had discussed these events among themselves but had been discouraged by adults from discussing them; or perhaps they found an assurance from my presence, so that these memories could, indeed, be narrated.

One of the children in our group was Avatar, an eleven-year-old who had a severely damaged eardrum and was described as being a deaf-mute. His mother often said to me, "He cannot speak, but he understands everything, and his actions can say more than words."

One day the van took a slightly different route and passed through a street we had not been in before. Suddenly Avatar became very excited and pointed to a tree. His shoulders were heaving and he gave the impression of jumping up and down on the seat, although he was, in fact, not moving at all. As he forced my attention toward the tree, pointing to that direction in agitated gestures even when the van had moved on, I asked him what had happened there. Then Avatar did a bit of mime: his hands first gripped an imaginary object and began to drag it, his face showing the resistance and the struggle of a person being dragged against his will to a terrible fate. He then stretched his hands as if over an imaginary rope, and made it into a lasso. The lasso was thrown over a branch of the tree, and, on the other side of the suspended rope, a noose was made that slipped around a neck. His face now became the face of a person around whose neck a noose is tightened, and then his head slumped forward, his face becoming that of a dead man. One of the children, who had perhaps watched the performance earlier (but I had no means of knowing, for I simply could not ask), told us that it was the tree from which his father had been hanged. "Were you watching?" I asked, and an emphatic nodding of the head affirmed his presence during this frightening episode. In the mime, it seemed to me, the hands had become those of the murderers and the face that of the victim. His body was a repository of knowledge and memory that surely must have been beyond him, for what he had been initiated into was a mode of dying. The scene of his instruction was not one in which he grew into a form of life, growing words as his world grew. Rather, it seemed to me that his body was the repository of knowledge not quite his to possess.

The children, for all their fights, always, always stood with each other in these remembrances. The more articulate ones often lent their voices to those who were numbed and could not speak. When remembering something, each would contribute words to the other so that memory became a collective event. For example, a little girl, who was perhaps five years old, would not speak at all. But whenever we passed a particular spot the children would say, "That is where Ballo's father was burned. The crowd left him to burn, and she ran to him, holding his hand while he died." Ballo would nod shyly to affirm what the children were saying, but could not be brought to put any of this into her own words.

Most children found a way of talking about their dead fathers or other relatives by creating figures of ghosts. Shanti's daughters would affirm that their mother came to them as a ghost. The youngest one was given to weeping much more than the older one. Her father's sister would threaten her, saying that if she did not stop crying, her mother's ghost would come and take possession of her body. The girl was terrified of this apparition and was unable to say anything at all. Once, when she was standing in a completely inert position, I asked her, "Are you thinking of your mother? Do her memories come to you?" She nodded and said, "Yes, but Bua (father's sister) says if you cry she will come and haunt you."

It seemed to me that in that period when I was involved with the children, I was constantly engaged in discussions of a fairly abstract character. Did political parties, the prime minister, the thugs belong to their worlds, or were they just playing at being mother, or being a local big man?[23] For example, one day as we were driving along in the van, Avatar excitedly pointed to the symbol of a hand painted on a wall. He then looked at me with expectation. "That is a hand," I said, and he nodded encouragingly. "It is a symbol of the Congress Party," I declared, for the slogan accompanying the hand asked you to vote for the Congress (I). His head moved from side to side in vehement denial. "It is not a symbol of the Congress Party?" I asked. He then showed me the palm of his hand and pointed to the wall, which had already disappeared from our view. "You are going to tell me what that hand meant?" Yes, he nodded. Then he proceeded to mime with his hands an episode from the life of Guru Nanak, the founder of Sikhism. One hand brought a boulder toward his head. Next, he mimed the coming of a ray of light from one hand with fingers of the other hand dancing and making patterns as the rays stopped the boulder in its way. Then his right hand was raised in the traditional gesture of protection, in which benevolent deities are iconically represented. For a moment he was the iconic representation of Guru Nanak. Then he raised his hand again and pointed to the wall where he had first spotted the hand. Now he was going to tell me the story of the Congress hand. A vicious, murderous look came on his face. Both hands became a flurry of movement—killing, dousing people with petrol and burning them alive. The hands and face were again a dialogue of gestures in which the hands portrayed the acts of killing, whereas the face represented the expressions and the pain of the dying. At the end of this performance Avatar showed us the auspicious hand of Guru Nanak and gestured protectively; then he switched to the hand of the Congress Party and mimed the brutalities to which that hand had subjected them. Possibly Avatar had heard some fragments of this discourse in the *gurudwara,* but I had not heard any adult put together such a story of contrasts.

Children developed a great curiosity about the external world. Names of countries that had resided in school textbooks and had been memorized just for passing exams became part of their lives. Hukam, another eleven-year-old, told me in great agitation one day that soon all the children of the Sikhs were going to be killed because Rajiv Gandhi, the prime minister, was going to Russia, where his mother had once gone. He would order the killing of all Sikhs—every child among them—so that his mother's soul could be avenged. I found myself vehemently assuring him that the prime minister had made no such statement before his departure, and that if he had heard this from someone, he should disregard it as rumor. It seems to me that part of this anxiety on the part of the children to interpret every sign in the political system for its relevance to their future mirrored the anxiety of the adults. The latter were constantly interpreting the signs according to which decisions about the future had to be made, and the children had simply picked up their anxiety. But it also seems that henceforth what politics would mean for them would be related to what it is to kill and be killed. I am not offering some kind of deterministic picture of what they would become as adults, but simply saying that their vision of the world and their place in it would perhaps always have to include such words as victim, riots, martyrs, terrorists—what these words are and what they can be made to do just as for those who grew up in the Gandhian world, politics were about *satyagraha,* civil disobedience, fasting, nonviolence. Will these words and these worlds come to cross each other? That would seem to be the challenge of democracy now.

In reading Cavell, I am struck that the figure of life is in movement—projections, unexpected regions of a word that I seem not to be able to share, revealing that you might be in my world but not of my flesh, my terror that whether our words can go on meaning what they do depends upon whether other people find it worth their while to continue to understand me, or that, finding a better bargain elsewhere, they might decide that they are not of our world.[24] So I offer two small exchanges to show how new and unexpected communications occurred. My relation to the men was more formal than my relation to the women and children. But I had made some friends among the men. I persuaded one of them, a Muslim, to accompany me one day to the police headquarters in Delhi to informally talk to a senior police officer. I had foolishly assumed that this was a safe place because it was far removed from the neighborhood. When we reached there and I handed over the pass that I had procured to gain entry, the constable gave me curious looks. Simultaneously my friend said, "Sister, where have you brought me? Don't you know my work is done at night?" As a matter of fact, I had not known this. To my relief, however, the fact that he was known to the police as a petty thief and pickpocket did not deter the senior police officer from hearing him out.

Later on another day, this friend said to me, "Do you have a VCR?"

"No."

"A television set?"

"Yes, a small one."

"Do you want a VCR?"

"No."

"A bigger color TV?"

"No, no, no—please no."

"Okay, then let me teach you how to hold your handbag. The way you hold it, I am surprised anything has remained in it. It is an invitation to pickpockets. Even I was tempted when you first started coming to the colony. You have done so much for people here—let me at least do this for you."

I am afraid that I was not a very good student—but that is another matter.

Another man, a truck builder, wondered about my past *karmas* that led me to be among them, hungry and thirsty, the whole day. I said jokingly that I was probably paying past debts, debts incurred in earlier lives, when he said, "You are wasting your time. Nothing is to be gained by this involvement. After all, our deaths do not mean anything. Alive, we are useful to the government for we can be hostages against the lives of the Hindus in Punjab. Dead, we are useful to the terrorists for we can become statistics in the list of Sikh grievances."

I know of no better words that would condense a whole philosophy in a drop, as it were.

ELEVEN

Revisiting Trauma, Testimony, and Political Community

TOWARD THE END OF CHAPTER 3, I alluded to the feeling that I was not able to name that which died when the citizens of the newly inaugurated nation in reclaiming their honor as husbands and fathers were simultaneously born as monsters—or at least that is how the literary figures I read saw the matter. I would like to imagine that this was not a straightforward assimilation of notions of trauma into the historical record in the sense that an unassimilated experience was coming to haunt the nation. I am not saying that there is nothing to be gained from such an understanding of history, but it seems to me that notions of ghostly repetitions, spectral presences, and all those tropes that have become sedimented into our ordinary language from trauma theory are often evoked too soon—as if the processes that constitute the way everyday life is engaged in the present have little to say on how violence is produced or lived with.

If the process of naming the violence presents a challenge, it is because such naming has large political stakes, and not only because language falters in the face of violence. The complex knotting of several kinds of social actors in any event of collective violence makes it difficult to determine whether the event should be named as an instance of "sectarian," "communal," or "state-sponsored" violence. Is it described appropriately in the framework of "riots," "pogroms," "civil disturbances," "genocide," or a combination of these? As Deepak Mehta has shown in meticulous detail, the term *riot* itself emerges in late nineteenth century as part of the colonial government's technology of control, and every kind of conflict that involved the imagination of unruly crowds is fitted within this protocol in official discourse, academic writing, and even individual testimony.[1]

The political scientist Paul Brass argues that neither *riot* nor *pogrom* effectively captures the dynamics of most violent occurrences involving large crowds.[2] Though the presumption is, he says, that riots are spontaneous acts of violence in response to a provocative event directed against an ethnic, religious, or linguistic group whereas pogroms are organized events of violence carried out through the agencies of the state, the boundaries between these are increasingly blurred. Naming the violence does not reflect semantic struggles alone—it reflects the point at which the body of language becomes indistinguishable from that of the world; the act of naming constitutes a performative utterance.

We can see the enormous stakes in these terms even in the structures of anticipation. For instance, in the wake of the recent violence (March 2002) against the Muslim minority in Gujarat in India, the prime minister at the time, Atal Bihari Vajpayee, is said to have warned the opposition in Parliament that they should not use the word *genocide* to describe the violence. "You should not forget," he said, "that the use of such expressions brings a bad name to the country, and it could be used against India in international platforms."[3] On the other hand, a group of legal activists in India were engaged in forming legal strategies to see if on the basis of arguments advanced in the international tribunals on Rwanda and the former Yugoslavia it was possible to argue in Indian courts that even though the Indian Constitution does not name genocide, such a crime can be read in the Constitution—hence the perpetrators of the violence should be tried for the crime of genocide. Others have tried different legal strategies, and though the outcomes remain to be seen in the face of great intimidation faced by survivors, it is clear that the struggle over naming reflects serious political and legal struggles. Allow me to reflect on these issues by recapitulating the experiences on which I base my observations.

I consider 1984 to be a major marker in the understanding of communal violence in India and the role of civil society in contesting the received pictures of what constitutes collective violence. This is not because academic studies were lacking earlier, but because the relation between the production of knowledge and the needs of immediacy was articulated in important ways for salvaging the democratic project in India in 1984. The reports prepared by civil rights organizations such as the People's Union for Democratic Rights and the People's Union for Civil Liberties were particularly important for their impact on popular opinion.[4] While the forms of action developed then were important for expanding the forms of mobilization, did this have any implication for our understanding of what constitutes ethnography?

In reflecting back, my own understanding of how to do an ethnography of the state evolved in entirely unexpected ways. This was because as members of the Delhi University Relief and Rehabilitation Team that was supported by *The Indian Express* but otherwise had a very ambiguous position, we had to operate within the cracks and schisms we could find in the state to be able to muster enough resources to carry out our work in the affected localities. In that sense, it was clear that even as many agents of the state were themselves engaged in breaking the law, it was still possible to use certain resources of the state because norms of secularism and democracy had been internalized by many actors in the system. I also found myself reflecting for years afterwards on what it meant for anthropological knowledge to be responsive to suffering—a point that is woven within the fabric of this book. On both these questions the issue was not that one divided one's activities into neat spheres to correspond to a division between academic and activist work, as Scheper-Hughes conceptualizes the issue[5]—but rather that the form of doing anthropology itself was shaped by the needs of immediacy or activism.

One important point was established about communal riots in India by the labors of various civil rights groups, lawyer activists, and university teachers (including myself) in 1984, namely that far from the state's being a neutral actor whose job was to mediate between already constituted social groups and their factional interests, several functionaries of the state were, in fact, actively involved as perpetrators of violence or, at the very least, were complicit with the violence against the Sikhs. In the process of writing this violence, however, it become evident to me that unless one understood the everyday life of the localities within which the riots occurred, it would be impossible to see how diffused feelings of anger and hate could be translated into the actual acts of killing. Because I brought the anthropologist's eye to the situation, I was able to show that the spatial pattern of the riots in the localities showed an intricate relation between local-level factors and the sense of national crisis created through the assassination of Mrs. Gandhi. Thus, while the official representation of communal violence in India continues to be dominated by the picture of crowds having gone insane in a natural reaction to some provocative action on the part of one group or another, the academic understanding of riots has changed considerably.

Unfortunately, though, there is still a tendency to work with models of clear binary opposites in the understanding of violence—state versus civil society, Hindus versus Muslims, global versus local, etc. Our involvement in 1984 with the actual practices of collecting data for purposes of rehabilitation, however, made me realize how complicated the divisions and connections between these binary entities were. There was a certain splitting in my own understanding of the state as we recognized that the various state actors were aligned differently in relation to the violence. For instance, while one faction of the Congress Party was actively engaged in abetting the riots in hopes of mobilizing support for their own leaders within the party hierarchy, others equally located within the state structures were appalled at the events. Thus, we were able to mobilize help from senior bureaucrats, police officers, and retired officials to create an aura of authority within the locality to undertake relief and rehabilitation. As in many other situations, dissimulation was an important part of our strategy to confuse the perpetrators of the violence, who had the support of local police officers and thus thought that they were above the law. The survivors as well as civil rights workers faced considerable threats and harassment from them. How, then, to function within that environment, except through camouflage?

To give an example of the strategies of dissimulation we deployed: a recently retired director of the Central Reserve Police Force helped us to organize the distribution of rations of food within a few days of the riots to the affected families who were not moved to relief camps.[6] He arrived with us in a truck accompanied by six policemen of the Reserve Force who were in uniform, and we set up appropriate procedures for identifying the affected families and getting rations to them while the police officers from the local stations watched.[7] Thus, when we subsequently did other kinds of work in the locality, the local police officers and many of the perpetrators could not decipher our social position. Were we part of an approved official machinery or part of some kind of opposition? Perhaps we were able to work and move around in the locality because it was not clear to anyone what risks it would entail to attack us. The dissimulation of our position, inserted into the uncertainty of relations in the locality, constituted the very conditions of the possibility for both rehabilitation work and the work of gathering evidence. Take another example: the mediation of a senior Home Ministry official resulted in our getting a police presence placed in the locality with personnel drawn from other police precincts. This ensured our security while we engaged in the distribution of compensation; it protected us from intimidation by local-level perpetrators; it allowed us to rebuild the houses of the victims; and it enabled freedom of movement within certain defined microspaces over which these selected policemen were able to establish surveillance. I could understand that the civil rights organizations and the lawyers needed to define themselves in purely oppositional terms to the state. My own position, however, constantly shifted between the need to gather evidence that could help in the legal processes and the processes of rehabilitation, on the one hand, and the broader understanding of the complex ways in which questions of agency and moral responsibility were implicated, on the other. This is the question faced by anthropologists, for they are professionally committed to a complex understanding of local context and yet must bring certain values to bear on the events they witness and record.[8] This question has serious implications for the public role that anthropology can play: the struggles around this are worth revisiting in thinking of this issue. They raise the question of how we, as anthropologists, inhabit the world with regard to contemporary events that elicit strong ethical concerns—yet we bring a certain ambiguity to the situation because of our commitment to understanding the local context that situates actions in ways that may seem incomprehensible from the outside.

It is twenty years now since the riots in 1984. In terms of events that I have felt compelled to respond to, there has been the terrible destruction of the Babri mosque, followed by riots in Bombay in 1992, the assassination of an extremely close friend in Colombo in 1999, the attacks in the United States of September 11, 2001, and then the atrocities against Muslims in Gujarat in March 2002. Surely there were other events of equal importance, but I can speak more easily about events that were significant in my own worlds.

I recognized with a sense of shock that many of the young persons, prominent and not so prominent, who struggled against the officially proclaimed narratives of the sectarian violence in Gujarat in 2002 were drawing on the repertoire of social action that had evolved in the organizations that were just getting established in 1984. Several newspaper editors and journalists in the print medium had taken considerable risks then to expose the complicity of prominent politicians and the police in the riots. In 2002, similarly, Barkha Dutt and Rajdeep Sardesai (of NDTV) exposed the lies of the state government by covering the riots, televising the mobs and the looting, thus facing enormous risks to their lives in the process.[9] In 1984 I brought the two young daughters of Shanti (whose husband and three sons were burned alive in the riots and who subsequently committed suicide) to live with me until we could make other arrangements for them. Her younger daughter would communicate only with my youngest son (Sanmay), who was then a little over four years old. Recently I read an account by Sanmay's childhood friend Bhrigu on some remarkable work he did with children in a camp for survivors in the area of Aman Chowk, in Ahmadabad.[10] I imagine that many of the young men who participated in the riots in March in Gujarat were similarly children in 1984. It is as if the various divides in forms of participation in the polity in India—one on the side of violence and one on the side of addressing this violence—take place through such initiations by fire. Does anthropology have any special role to play in this scene, apart from lending itself to the larger projects through which testimony for legal indictments is gathered, the work of rehabilitation is undertaken, and the victims and survivors are given some succor? Is it even important that there be any boundaries between disciplines or between professions, or between activism and scholarship? What I offer here is profoundly shaped by my own biography—I want to state clearly that it is not more or less virtuous to be engaged in doing anthropology in this manner. Nevertheless, when faced with the kind of trauma that violence visits on us, we have to be engaged in decisions that shape the way that we come to understand our place in the world. The relation between anthropology and the making of the public sphere can result from different kinds of intersections. It is only by being attentive to these different projects that we can escape a complete instrumentalization of knowledge, alternately demanded by the state and the market—and yet keep the demands of immediacy and the demands of the long term in some balance. There is also the matter of too much being at stake in speaking carelessly or without tact on these matters. The boundaries between doing and saying, implicit in the division of labor between what Kant called the "higher" faculties of theology, law, and medicine and the "lower" faculty of philosophy, are not so easily maintained.

The rest of this chapter is organized as follows. In the first section, I consider the criticism that concentrating on trauma results in the creation of communities of ressentiment. It is not clear to me whether the claim is that emphasis on the suffering of victims within a popular wound culture makes it difficult to acknowledge the past and hence to engage in self-creation in the present—or whether this ressentiment is seen as the inevitable fate of an attempt to address the issue of suffering and recovery. I do not deny that there is plenty of evidence of stories of victims and survivors that hook into a popular culture in which the trope of the "innocent" victim provides the cover to engage in voyeurism. At the very least, this has the potential to open up suspect spaces in which stories of suffering are deployed in the dividing practices of separating "innocent" victims from "guilty" ones. But I still ask whether a different picture of victims and survivors is possible in which time is not frozen but is allowed to do its work. In the second section, I consider what it means to engage in an ethic of responsibility or to speak responsibly within the anthropological discourse. I try to defend a picture of anthropological knowledge in relation to suffering as that which is wakeful to violence wherever it occurs in the weave of life, and the body of the anthropological text as that which refuses complicity with violence by opening itself to the pain of the other.

VICTIMHOOD, TESTIMONY, AND COMMUNITIES OF RESSENTIMENT

A good place for me to enter the debate on the different ways in which the idea of suffering and testimony is placed in the making of political community is to evoke the contrast between prophetic and diagnostic modes of criticism as developed by Reinhart Koselleck.[11] I wish then to use this contrast to engage with some important arguments made by Achille Mbembe on the issue of suffering and self-creation.[12] I take Mbembe because he represents an important break from the kind of scholarship on violence and suffering that has remained content with explanations couched in terms of inherent properties of a particular culture to produce violence. What is notable in the latter kinds of explanations is that they are completely oblivious of work in literary criticism that looks at the production of violence for consumption in the public sphere in the Western countries as a sign of a *pathological public sphere*—yet when cultural productions such as cartoons or advertisements appear in newspapers in Burundi or Rwanda or Sri Lanka that are embedded in notions of kingship or demons, this is quickly taken as a sign of the normal development of a cultural repertoire in the age of mechanical reproduction. How is criticism to be articulated in the context of such ideas of the normal and the pathological? How is one to distinguish between the normal and the normative— how to recognize that normalization might provide a lens to the pathological rather than the normative? Throughout this book I have tried to remain attentive to the idea of suffering as a concern with life and not with either the given and ready-made ideas of culture or a matter of law or norms alone.

To return to Koselleck, as I understand it, the prophetic mode of criticism is anchored to the genre of a dramatic denunciation of the present since the prophet (in contrast to the priest) speaks on behalf of the future community. In contrast we speak of a critical state in medical diagnosis when the disease takes a turn for the better or the worse—it requires careful reading of signs and symptoms and a watchful relation to the minutiae through which the disease manifests itself. I submit that communities of ressentiment are much more likely to be created when the stance toward suffering is a prophetic one, though prophecy is often masked as if it were diagnosis based upon the close reading of symptoms. With this framing of the question, I turn to Mbembe's recent provocative enunciation of what he calls the failure of the collective imaginaire of Africa to arrive at a distinctly African mode of writing the self. Mbembe's formulation of the issues obviously takes inspiration from the recent concern with questions of reading social relations and the self through a certain kind of aesthetic. How do pictures of disintegration, violence, and impossibility of a future fold into this aesthetic? Meditating on the experience of Africa, I hope, will allow me to bring some of my own questions into play with scholars who see the self as increasingly the site of hallucinatory writing.

Mbembe refers to the fateful descriptions of Africa as a site of failed states, of wars and new epidemics, and faults current social theory as being completely out of its depth in conceptualizing these crises. My concern is not so much to save social theory as to be as attentive as I can to the diagnosis offered. Mbembe contends that writing of a collective subject in Africa that could be considered "authentic" or true to experience has been blocked by the way in which the discourse of victimhood has been deployed to make the historical experience of slavery, colonization, and apartheid count. He argues that genuine philosophical inquiries have been neglected in African criticism and that the neglect is responsible for the fact that unlike the Jewish experience of the Holocaust, which has yielded genuine philosophical inquiry, African criticism has not been able to address suffering in history in a manner that could lead to the birth of the subject. In Mbembe's words:

> The first question that should be identified concerns the status of
> suffering in history—the various ways in which historical forces inflict

psychic harm on collective bodies and the ways in which violence shapes subjectivity. It is here that a comparison with other historical experiences has been deemed appropriate. The Jewish Holocaust furnishes one such comparative experience. Indeed, the Holocaust, slavery, and apartheid all represent forms of originary suffering. They are all characterized by an expropriation of the self by unnamable forces. . . . *Indeed, at their ultimate foundation, the three events bear witness against life itself. . . . Whence the question: How can life be redeemed, that is, rescued from this incessant operation of the negative?*[13]

Despite the reference Mbembe makes to the events of the Holocaust, slavery, and apartheid as bearing witness against life, the figure of life is left relatively unexplored. Instead, Mbembe creates a discourse in which the obstacles to the recovery of the self in the collective imaginaire of Africa are traced to a series of denials. The most powerful of these denials for him is the African inability of self-representation, itself based on a ritualistic reiteration of such terms as "speaking in one's own voice" or recovering an authentic "African" identity based upon one or another version of nativism. Mbembe offers three critiques of the African attempts at self-recovery, of which I take up only the last for discussion here: "In the critique that follows, I will be arguing that . . . their privileging of victimhood over subjecthood is derived, ultimately, from a distinctively nativist understanding of history—one of history as sorcery." For Mbembe, history as sorcery is premised on the further notion that unlike the Jewish memory of the Holocaust, there is properly speaking no African memory of slavery, which at best is experienced as a wound whose meaning belongs to the domain of the unconscious, more in the realm of witchcraft than history.[14]

Among the reasons for the difficulty in the project of recuperating the memory of slavery, Mbembe identifies the shadowy zone in which the memory of slavery between African Americans and continental Africans hides a rift. For the Africans this is a silence of guilt and the refusal of Africans to face up to the troubling aspect of the crime that engages their own responsibility in the state of affairs. He argues further that the erasure of this aspect of the suffering of modern Black slavery manages to create the fiction (or illusion) that the temporalities of servitude and misery were the same on both sides of the Atlantic: "This is not true. And it is this distance that prevents the trauma, the absence, and the loss from ever being the same on the two sides of the Atlantic. As long as continental Africans neglect to rethink slavery—not merely as a catastrophe of which they were but the victims, but as the product of a history that they have played an active part in shaping—the appeal to race as the moral and political basis of solidarity will depend, to some extent, on a mirage of consciousness."

There are several important assumptions here about the obligation to render the originary meaning of memory for forging collective identity that have relevance for our understanding of what unites and what divides anthropology from the scenes of recovery in these terms. First, it is clear that the Holocaust is cast as a model with reference to which the "failure" of the African project of self-writing is posed, and with this Mbembe introduces all the assumptions of trauma theory about unclaimed experience that awaits belated completion. Thus it is assumed that the making of collective identity is closely tied with the task of recovery of memory that constructs one's role in it as agent rather than victim. Third, self-creation is conceptualized as a form of writing. Though Mbembe does not state this explicitly, I imagine that writing the self points to a promise—the creation of a future community. He seems to reject any notions of the self in terms of other metaphors such as those of finding or founding, or finding *as* founding, because of his suspicion of models of the self located in a discovery of the past. Yet one is also left with a suspicion that Mbembe's notions of the past are located in a linear conception of time since he seems to refuse the possibility that one could occupy the space of devastation by making it one's own not through a gesture of escape, but by occupying it as the present in a gesture of mourning. If writing the self refers to the making of a future community, then its meaning both in the literal and in the figurative sense is left unexplored.[15] Finally, new forms of the self are said to emerge in the practices of war that in the African scene are now part of everyday reality rather than constituting a state of exception. These new forms of writing the self are related, for Mbembe, in failed projects of recovering memory. The last seems evident, for example, in the statement that follows: "Trembling with drunkenness, he or she becomes a sort of work of art shaped and sculpted by cruelty. It is in this sense that the state of war becomes part of the new African practices of the self. Through sacrifice, the African subject transforms his or her own subjectivity and produces something new—something that does not belong to the domain of a lost identity that must at all costs be found again, but rather something radically different, something open to change and whose theory and vocabulary remain to be invented." And further on, "there emerges an original imaginaire of sovereignty whose field of exercise is nothing less than life in its generality. That latter may be subject to an empirical, that is, biological death. But it can also be seen to be mortgaged in the same way that objects are, in a general economy whose terms are furnished by massacres and carnage, in the manner of capital and labor and surplus value as is posed in the classical Marxist model."

The figure of life again makes an appearance, but this time it is mortgaged in the attempt to "write" the self through practices of war and cruelty.[16] Earlier in this essay I had drawn attention to the concern with "how can life be redeemed, that is, rescued from this incessant operation of the negative"—but apart from a reference to the "thickness" of the African present and the stylization of conduct and life, we get no analysis of how the figure of *life* is to be distinguished from the doomed projects of recovery of identity.

It is not my intention to carry the argument with Mbembe further in the register in which he has chosen to write, because I am unclear about the project of *writing the African self* and especially because of Mbembe's earlier evocation of writing as a hallucinatory project.[17] Nevertheless, I am very interested in his question of how one would address violence that is seen as a witness against life itself (rather than, say, against a particular kind of identity). Are there other paths on which self-creation may take place, through occupying the same place of devastation yet again, by embracing the signs of injury and turning them into ways of becoming subjects? Instead of the register of the prophetic pronouncement, let me turn to the register of the everyday through which one may attempt to redeem life. What is it to take up this challenge, writing within the genre of anthropological inquiry? I simply take this as an opportunity to lay out the different way in which I see the issues that are at stake in the project of anthropology in relation to violence and suffering. As I hope to show, it is not that ghosts stand expelled in the scenes of violence I describe, but rather that everyday life is not expelled.

In the first chapter of this book, I tried to define the way that my own relation to questions of violence and recovery was framed by the ethnographic context so that the violence of the Partition as part of people's lives dawned upon me, whereas in the case of the violence in 1984, I was propelled into it. For women such as Asha and Manjit, I became an unwitting collaborator, perhaps an alternate self, through whom the past could be visited while retaining a proximity to the projects of the present. While the events of the Partition formed a field of force within which the stories moved even as these were not explicitly articulated, I do not think that I could speak of the Partition as a spectral presence. In the case of 1984, the immediacy of the violence meant that what constituted the work of ethnography was located in the concrete issues of ensuring that the survivors could inhabit that space again, sometimes literally, sometimes figuratively. There is no pretense here at some grand project of recovery but simply the question of how everyday tasks of surviving—having a roof over your head, being able to send your children to school, being able to do the work of the everyday without constant fear of being attacked—could be accomplished. I found that the making of the self was located, not in the shadow of some ghostly past, but in the context of making the everyday inhabitable. Thus, I would suggest that the anthropological mode of knowing the subject defines it in terms of the conditions under which it becomes possible to speak of experience. Hence there is no unitary collective subject (such as the African self or the Indian self) but forms of inhabiting the world in which one tries to make the world one's own, or to find one's voice both within and outside the genres that become available in the descent into the everyday. Thus, testimony of the survivors as those who spoke because the victims could not was best conceptualized for me, not through the metaphor of writing, but rather through the contrast between saying and showing.

For one brief moment, let us go back to the picture of women sitting in stillness in the street of Sultanpuri, refusing to provide the spectacle of an ordered body and ordered space through which normality was to be staged for visiting dignitaries such as Mother Teresa. Recall that the women who had been sitting in mourning did not engage in any discussion—they simply refused to present a clean facade. As I argued, to one schooled in the cultural grammar of mourning, the women were presenting their bodies as evidence of their grievous loss. On the one hand, they could not make their bodies speak to bring forth the traditional laments. Yet, on the other hand, the pollution they insisted on embodying was "showing" the loss, the death, and the destruction. As I said, I was reminded of the powerful figure of Draupadi in the Mahabharata, who had been disrobed in the court of the King Duryodhana when she was menstruating because her husband staked her in a gamble with the king. The text has it that for fourteen years she wore the same cloth stained by her blood and left her hair wild and uncombed.

Clearly, the women were not embodying pollution as a direct act of mimesis of the figure of Draupadi, nor were they engaged in an act of "showing" after any reasoned engagement with the question of how to contest the denial in the official narrative that a large number of Sikhs had been killed. Yet their testimony can be constructed from the new way in which they occupied the space of symbolic representations in the collective imaginaire. It seems to me that this form of creating oneself as a subject by embracing the signs of subjection gives a very different direction to the meaning of being a victim compared to what Mbembe suggests. For what the women were able to "show" was not a standardized narrative of loss and suffering but a project that can be understood only in the singular through the image of reinhabiting the space of devastation *again*. Thus far, from the opposition between the experience of violence as a victim/survivor and that of the subject, it was the ability to recraft the symbols and genres of mourning that made them active in the highly contested domain of politics. This gave the women and us (in their company) the ability to engage a wider public on the meaning of this violence. Anthropologists have been accused of making the social so complex as to make it useless for any policy purposes that demand some reduction of complexity. However, in my experience it is precisely when anthropologists are able to covey the meaning of an event in terms of its location in the everyday, assuming that social action is not simply a direct materialization of cultural scripts but bears the traces of how these shared symbols are worked through, that it can be most effective. Now, Mbembe is surely right to insist that the transformation of war in many African countries has made it concomitant with the social itself rather than something set apart from the social. Yet his description has a unitary character—nothing is broken in that smooth flow of moment of sculpting oneself in cruelty because there is no temporality to this creation of the self. But even more fundamental is the fact that in rendering the "truth" of the African self writing in these terms, Mbembe also seems to strip the actors of a certain form of concealment, call it their separateness—whereas my own sense of understanding of ethnography is that it is at its very best a record of our having reached the kind of limit that allows us to say that my spade is turned.

Anthropologists have deployed the idea of narrativization as a mode through which experience is given shape, but stories, like other social phenomena, have unanticipated consequences. In an earlier paper I wrote with Arthur Kleinman that "The social space occupied by scarred populations may enable stories to break through routine cultural codes to express counterdiscourse that assaults and even perhaps undermines the taken-for-granted meaning of things as they are. Out of such desperate and defeated experiences stories may emerge that call for and at times may bring about change that alters utterly the commonplace—both at the level of collective experience and at the level of individual subjectivity."[18] As opposed to the dramatic potential of stories in the media that are successful in focusing attention on a catastrophic event, the potential of anthropology lies in showing both (a) how it is that something can build into a crisis and (b) how events can be carried forward and backward in time. This is, in turn, related to the capacity of seeing and documenting the eventfulness of the everyday. In our thoughts on the experience of communities devastated by violence, as well as the soft knife of everyday oppressions, Kleinman and I wrote the following:

> Clearly a double movement seems necessary for communities to be able to contain the harm that has been documented in these accounts: at the macrolevel of the political system it requires the creation of a public space that gives recognition to the suffering of survivors and restores some faith in the democratic process, and at the microlevels of community and family survivors it demands opportunities of everyday life to be resumed. This does not mean that success would be achieved in separating the guilty from the innocent through the working of the criminal justice system, for in most cases described here it is not easy to separate the guilty and to pinpoint the legal responsibility, but it does mean that in the life of a community, justice is neither everything nor nothing—that the very setting-into-process of public acknowledgement of hurt can allow new opportunities to be created for resumption of everyday life.

In other words, I am suggesting that self-creation on the register of the everyday is a careful putting together of life—a concrete engagement with the tasks of remaking that is mindful of both terms of the compound expression: *everyday* and *life*. It points to the eventfulness of the everyday and the attempt to forge oneself into an ethical subject within this scene of the ordinary.

ANTHROPOLOGY AND THE ETHICS OF RESPONSIBILITY

In his essay on "Science as Vocation," Max Weber named the type of ethics that marks the pursuit of science as the ethics of responsibility.[19] But the question of responsibility in relation to anthropology is not easy to define in terms of the contrast between doing and saying. In the *Current Anthropology* forum on anthropology in public, Charles Hale put the matter in the following way: "We must make our way among highly charged accounts of what happened producing versions of our own that are inevitably partial and situated. Alternately, by choosing not to delve into that recent history we run the risk of complicity with powerful interests that are well served by official amnesia."[20] Hale is right on target that to expose the official lies is both an act of saying and an act of doing. In such heroic moments when the anthropologist has the resources to expose the official lies, the ethical imperative seems clearer than when one follows the trajectory of what happens to victims or perpetrators over time. I refer not simply to the transformation when victims become killers as Mahmood Mamdani has argued in his recent book,[21] but when violence becomes so embedded into the fabric of the social that it becomes indistinguishable from the social. I referred earlier to Mbembe's argument that wars in Africa have become part of the everyday life but was hesitant to accept his formulation that this was the result of the past that is not mastered and hence comes to haunt the living.

There is an interesting lead given by Diane Nelson on this point in some of her recent work on Guatemala when she asks how it is that the same state that was experienced as the agent of massacres and the scorched-earth policy could now be viewed as the object of desire.[22] The state, she argues, comes to be understood as two-faced, bamboozling, desirable, deceptive, and dangerous. Thus turning on its head the stereotypical image of the masked mimicry of the state by cunning two-faced natives, Nelson's ethnography of the state puts it on a highly mobile trajectory in which it is both feared and desired. After twenty years of the worst of the counterinsurgency politics, the work of time seems to obliterate the strict divisions between the state as oppressor and the people as oppressed. To take one such event: General Rios Montt was named a party to genocide in the Guatemalan civil war by the United Nations Truth Commission in 1999. After taking power in the 1982 coup d'état his government oversaw scorched-earth campaigns and massacres throughout the country. Yet, a few months after the Truth Commission's findings, Rios Montt's political party was elected, and he became the elected head of Congress. What should have been a fixed position (resentful victims) became uncannily mobile. Rather than clarity of the picture of the state as oppressor that stands apart from innocent victims, we encounter the idea that nothing is as it seems. The fighters of yesterday are the collaborators of state projects today. These are typically the sites of rumor, gossip, and a pervading sense of corruption by both those who embody the state and those who are presented as the ones offering resistance to it.

Perhaps one can get an idea of the distance between a theoretical stance that locates questions of sovereignty in some version of the idea of consent and truth-telling practices around it and the ethnographic take on this. In their general formulation of what they call the general passage from a paradigm of modern sovereignty toward a paradigm of imperial sovereignty, Hardt and Negri have commented upon the limitations of a perspective that criticizes Enlightenment notions of truth in the following terms:

> In the context of state terror and mystification, clinging to the primacy of the concept of truth can be a powerful and necessary form of resistance. Establishing and making public the truth of the recent past—attributing responsibility to state officials for specific acts and in some cases exacting retribution—appears here as ineluctable precondition for any democratic future. The master narratives of the Enlightenment do not seem particularly repressive here, and the concept of truth is not fluid or unstable—on the contrary! The truth is that this general ordered the torture and assassination of that union leader, and this colonel led the massacre of that village. Making public such truths is an exemplary Enlightenment project of modernist politics, and the critique of it in these contexts could serve only to aid the mystificatory and repressive powers of the regime under attack.[23]

Unlike the nostalgia for a public space marked by the clear separation of the perpetrators and victims, most close studies of truth commissions have shown how much the notion of testimony excluded certain other models of testimony and remembrance.[24] Thus, truth-telling practices may emerge not as the exemplary Enlightenment project with the emphasis on Truth with a capital *T*, but simply as a way for local communities caught between the violence of the state and the guerrillas to carve out a public space for themselves. If the commitment to Enlightenment rationality is the condition for building democracies in societies steeped in long-term wars and insurgency/counterinsurgency operations, then we are in effect denying the attempts to build democracies in the messy worlds in which transformations of this kind are taking place.

Anthropologists cannot take comfort in any simple notion of innocent victims or the work of culture as a pregiven script. Culture pertains not only to a conventionalized or contractual sense of agreement among members of a society, but also refers to a mutual absorption of the social and the natural. Violence of the kind that was witnessed in the Partition riots in India calls into question the very idea of life—we reach not the end of some intellectual agreement but the end of criteria. Consider the production of bodies through violence in which women were stripped and marched naked in the streets, or the fantasy of writing political slogans on their private parts, and most recently in Gujarat, the stories of tearing open the womb of a pregnant woman to rip apart the fetus in the act of killing.

Manjit taught me that while the violence that lived within the kinship universe was sayable, other forms of violence, such as that of the Partition riots, was such that any claim over culture became impossible. She taught me that one could utter words to describe it, but "it was as if one's touch with these words and hence with life itself had been burned or numbed." Manjit also taught me that there is deep moral energy in the refusal to represent certain violations of the human body. In allowing her pain to happen to me, she taught me that to redeem life from the violations to which she had been subjected was an act of lifelong engagement with poisonous knowledge; in digesting this poison in the acts of attending to the ordinary, she had been able to teach me how to respect the boundaries between saying and showing. This is how I see the public role of anthropology: acting on the double register in which we offer evidence that contests the official amnesia and systematic acts of making evidence disappear, but also witnessing the descent into the everyday through which victims and survivors affirm the possibility of life by removing it from the circulation of words gone wild—leading words home, so to speak. My sense of indebtedness to the work of Cavell in these matters comes from a confidence that perhaps Manjit did not utter anything that we would recognize as philosophical in the kind of environments in which philosophy is done . . . but Cavell's work shows us that there is no real distance between the spiritual exercises she undertakes in her world and the spiritual exercises we can see in every word he has ever written. To hold these types of words together and to sense the connection of these lives has been my anthropological kind of devotion to the world.

NOTES

I. THE EVENT AND THE EVERYDAY

1. I start with a simple notion of event as a historical construct that constitutes a rupture. This was the sense in which it was used in the controversy among historians in the 1960s and 1970s as to the merits of an event-centered history versus history of everyday life. As I move through the text, I hope it will be evident that the notion of event becomes analytically more complex as its relation to language and to everyday life begins to unfold. On the notion of event as a historical construct, see Thomas Flynn, "Michel Foucault and the Career of the Historical Event," in *At the Nexus of Philosophy and History*, ed. B. P. Dauenhaeur (Athens: University of Georgia Press, 1987), 178–200. In my earlier work I thought of an event as critical when it could not be subsumed within the existing repertoires of thought and action. See Veena Das, *Critical Events: An Anthropological Perspective on Contemporary India* (Delhi: Oxford University Press, 1995). On the relation between event and language, Gilles Deleuze's notion that the event is expressible in a proposition only as enveloped by the *verb* points to the moving and incorporeal character of the event. See Gilles Deleuze, *The Logic of Sense*, trans. Mark Lester with Charles Stivale (New York: Columbia University Press, 1990), 182.

2. In the aesthetic theory of an audience in Sanskrit, from which I derive my fantasy of a reader, the performance speaks to one who is *sahridaya* or of a similar or even shared heart. Yet the community of the writer and the reader is not necessarily a community of comfort, for sharing a heart means that something

in both, the writer and the reader, dies between the writing and the reading. There is a rich tradition of anthropologists engaging with Wittgenstein, but I am not interested here in providing a general picture of this relationship. For some of those concerns, see Veena Das, "Wittgenstein and Anthropology," *Annual Review of Anthropology* (1998) 27: 171–95.

3. See Marilyn Strathern, *The Relation* (Cambridge: Prickly Pear Press, 1995), 11, 13.

4. Strathern makes the subtle point that relations might appear as versions of one another as when affines become exchange partners, thus adding a new dimension to the relationship, augmenting it and allowing one to see each from the perspective of the other. See Marilyn Strathern, *Partial Connections* (Savage, MD: Rowman & Littlefield, 1991).

5. See Ludwig Wittgenstein, *Tractatus Logico-Philosophicus,* trans. C. K. Odgen (London: Kegan Paul, 1932), especially propositions 5.61 and 5.62. Note that Wittgenstein does not use the idea of world as some kind of systematic whole; hence the limits are not the limits of the factual. I have read the text but do not know it well and so am indebted to Eli Friedlander, *Signs of Sense: Reading Wittgenstein's Tractatus* (Cambridge, MA: Harvard University Press, 2001) especially ch. 8.

6. One could also consider Wittgenstein's thought that experience does not happen *to* the subject, for the subject is the condition for experience by drawing upon the analogies he alludes to. Thus, "I should almost like to say: One no more feels sorrow in one's body than one feels seeing in one's eyes." Ludwig Wittgenstein, *Zettel,* ed. G. E. M. Anscombe and G. H. von Wright, 2nd ed. (Oxford: Blackwell, 1981), para. 419; quoted again in *Remarks on the Philosophy of Psychology, Volume II,* ed. G. E. M. Anscombe and G. H. von Wright (Oxford: Blackwell, 1980), para. 327.

7. This does not imply that Wittgenstein is defining anything like a human essence that is given in advance, though the question of how the natural and the social are mutually absorbed in each other is of the utmost importance in his writing. As the later chapters will make clear, the scale and complexity of the human cannot be determined outside and in advance of our experience as beings who are complicated enough to be embedded in language.

8. Eric L. Santner, *Stranded Objects: Mourning, Memory and Film in Postwar Germany* (Ithaca: Cornell University Press, 1990), 7. This rhetoric of mourning does not imply for me that the idea of some kind of moral education of the self is given up, but that it has to grow out of the everyday rather than through some fantasy of acting upon complete knowledge and its related rational action. Cavell thinks of such moral education through the figure of transfiguration.

9. Stanley Cavell, *A Pitch of Philosophy: Autobiographical Exercises* (Cambridge, MA: Harvard University Press, 1994), 75–76.

10. See para. 120 in *Philosophical Investigations*, "When I talk about language (words, sentences, etc.) I must speak the language of every day. Is this language somehow too coarse and material for what we want to say? *Then how is another one to be constructed?*—And how strange that we should be able to do anything at all with the one we have!" Ludwig Wittgenstein, *Philosophical Investigations*, trans. G. E. M. Enscombe (New York: Macmillan, 1953), para. 120, emphasis in original.

11. Stanley Cavell, "Something Out of the Ordinary," *Proceedings and Addresses of the American Philosophical Association* 71, no. 2 (November 1997): 26.

12. See Das, "Wittgenstein and Anthropology," 171–95, and Veena Das, "The Event and the Everyday: Notes on Illness, Despair and Hope," Wertheim Lecture delivered at the Center for Asian Studies, Amsterdam, October 2003.

13. The sense that my speech might not be my voice is expressed with great sensitivity in a Hindi novel by Krishna Baldev Vaid: "*mere muh se jo awaz niklegi, voh meri nahin hogi, ya kisi ko sunai nahin degi, ya kisi se pahchani nahin hogi*"—the voice that emanates from my mouth will not be mine, or no one will hear it, or no one will recognize it; cited in Annie Montaut, "La poétique du vide chez Vaid et la résistance à la violence communautaire," *Puruṣārtha: Special Issue, Littérature et Poétiques Pluriculturelles en Asie du Sud*, ed. Annie Montaut, 24 (2000): 113–55.

14. Jacques Derrida, "Signature, Event, Context," in *Limited Inc.*, ed. G. Graff (Evanston: Northwestern University Press, 1988), 1–25. Hent de Vries explains this impulse in Derrida with reference to the relation between prayer and the founding of theology: "Derrida leaves no doubt that prayer owes its very existence to a possible contamination. If prayer did not contain the risk of being lost (in predication, citation, mechanical repetition, . . .) and thus of missing its mark—no theology, positive or negative would be possible." This scene of prayer becoming lost captures the danger of words not finding their home. Perhaps the acceptance of this fact rather than a search for guarantees might give us peace. See Hent de Vries, *Minimal Theologies: Critiques of Secular Reason in Adorno and Levinas* (Baltimore: Johns Hopkins University Press, 2005), 656.

15. Both Deborah Poole and Pradeep Jeganathan have given us masterly analyses of the fear generated in the mode of anticipation and how the state is implicated in that temporality. See Pradeep Jeganathan, "Checkpoint: Anthropology, Identity and the State," and Deborah Poole, "Between Threat and Guarantee: Justice and Community in the Margins of the Peruvian State," in *Anthropology in the Margins of the State*, ed. Veena Das and Deborah Poole (Santa Fe: SAR Publications and Delhi: Oxford University Press, 2004), 35–67, 67–81.

16. See Veena Das, "Masks and Faces: An Essay on Punjabi Kinship," *Contributions to Indian Sociology* 1 (1976): 1–30.

17. Pamela Reynolds's analysis of the implications of changing residential configurations for the understanding of violence in young people's lives in

South Africa offers methodological and theoretical insights of the utmost importance on this problem. See her essay "The Ground of All Making: State Violence, the Family, and Political Activists," in *Violence and Subjectivity,* ed. Veena Das, Arthur Kleinman, Mamphela Ramphele, and Pamela Reynolds (Berkeley: University of California Press, 2000): 141–71.

18. On the axiom of kinship amity, see Meyer Fortes, *Kinship and Social Order: The Legacy of Lewis Henry Morgan* (Cambridge: Cambridge University Press, 1971), ch. 7.

19. For an outstanding example of such a methodology of fieldwork, see Janet Carsten, *The Heat of the Hearth: The Process of Kinship in a Malay Fishing Community* (Oxford: Clarendon Press, 1997). Carsten was completely incorporated as a daughter within the village community she studied so that her account of the kinship system is almost visceral. Her discussion shows how this was not so much a strategy on her part as a response to certain ways of incorporating outsiders that seemed normal to the villagers.

20. The use of the word *buried* might convey the impression that the violence was repressed. I use the term buried here in the sense in which a text may bury a certain memory as, for instance, in Cavell's interpretation of Emerson's text on dawning, as burying the name of Emerson's dead son through its dispersal in the text. The memory here does not have to be exhumed: it is like the background pattern in a weave, ever present and yet not fully visible.

21. The sense of a funereal landscape is found in many ethnographies of violence. Here is Mark Whitaker writing on his revisit to Batticaloa: "Ethnographic fragments such as the ones above present a problem for a constructivist anthropologist like myself. I wrote them to be, however inadequately, like something that I had witnessed. In a way, I can feel the harsh gaze of all that watching even now, staring out at me from the photographs of dead warriors, whom I remember as children, or etched in that ugly moonscape between Polonavura and Batticaloa, now with its abandoned and looted houses and paddy fields burned out and raked over by the various armies that one elderly Tamil woman I talked to called 'the centipedes of war.'" Whitaker takes his notion of fragment in a very different direction than mine, for he ties the idea of the fragment with the impossibility of representation, while for me the connection is with mourning. Mark Whitaker, "Ethnography as Learning: A Wittgensteinian Approach to Writing Ethnographic Accounts," *Anthropological Quarterly* 69, no. 1 (1998): 1–13.

22. See Veena Das, "The Anthropology of Violence and the Speech of Victims," *Anthropology Today* 4, no. 3 (1987): 106–9.

23. I am aware that some activists such as Madhu Kishwar gave evidence before the People's Commission of Inquiry, which was appointed by citizen groups, attesting that women had been raped. When I initially went into Sultanpuri some women who lived in the relatively less affected areas such as

D Block told us that some women had been raped. However, after more than a year's sustained work in the worst affected blocks in this area, I can say with some confidence that men were killed and property was looted, but women were not raped in Sultanpuri. In fact, survivors made this point to distinguish it from the Hindu-Muslim riots, about which they had the kind of tacit knowledge that is available in these communities. A detailed analysis follows in chapter 8.

24. Veena Das, "Communities, Riots and Survivors," in *Mirrors of Violence: Communities, Riots and Survivors in South Asia* (Delhi: Oxford University Press, 1990), 1–35.

25. See Deepak Mehta and Roma Chatterji, "Boundaries, Names, Alterities: A Case Study of a 'Communal Riot' in Dharavi, Bombay," in *Remaking a World: Violence, Social Suffering, and Recovery,* ed. Veena Das, Arthur Kleinman, Margaret Lock, Mamphela Ramphele, and Pamela Reynolds (Berkeley: University of California Press, 2001), 201–50.

26. See Sudhir Kakar, *Colour of Violence: Cultural Identities, Religion and Conflict* (Delhi: Penguin Books, 1995).

27. For the varied ways in which the idea of Partition is realized, see the various essays in *Transeuropéennes: Divided Countries, Separated Cities,* no. 19/20 (2000–2001).

28. For instance, Clifford Geertz, who is pleased to acknowledge Wittgenstein as one of his masters, speaks of the importance of the concept of forms of life as opening a pathway to "trying to discover how in the midst of talk, people, individual people, people as a whole—put a distinct and variegated voice together." See Clifford Geertz, *Available Light: Anthropological Reflections on Philosophical Topics* (Princeton: Princeton University Press, 2000), xii. Surely this move was extremely productive for anthropology, but it attests more to the freedom it promised from overly deterministic models of knowledge in which the personality of the researcher is converted into a neutral observer rather than to the specificity of thought on the connection between forms and life. This is not as much a criticism of Geertz as a way of acknowledging how difficult it is to absorb this concept.

29. Stanley Cavell, "Declining Decline: Wittgenstein as a Philosopher of Culture," in *This New Yet Unapproachable America: Lectures after Emerson after Wittgenstein* (Chicago: University of Chicago Press, 1988), 41.

30. The question of whether there is sharp division between humans and animals in Wittgenstein's conception is a complicated one. While I touch on this question lightly in some parts of this text, I cannot take it up in any detail. The presence of various animals in *Philosophical Investigations,* such as the lion, the dog, the bee, the spider, the fly, and even the cow might alert us to this problematic. I wanted to write on the tracks animals leave in texts, to acknowledge our dog, Iota, who often guided my thoughts, but must postpone it for now.

31. Giorgio Agamben, *Homo Sacer: Sovereign Power and Bare Life,* trans. D. Heller Roazen (Stanford: Stanford University Press, 1998).

32. George C. F. Bearn, *Waking to Wonder: Wittgenstein's Existential Investigations* (Albany: State University of New York Press, 1997).

33. Ludwig Wittgenstein, *Culture and Value,* ed. G. H. von Wright, trans. Peter Winch (Oxford: Blackwell, 1980), 44; quotation from para. 217.

34. Some scholars interpret forms of life as those that remain after explanations are exhausted, and social science as the discipline that explains "the normative patterns of behavior." They conclude, therefore, that there is a paradox in using this idea within a social science paradigm: for example, Paul Seabright, who starts his essay on this Wittgensteinian "paradox" by stating that "forms of life" refer to shared practices, customs, or institutions. I hope my discussion shows that this is a very impoverished view of the idea of forms of life, for it contains no reflections on the notion of "life." It also endorses a view of social science and of culture that many anthropologists have done much to overcome. Paul Seabright, "Explaining Cultural Divergence: A Wittgensteinian Paradox," *Journal of Philosophy* 84, no. 1 (1987): 11–27.

2. THE FIGURE OF THE ABDUCTED WOMAN

1. Gyanendra Pandey, "The Prose of Otherness," in *Subaltern Studies,* ed. David Arnold and David Hardiman (Delhi: Oxford University Press, 1994), vol. 8, 188–221, quotation from 205.

2. It is, however, important to note that despite the gesture toward the ordinary, what is at stake in this testimonial literature is not the history of the ordinary but, rather, the retelling of the story from the perspective of ordinary people in extraordinary times. Hence, the emphasis is on remembering the Partition and not on how it folds into everyday life in the present. See Gyanendra Pandey, *Remembering Partition: Violence, Nationalism and History in India* (London: Cambridge University Press, 2003). Among the most important contributions within this genre of writing are Urvashi Butalia, *The Other Side of Silence: Voices from the Partition of India* (Durham: Duke University Press, 1998) and Ritu Menon and Kamla Bhasin, *Borders and Boundaries: Women in India's Partition* (New Brunswick, NJ: Rutgers University Press, 1998). See also Sukeshi Kamra, *Bearing Witness: Partition, Independence and the End of the Raj* (Calgary: University Press of Calgary, 2002).

3. Rada Ivekovic has analyzed the manner in which gender hierarchies in ordinary times are further utilized in times of war and ethnic strife to create new hegemonies although she is mindful of the way that the future can be opened up in these very times. See Rada Ivekovic, *Le sexe de la nation* (Paris: Non & Non, Éditions Léo Scheer, 2003).

4. The fact-finding report commissioned by the government never saw the light of day.

5. Speaking of the Eichmann trial, Shoshana Felman says, "The trial was a conscious legal effort not just to give victims a voice and a stage, to break the silence of the trauma, to divulge and to uncover secrets and taboos, but to transform these discoveries into one national, collective story, to assemble consciously, meticulously, diligently, an unprecedented public and collective legal record of mass trauma that formerly existed only in the repressed form of a series of untold, fragmented private stories and traumatic memories." See Shoshana Felman, *The Juridical Unconscious: Trials and Traumas in the Twentieth Century* (Cambridge, MA: Harvard University Press, 2002), 7. At this point I will say only that Felman's formulation does not allow for many situations in which the public telling and the attempt to create a *national* story of a wound can itself take on the character of rumor, of words gone wild, and could convert justice into vengeance. A good example is the speech Felman quotes from George Bush after September 11th in which he said, "I will never forget the wound to our country and those who inflicted it. . . . Our grief has turned to anger and anger to resolution. Whether we bring our enemies to justice or justice to our enemies, justice will be done" (quoted in Felman, 3). What is interesting is that Felman concludes that "the promised exercise of *legal* justice—of justice by trial and by law—has become civilization's most appropriate and most essential, most ultimately meaningful response to the violence that wounds it" (3, emphasis in the original). Yet this speech was not about justice but about justice as *vengeance,* as the reference to enemies clearly implies and strangely this goes unnoticed in Felman's account. Subsequent events have shown more clearly that naming the tragic events of September 11th as acts of *war* rather than *crimes* shows the easy slippage between these categories. The attempt to create a national story of hurt can take the form of rumor rather more easily than Felman allows for. In that sense the Eichmann trial was exceptional rather than paradigmatic, because the line between victims and perpetrators was so clear—those lines become blurred in most situations of ongoing violence, as the experience of truth and reconciliation commissions in various countries have shown. See Fiona Ross, *Bearing Witness: Women and the Truth and Reconciliation Commission in South Africa* (London: Pluto Press, 2003); Richard Wilson, *The Politics of Truth and Reconciliation in South Africa* (Cambridge: Cambridge University Press, 2003).

6. G. D. Khosla, *Stern Reckoning: A Survey of the Events Leading Up to and Following the Partition of India* (Delhi: Oxford University Press, 1989; first published in 1949).

7. It is worth quoting Pandey in detail on this pattern: "On the basis of published and unpublished materials and oral evidence provided to him by officials and non-officials in Pakistan, Symonds declared that, 'at the lowest estimate' half a million people perished and twelve million became homeless. . . . Nothing

in the surviving records, in the calculations made at the time, or in the contentious debates that have gone on since then, gives us anything like a persuasive basis for such an inference. Is it, rather, a question of what we can live with? Yet, it is not entirely clear why it is easier to live with 500,00 dead than with a larger or smaller figure. Is it the 'median' that allows one to emphasize the enormity of Partition and point to our surviving humanity at the same time? Or is it a figure that has gained credibility in academic circles simply by repetition?" (Pandey, *Remembering Partition*, 90–91). It seems to me that the issue is not one of our surviving humanity or of arriving at some kind of an average from widely discrepant numbers, but rather of tracking how official discourse functions as rumor and asking what this authorizes. I argue that the reference to the enormity of the numbers involved authorizes the idea of unprecedented violence that has unsettled the very possibility of the social contract because the sexual contract is not in place.

8. The form of this story is an ancient one, as, for instance, in the epic depictions of Sita and Draupadi in the Ramayana and the Mahabharata. The movement of this story to a new register that makes it a state obligation to recover abducted women is, however, a new way of anchoring the state to the mythological imagination. For an analysis of the movements of gift and counter-gift, marriage and abduction in the stories, see Veena Das, "Narrativizing the Male and the Female in Tulasidas's Ramacharitamanasa," in *Social Structure and Change: Ritual and Kinship*, vol. v, ed. A. M. Shah, B. S. Baviskar, and E. Ramaswamy (Delhi: Sage Publications, 1998), 67–93.

9. *Proceedings of the Indian National Congress 1946–1947* (New Delhi: Government of India, 1947).

10. *Proceedings of the Indian National Congress 1946–1947.*

11. Khosla, *Stern Reckoning*, 234.

12. Rajashree Ghosh, "The Constitution of Refugee Identity," unpublished M. Phil. dissertation, University of Delhi, 1991.

13. Kamlabehn Patel, *Mula Suta Ukhledan* (Bombay: R. R. Seth, 1985).

14. The following quotations from these discussions are taken from *Constituent Assembly of India (Legislative) Debates* (New Delhi: Government of India, 1949).

15. The mythic motif of the abduction of the innocent Sita by Ravana and her subsequent banishment by Rama was evoked as a metaphor in popular literature as well as popular Hindi films.

16. Veena Das, "Sexual Violation and the Making of the Gendered Subject," in *Discrimination and Toleration*, ed. K. Hastrup and G. Urlich (London: Kluwer Law International, 2002), 257–73, quotation from 271.

17. The text of the Abducted Persons (Recovery and Restoration) Act, 1949 (Act No. LXV of 1949), is reproduced as Appendix 1 in Menon and Bhasin, *Borders and Boundaries*, 261.

18. On the relative weight given to men and women in the procreative process in Punjabi kinship, see Das, "Masks and Faces." There is a vast literature in anthropology that shows how theories of procreation codify ideologies of kinship. Much of this was published in the late 1960s and early 1970s under the category of virgin birth debate. As an example, see Edmund Leach, "Virgin Birth," *Proceedings of the Royal Anthropological Institute of Great Britain and Ireland* (1966): 39–49.

19. In an astute analysis of the sexual violence and creation of public memory in the Bangladesh Liberation War of 1971, Nayanika Mookherjee shows the subtle changes in the nature of reproductive (in addition to sexual) violence against women. She shows that one of the purported reasons for violence against Bengali women by Pakistani soldiers was to improve the genes of the Bengali people and to populate Bangladesh with a race of "pure" Muslims. This eugenic ring was completely absent in the case of Hindu-Muslim violence and shows that the image of Hinduized Muslims could be mobilized for hate in the Bangladesh war. Thus creation of boundaries is part of the shifting discourses of community rather than something pregiven and held in perpetuity. See Nayanika Mookerjee, "'A Lot of History': Sexual Violence, Public Memories and the Bangladesh Liberation War of 1971," unpublished Ph.D. dissertation, School of Oriental and African Studies, University of London, 2002.

20. I owe this insight to the important work of P. K. Dutta and Charu Gupta.

21. See Veena Das, "Paternity, Sovereignty and the Argument from Nature," in *Powers of the Secular Modern: Talal Asad and His Interlocutors,* ed. David Scott and Charles Hirschkind (Stanford: Stanford University Press, 2006, 93–113). Gauri Viswanathan argues that the convert was subjected to social death and thus denied all earlier forms of sociality. I see this to be a more complicated question. The notion of fatherhood was at the center of theological and political debates in eighteenth-century Europe. The core of the disagreement was on the kind of "natural" rights that the father had over the son. Thus, even with conversion the rights of the father did not automatically disappear since conversion affected the *social* position of the convert but not necessarily the relations that were seen to derive from nature.

22. See Paola Bachetta, *La construction des identités dans les discours nationalists hindous (1939–1992): le Rahstriya Swayamsevak Sangh et la Rashtriya Sevika Samiti* (Lille: ANRT, Université de Lille III, 1996), and Charu Gupta, *Sexuality, Obscenity, Community: Women, Muslims, and the Hindu Public in Colonial India* (New York: Palgrave, 2002; first published, Delhi: Permanent Black, 2001). Page references are to the Palgrave edition.

23. Gupta, *Sexuality, Obscenity, Community,* 248.

24. Gupta, *Sexuality, Obscenity, Community,* 267.

25. Claude Lévi-Strauss, *The Elementary Structures of Kinship*, rev. ed. trans. J. H. Bill and J. R. von Sturmore, ed. Rodney Needham (London: George Allen & Unwin, 1969).

26. Mary Laura Severance, "Sex and the Social Contract," *Journal of English Literary History*, 67, no. 2 (2000): 453–513. I remind the reader that in Filmer's theory fatherly power is the basis for kingly power—hence, the father had the right to kill the son without incurring any legal penalty. See Sir Robert Filmer, *Patriarcha and Other Writings* (Cambridge: Cambridge University Press, 1991; first published in 1680). I discuss this in some detail in my essay "Paternity, Sovereignty and the Argument from Nature."

27. Severance, "Sex and the Social Contract," 456.

28. Jean-Jacques Rousseau, *Émile* (New York: Everyman's Library, 1974; first published in 1911). Page numbers are from the 1974 Everyman's Library edition.

29. Das, "Paternity, Sovereignty and the Argument from Nature."

30. Rosseau, *Émile*, 448, emphasis added.

31. Rosseau, *Émile*, 325.

32. Mario Feit has examined the implications of Rousseau's theory of the relation between sexuality and mortality for same-sex marriage in an innovative and interesting way. While I see that there are important implications of Rousseau's thesis of citizenship for non-normative forms of sexuality, I am much more interested here in the way in which the figure of the father places Rousseau in the debate on fatherhood in Filmer, Hobbes, and Locke. I have learned much from Mario Feit's discussion on population: Mario Feit, "Mortality, Sexuality, and Citizenship: Reading Rousseau, Arendt, and Nietzsche," unpublished Ph.D. dissertation, Johns Hopkins University, 2003.

33. This quote is from a Hindi vernacular tract from 1927, cited in Gupta, *Sexuality, Obscenity, Community*, 292 (translation by Gupta). Gupta does not explore the similar Urdu language popular culture, but it would have been very interesting to see what tropes were used to delegitimize popular practices of women in the attempt to purify the Muslim community of Hindu influence.

3. LANGUAGE AND BODY

1. See Veena Das, "Language and Body: Transactions in the Construction of Pain," in *Social Suffering*, ed. Arthur Kleinman, Veena Das, and Margaret Lock (Berkeley: University of California Press, 1997), 67–91.

2. Michel Foucault, "Foucault Live: Collected Interviews, 1961–1984," ed. Sylvère Lotringer, *Semiotext(e)* (1989): 308.

3. Stanley Cavell, *Philosophical Passages: Wittgenstein, Emerson, Austin, Derrida* (Oxford: Basil Blackwell, 1995).

4. Ludwig Wittgenstein, *The Blue and Brown Books* (Oxford: Basil Blackwell, 1958), 49.

5. Stanley Cavell, "Comments on Veena Das's Essay 'Language and Body: Transactions in the Construction of Pain,'" in Kleinman et al., *Social Suffering,* 93–99.

6. Rabindra Nath Tagore, *Ghare Baire,* Rabindra Rachnabali, vol. 8 (Calcutta: Vishvabharati, 1941). The version in English is entitled *The Home and the World,* trans. Surendranath Tagore (New Delhi: Penguin Books, 1985; first published in 1919). I have used the Bengali text; all translations are mine. The *swadeshi* movement arose as a protest movement in Bengal in 1903 against the decision of the colonial government to partition Bengal. It was led primarily by upper-caste Hindus to boycott all British goods. It grew later into other movements such as the noncooperation and civil disobedience movements of Gandhi. See, e.g., Sumit Sarkar, *The Swadeshi Movement in Bengal, 1903–1908* (New Delhi: People's Publishing, 1973), and more recently, Sankari Prasad Basu, *Swadeshi Movement in Bengal and Freedom Struggle of India* (Calcutta: Papyrus, 2004).

7. I have used the original Bengali version with my own translations. As Tapobrata Ghosh shows, the original Bengali text and its English translation differ in significant respects so that the primacy of character gives way to primacy of plot in the English translation. See Tapobrata Ghosh, "The Form of the Home and the World," in *Rabindra Nath Tagore's* The Home and the World: *A Critical Companion,* ed. P.K. Datta (Delhi: Permanent Black, 2003), 66–81. The original paper was translated from Bengali into English by Sunanda Das. P.K. Datta's introduction to this volume (1–27) gives a succinct description of the issues raised in literary criticism and history around this book.

8. If Sandip sounds like a textbook, this is precisely what is intended. This point was completely missed by many critics of Tagore.

9. All these adjectives describe the goddess and were taken by Bankimchandra to describe the nation as mother in his famous poem "Vande Matram" (I bow to the mother). The poem has the form of a *strotra,* or hymn of praise—it appeared first within the novel *Anandamath,* and as Julius Lipner has shown, subsequently it took on a life of its own. Lipner says that in the novel the hymn is supposedly sung in a plaintive mood, shown by the reference to the *raga* Malhar with its tones of longing, but later Tagore sang it in a public gathering in the *raga* Desh set to a Qawalli beat. The subsequent usage has turned this poem into a militant song now widely used to intimidate non-Hindus, especially Muslims, by militant organizations such as the RSS and other organizations of Hindu militants loosely referred to as the Sangh Parivar. Julius Lipner, "Vande Matram: The Genesis and Power of a Song," paper presented to the Conference on Political Hinduism, UCLA Center for the Study of Religion, May 6–7, 2005.

10. The use of the affectionate diminutive shows that she is not expelled from his heart.

11. It would be obvious that my interpretation of this text differs considerably from the interpretation offered by Ashis Nandy, *The Illegitimacy of Nationalism: Rabindranath Tagore & the Politics of Self* (Delhi: Oxford University Press, 1994). Nandy argues that Tagore's women stand for an authentic, unencumbered relation to tradition and hence are the defense that the culture puts up in response to both colonialism and an illegitimate nationalism that is modeled on the colonial image. For me, Tagore has a more complex relation to both tradition and nation, as is evident in Nikhil's sense of defeat when Bimala insists in offering him her worship. It is interesting to note that Tanika Sarkar, who gave a somewhat impoverished reading of the text in her earlier work, finding the novel to be "politically compromised," has now developed a more nuanced reading of the text. See Tanika Sarkar, "Many Faces of Love: Country, Woman, and God in *The Home and the World,*" in *Rabindranath Tagore's* The Home and the World: *A Critical Companion,* 27–45. On the general issue of the place of the family as some kind of inner sanctuary against colonial domination, recent historical scholarship shows this to be more a male fantasy than a description of the domestic. As Sumit Guha puts it, "The interior space of the family that Partha Chatterjee sees Indian nationalists constructing as an inviolable sanctum of national identity was a very novel space, and no archaic sanctuary." Sumit Guha, "The Family Feud as a Political Resource in Eighteenth-Century India," in *Unfamiliar Relations: Family and History in South Asia,* ed. Indrani Chatterjee (New Brunswick, NJ: Rutgers University Press, 2004), 46–73, quotation from 47.

12. See Veena Das and Ashis Nandy, "Violence, Victimhood and the Language of Silence," in *The Word and the World: Fantasy, Symbol, and Record,* ed. Veena Das (Delhi: Sage Publications, 1986). The original story appears in Sa'adat Hasan Manto, *Nimrud Ki Khudai* (Delhi: Saqi Book Depot, 1990; first published in 1950). An English translation is included in an anthology of stories on the Partition by Alok Bhalla. See Alok Bhalla, ed. and trans., *Stories about the Partition of India,* vols. 1–3 (Delhi: Indus Publications, 1994). Though I admire the tireless work Bhalla has done in making these stories available, there are some problems with the translation of this story, as I have pointed out elsewhere. See Veena Das, "Review of *Stories about the Partition of India,*" *Seminar: Special Issue on Memories of Partition* 420 (1994): 56–58.

13. See my account of the narration by a man on how he had felt compelled to kill his favorite sister because he thought that the other modes of dying in the hands of a crowd would be too painful for her. See Das, *Critical Events.*

14. For a description of the transformation of Manto's stories in powerful art installations in the work of the painter Nalini Malani, see Ashish Rajadhyaksha, "Spilling Out: Nalini Malani's Recent Video Installations," *Third Text* 17, no. 1 (2003): 53–61. Sahar Jalal, the miniature painter, has rendered Manto's story into a stunning miniature painting.

15. See Jonathan Parry, "The Aghori Ascetics of Benares," in *Indian Religions,* ed. Richard Burghart and Audrey Cantlie (London: Curzon Press, 1985), 51–78. Commenting on this paper, A. Piatogorsky opines that for the Aghoris, it is death itself that is the focus of the religious consciousness. Their rituals and their meditation are based upon the distinction, Piatogorsky says, between three components of the universe—that which dies naturally or timely death, that which dies unnaturally or untimely death, and that which has always been, as it were, already dead and that is therefore within death. A. Piatogorsky, "Some Phenomenological Observations on the Study of Indian Religion," in *Indian Religions,* 208–58. I find this remark to be of profound importance in thinking about unnatural or untimely death and the responsibilities of the living toward these deaths in a way that is very differently conceptualized than in, say, trauma theory. Rather, it seems that for the Aghoris, the question is how they as specialists on death can absorb the residues, the poisons of untimely deaths, in a way that they might protect future generations.

16. C. Nadia Seremetakis, *The Last Word: Women, Death and Divination in Inner Mani* (Chicago: University of Chicago Press, 1991), 101.

17. See also Charles L. Briggs, "Personal Sentiments and Polyphonic Voices in Warao Women's Ritual Wailing: Music and Poetics in a Collective Discourse," *American Anthropologist* 95, no. 4 (2003): 929–57. For a subtle analysis of funeral laments as related to both life and death, see Stefania Pandolfo, *Impasse of the Angels: Scenes from a Moroccan Space of Memory* (Chicago: University of Chicago Press, 1997). See also Lila Abu-Lughod, "Islam and the Gendered Discourse of Death," *International Journal of Middle East Studies* 25, no. 2 (1993): 187–205.

18. See Veena Das, "The Work of Mourning: Death in a Punjabi Family," in *The Cultural Transition: Human Experience and Social Transformation in the Third World,* ed. Merry I. White and Susan Pollock (London: Routledge & Kegan Paul, 1986), 179–210.

19. Loring Danforth, *The Death Rituals of Rural Greece* (Princeton: Princeton University Press, 1982). This is not to suggest any underlying similarity in the theoretical frames used by Seremetakis and Danforth. See also Margaret Alexiou, "Reappropriating Greek Sacrifice: Homo Recans or Anthropos Thysiazon?" *Journal of Modern Greek Studies* 8 (1990): 97–123. For a detailed discussion of the structure of these rituals and the manner in which caste and kinship categories are utilized, see chapter 5 in Veena Das, *Structure and Cognition: Aspects of Hindu Caste and Ritual* (Delhi: Oxford University Press, 1977) and my paper "The Work of Mourning."

20. For a masterly description of how laments might give expression to complaints that break the silences imposed by power, see James M. Wilce, "The Pragmatics of 'Madness': Performance Analysis of a Bangladeshi Woman's 'Aberrant' Lament," *Culture, Medicine and Psychiatry* 22, no. 1 (1998): 1–54.

Margaret Trawick Egmore's classic paper on the relation between genre and voice remains one of the most important contributions to this topic. See Margaret Trawick Egmore, "Internal Iconicity in Paraiyar Crying Songs," in *Another Harmony: New Essays on the Folklore of India,* ed. S. H. Blackburn and A. K. Ramanujan (Delhi: Oxford University Press, 1986), 294–344.

21. See Veena Das, "Composition of the Personal Voice: Violence and Migration," *Studies in History* 7, no. 1 (1991): 65–77.

22. Das, "Narrativizing the Male and the Female in Tulasidas's Ramacharitamanasa."

23. Jenny Sharpe, *Allegories of Empire: The Figure of Woman in the Colonial Text* (Minneapolis: University of Minnesota Press, 1993), 64.

24. Here I refer to the haunting images that Khwaja Ahmad Abbas, the Urdu writer, used to refer to the atrocities perpetrated on women. "Did the English whisper in our ears that you may chop off the head of whichever Hindu you find, or that you may plunge a knife in the belly of whichever Muslim you find? Did the English also educate us into the art of committing atrocities with women of other religions right in the market place? Did they teach us to tattoo Pakistan and Jai Hind on the breasts and secret organs of women?" Khwaja Ahmad Abbas, "Prastavna," in *Ramanad Sagar, Aur Insan Mar Gaya* (Delhi: Rajkamal Prakashan, 1977), original in Hindi, my translation.

25. Menon and Bhasin, *Borders and Boundaries.*

26. "Within the body, growing as a graft, indomitable, there is an other. And no one is present, within that simultaneously dual and alien space, to signify what is going on. 'It happens but I am not there.' 'I cannot realize it but it goes on.' 'Motherhood's impossible syllogism.'" Julia Kristeva, "Motherhood according to Giovanni Bellini," in Julia Kristeva, *Desire in Language: A Semiotic Approach to Literature and Art,* trans. Thomas Gora, Alice Jardine, and Leon S. Roudize (New York: Columbia University Press, 1980; first published 1977): 237–71, quotation from 237.

27. I accept Linda Wentink's translation of the word *fundanen* as tassels, though earlier I had translated it as the inelegant "pompoms." Wentink's translation appears in *Journal of South Asian Literature* 20, no. 2 (1985): 107–12. An interesting discussion of some of the issues on literature and remembering may be found in Shashi Joshi, "The World of Sa'adat Hasan Manto," *Annual of Urdu Studies* 11 (2001): 141–53, available at www.urdustudies.com/pdf/11/13world.pdf, though there is an intrusive influence of the Holocaust model in her interpretation that takes away from the force of the specificity of the daughter's gesture in *Khol Do*. Michael Jauch does a subtle reading of this point in the narrative. See his "Witnessing Violence: Perspectives on Sa'adat Hasan Manto's 'Khol Do' and Rajinder Singh Bedi's 'Lajvanti,'" *Annual of Urdu Studies* 13 (2003): 189–202, available at www.urdustudies.com/pdf/13/15jaunchwitness.pdf.

28. Jacques Lacan, "The Splendor of Antigone," in *The Ethics of Psychoanalysis: The Seminars of Jacques Lacan, Book VII,* ed. Jacques-Alain Miller, trans. Russell Grigg (New York: W. W. Norton, 1997), 7, 243–57.

29. Aamir R. Mufti makes the subtle point that in the lyrical poetry of Faiz Ahmad Faiz, the Pakistani poet whose poetry was read and widely admired on both sides of the border, terms such as *watan* or *quam* (nation, people) do not have a direct referent. "It might even be said," writes Mufti, "that to speak of watan and quam (nation/people) in the context of Faiz is to remain meaningfully silent about the object towards which they point. . . . Where exactly, in other words, is the poet's home?" Aamir R. Mufti, "Towards a Lyric History of India," *Boundary* 31, no. 2 (2004): 245–74. Mufti also argues that in this poetry the motif of the separation from the beloved is made the modality of collective selfhood. Mufti introduces a much more complex rendering of the idea of the Partitioned nation than historians such as Pandey.

4. THE ACT OF WITNESSING

1. See Judith Butler, *The Psychic Life of Power: Theories in Subjection* (Stanford: Stanford University Press, 1997), and J. Mohanty, "The Status of the Subject in Foucault," in *Foucault and the Critique of Institutions,* ed. John Caputo and Mark Young (University Park: Pennsylvania State University Press, 1993).

2. Some anthropologists have questioned whether the notion of witnessing can be deployed as an analytical place from which to write because they argue that the strong Christian underpinnings of this concept make it an unsuitable and even suspicious category for anthropological work. I find this view excessively constraining, as if other cultures (e.g., Islam and Hinduism) did not have notions of witnessing. First of all, notions of witnessing carry somewhat different meanings in these religions—e.g., *shahadat* in Islam and the relation between *sakshi* and *sakhi* in the Bhakti traditions in Hinduism. In any case a concept does not become illegitimate because its origins can be located in an adjacent discourse, be that of religion or science, unless we can show the specific ways in which it impacts upon description. For my part, the notions of witnessing are deployed here not to attest to faith in the face of a mutilated body but to the creativity of life. This is not to say that other notions of witnessing as in the case of the Nazi camps are not extremely powerful. See, especially, Giorgio Agamben, *Remnants of Auschwitz: The Witness and the Archive,* trans. Daniel Heller-Roazen (New York: Zone Books, 1999). Not all forms of violence and remembering can be recounted through this model, though.

3. George W. F. Hegel, *The Philosophy of Fine Art,* vol. 2, trans. F. P. B. Osmaston (London: G. Bell & Sons, 1920).

4. Hegel, *The Philosophy of Fine Art,* 210.

5. Lacan, "The Splendor of Antigone."

6. Lacan, "The Splendor of Antigone," 255.

7. Lacan, "The Splendor of Antigone," 278.

8. See Martin Jay, *Downcast Eyes: The Denigration of Vision in Twentieth-Century French Thought* (Berkeley: University of California Press, 1993), and J. F. MacCannell, *Figuring Lacan: Criticism and Cultural Unconscious* (London: Croomhelm, 1986).

9. In some sense, Antigone's figure speaks to the work of mourning that we discussed in the last chapter. For Hegel, community comes into being by its interference with the family and thus with women, for women's positioning perverts community—they are the internal enemy. As Tina Chanter puts it, the irony of women's position in Hegel is that they make possible the integrity of the polis, and yet they must remain defined in opposition to it as outsiders who threaten its integrity. Tina Chanter, *Ethics of Eros: Irigaray's Re-writing of the Philosophers* (New York: Routledge, 1995). Luce Irigaray speaks to these issues eloquently: "Their [i.e., women's] inherent duty is to *ensure burial for the dead*, thus changing a natural phenomenon into a spiritual act. One more step (into negation) and we see that it is the task of womankind, as guardian of the blood ties, to gather man into his final figuration, beyond the turmoil of contingent life and scattered moments of Being-there." Luce Irigaray, *Speculum of the Other Woman,* trans. Gillian C. Gill (Ithaca: Cornell University Press, 1985). For an important discussion of these issues, see also Carol Jacobs, "Dusting Antigone," *Modern Language Notes,* 111, no. 5 (1996): 890–917. It would be clear from the last chapter that mourning rituals in India assume a much more complicated division of voice and of labor between men and women.

10. Wittgenstein, *Philosophical Investigations,* para. 103. See also para. 97, where he speaks of a humble use of words as a way of being able to shake the idea of a perfect language awaiting construction.

11. As in the case of other names, this is a pseudonym, coined by my own investment in her. Literally the term means "hope."

12. The literal expression in Punjabi is *man nahin lagda,* and depending upon context it can express mild boredom to serious disengagement with life.

13. Hans-Georg Gadamer, "The Hermeneutics of Suspicion," in *Phenomenology and the Human Sciences,* ed. J. N. Mohanty (Boston: Martinus Nijhoff, 1985), 73–85.

14. Robert Desjarlais, *Sensory Biographies: Lives and Deaths among Nepal's Yolmo Buddhists* (Berkeley: University of California Press, 2003), 107.

15. The genre of women's songs, especially those that take the voice of the younger sister, articulate this hurt and are common in many regions of India. See Egmore, "Internal Iconicity in Paraiyar 'Crying Songs,'" and Ann G. Gold and Gloria G. Raheja, eds., *Listen to the Heron's Words: Reimagining Gender and Kinship in North India* (Berkeley: University of California Press, 1994).

16. I am not using this term in a technical sense, but then part of the burden of this book is to offer other ways of looking at the experience of violation, hurt, and trauma.

17. Compare Lynn Bennett, *Dangerous Wives and Sacred Sisters: Social and Symbolic Roles of High-Caste Women in Nepal* (New York: Columbia University, 1983), for a similar argument in the case of Rajasthan.

18. If I may draw attention to the beautiful way Desjarlais puts such matters— he says of his interlocutor, Kisang, that "When it comes to the various takes on dying, it is better to think of them not as directly mirroring or windowing any 'lived experience' of hers but as engaging existential domains, spun out of spoken words and private thoughts that she could invoke or inhabit from time to time." Desjarlais, *Sensory Biographies*, 361. As we shall see later in the narrative, Asha too lived something in this telling, and so I ask what am I in relation to her—a discussion I engage later in the book.

19. The *pagdi* is the sign of honor—whiteness here refers to unsullied honor.

20. Gananath Obeyesekere, *The Cult of the Goddess Pattini* (Chicago: University of Chicago Press, 1984).

21. Compare the similar analogy by which divorce is represented as a relation not fully realized rather than one that tears two people apart in the kinship system in Bengal. Ralph W. Nicholas, "The Effectiveness of the Hindu Sacrament *(samaskara)*: Caste, Marriage and Divorce in Bengali Culture," in *From the Margins of Hindu Marriage: Essays on Gender, Religion and Culture*, ed. Lindsey Harlan and Paul B. Courtright (New York: Oxford University Press, 1995).

22. See Das, "Composition of the Personal Voice."

23. I think what might have been a vague knowledge sensed as a child probably became certainty as she reflected and worked on this memory as an adult. In the next chapter I discuss how she encoded this knowledge in her story.

24. The English word "taunt" was incorporated in Punjabi especially as a form of doing, e.g, *bada taunt karde si'* (they did very much taunting).

25. Byron Good, *Medicine, Rationality and Experience: An Anthropological Perspective* (Cambridge: Cambridge University Press, 1994); Desjarlais, *Sensory Biographies*.

26. Martha C. Nussbaum, *The Fragility of Goodness: Luck and Ethics in Greek Tragedy and Philosophy* (Cambridge: Cambridge University Press, 1986), 46. I am aware that this quotation might capture a sensitivity more appropriate to an earlier avatar of Nussbaum—yet, it cannot go without saying that her sensitivity to complex questions of ethics in the Greek case is exquisite even though in the case of contemporary India she is not willing to offer the same.

27. Is it necessary to emphasize that we can understand the moral stakes for Asha only if we can enter a life, a world, in which she felt that her eternity was in jeopardy? A passing comment by a reader who was puzzled as to how the presence of a "horny" brother-in-law could cause such a major dilemma to Asha

makes me want to revisit the point that the temporal depth in which Asha saw her relationships—e.g., her conviction that her relation with her second husband was a momentary alliance of interests, but that in some future life, her relation to her first husband to whom she had been married with the sacred fire as witness would be resumed—shows that the moral stakes in her lifeworld cannot be understood outside that frame. This is not to deny that this story is also about the way that patriarchy structures the "inner" in Hindu society.

28. Pierre Bourdieu, *The Logic of Practice* (Stanford: Stanford University Press, 1990).

29. Stanley Cavell, *Disowning Knowledge in Six Plays of Shakespeare* (Cambridge: Cambridge University Press, 1987). See especially chapter 6 and the discussion on pages 196–97. The idea of poisonous knowledge is again found in the fantasy of writing as poisonous. See Cavell's analysis of Edgar Allen Poe's stories "The Imp" and "The Black Cat": "Both the fiction of the writer's arresting himself and wearing fetters and tenanting the cell of the condemned and the fiction of providing a poisoned wax light for reading are descriptions or fantasies of writing, modeled by the writing before us. . . .What is it to fantasize that words are fetters and cells, and to read them, to be awake to their meaning, or effect, is to be poisoned? Are we being told that writer and reader are one another's victims? Or is the suggestion that to arrive at the truth something in the reader as well as the writer must die? Does writing ward off or invite the angel of death?" Stanley Cavell, *In Quest of the Ordinary: Lines of Skepticism and Romanticism* (Chicago: University of Chicago Press, 1988), 123. This speaks to me also as a description of the ethnographic experience in which forms of knowing are offered that put the self of the anthropologist and her interlocutor in jeopardy. This is not anthropological machismo or simply an exercise of authority but one way of knowing the world that, like all knowledge, carries its risk of infection, contagion, poison.

30. Here I would say that everyday sensibilities are the opposite of the mythical fantasies of revenge. The classical example in India is Draupadi's refusal to change her clothes strained with menstrual blood or comb her hair until her dishonor is avenged. The classic paper on this is Alf Hiltebeitel, "Draupadi's Hair," in *Autour de la déesse hindoue,* ed. Madeleine Biardeau, *Puruṣārtha* 5 (1981): 179–214.

31. Michel Foucault, *Discipline and Punish: The Birth of the Prison* (New York: Pantheon Books, 1977), 30.

32. Cavell, *In Quest of the Ordinary.*

5. BOUNDARIES, VIOLENCE, AND THE WORK OF TIME

1. It is particularly striking that while the consumption of violence in the form of public spectacle in the North American context has been rendered by its most sensitive observers as creating a pathological public sphere, similar spectacles

of consumption of torn and mutilated bodies in other societies across the civilized/savage divide are rendered as an expression of cultural values. For the formulation of the idea of a pathological public sphere, see Mark Seltzer, *Serial Killers: Death and Life in America's Wound Culture* (New York: Routledge, 1998).

2. Henri Lefebvre, *Dialectical Materialism,* trans. John Sturrock (London: Cape, 1968).

3. Cavell, "Declining Decline."

4. Michael Gilsenan, *Lords of the Lebanese Marches: Violence and Narrative in an Arab Society* (Berkeley: University of California Press, 1996), 64.

5. See Veena Das and Ranjit Singh Bajwa, "Community and Violence in Contemporary Punjab," in *Violences et non-violences en Inde,* ed. D. Vidal, G. Tarabout, and E. Mayer, special issue of *Puruṣārtha* 16 (1994): 245–59.

6. This pseudonym means "one who can win hearts." I should emphasize that the story, if it ever surfaced, hinted that she was abducted, but that the army immediately rescued her so that there was never any discussion of whether or not she was raped or otherwise abused.

7. For an account of different kinds of strategies used by families to meet this collective misfortune, see Das, "Masks and Faces."

8. This is a common phrase, *taunt karde si*—he would taunt me. The Punjabi equivalents—*tane dena, boliyan sunana*—are common in the everyday rhetoric of women's speech, but the English word is also frequently used, as I described in the last chapter.

9. The conjunction of good–bad is the euphemism used when one wants to implicate one's own relatives in having used discourteous or insulting utterances about one. There are subtle horizontal differences that mark other expressions like *gali* (abuse), or *bak-bak* (nonsense)—their implications in the verbalization of honor–shame strategies are quite different. By horizontal differences I mean the kind of differences between such pairs of words as coronation/inauguration, promising/intending, etc. I follow Cavell in this usage; see Cavell, "Declining Decline."

10. James Scott, *Domination and the Arts of Resistance: Hidden Transcripts* (New Haven: Yale University Press, 1990).

11. It was an acceptable practice for a Hindu girl to be married to a Sikh man or even for one son to be given over to the Sikh faith in fulfillment of a vow before the Sikh Gurus to avoid some misfortune.

12. There is an extensive literature on the emotional investment in joint family living in India. Though partition of the family is part of the normal developmental cycle of the domestic group, it is fraught with emotional turmoil similar to a divorce in the family in North America, as if a language of division is being brought to bear on that which should never have been divided. For a review of the literature, see Patricia Uberoi, "Beyond the Nuclear/Joint Family Debate," in *Oxford India Companion to Sociology and Social Anthropology,* ed. Veena Das (Delhi: Oxford University Press, 2001).

13. The most sensitive depiction of this process may be found in Krishna Sobti, *Zindaginama* (Delhi: Rajkamal Publications, 1972).

14. This particular story of Thaoa Khalsa has been canonized in survivor accounts. The story was about the collective suicide of about ninety women and children—it was cited in citizen petitions and recounted to the feminist historians Urvashi Butalia and Sudesh Vaid. Butalia and Vaid give the account as survivor testimony but do not ask themselves how the genre of heroic sacrifice might have influenced the telling. See Urvashi Butalia, "Community, State and Gender," in *Economic and Political Weekly, Review of Women's Studies* 17 (1993): WS12–WS24, and *The Other Side of Silence.* Pandey provides an interesting discussion of how this story circulated between official accounts and popular accounts; see Pandey, *Remembering Partition,* 84–88. Manjit's account suggests that what circulates as general memory, not necessarily related to events that are part of one's own experience, may become incorporated into specific memories.

15. Rameshwari Nehru offered the analogy between Padmini's sacrifice and the sacrifice made by these women. See Rameshwari Nehru, "Punjab ka bhayankar hatyakand" (The terrifying event of mass murder in Punjab), *Deshdut,* December 28, 1947, cited in Pandey, *Remembering Partition, 87.*

16. I do not mean to say that it is therefore passively accepted—indeed, the whole story of Manjit shows that it is deeply resented. Nor is it my contention that these forms of violence are always narratable across human societies.

17. See chapter 2.

18. Gilles Deleuze, *Pure Imminence: Essays on a Life* (New York: Zone Books, 2001).

19. Deleuze, *Pure Imminence,* 28.

20. Stanley Cavell, *Contesting Tears: The Hollywood Melodrama of the Unknown Woman* (Chicago: University of Chicago Press, 1996), 81–115.

21. Cavell, *Contesting Tears,* 81.

22. Cavell, *Contesting Tears,* 108.

23. Wittgenstein, *Philosophical Investigations,* para. 363.

24. This complicated relation between word and gesture points to a different region of thought than, say, in thinking of pictures in relation to words as in W. J. T. Mitchell's fascinating discussion of what he calls "imagetexts." See Mitchell, *Picture Theory: Essays on Visual and Verbal Interpretation* (Chicago: University of Chicago Press, 1994).

6. THINKING OF TIME AND SUBJECTIVITY

1. See Alfred Gell, *The Anthropology of Time: Cultural Constructions of Temporal Maps and Images* (Oxford: Berg, 1992).

2. E. Evans-Pritchard, "Nuer time Reckoning," *Africa* 12 (1939): 189–216 and the discussion on Balinese calendars in Clifford Geertz, "Person, Time

and Conduct in Bali," in *The Interpretation of Culture* (New York: Basic Books, 1973).

3. Nelson Goodman, "Twisted Tales: or Story, Study, and Symphony," *Critical Inquiry* 7, no. 1 (1980): 103–19.

4. The labels A series and B series are elaborated by R. Gale, *The Philosophy of Time* (New York: Doubleday, 1967) and *The Language of Time* (London: Routledge, 1968), but the ideas according to Gell are first formulated in the context of a paper on the unreality of time by the early-twentieth-century philosopher J. E. M. McTaggart. See McTaggart, "The Unreality of Time," *Mind* (1908): 457–74.

5. Gell, *The Anthropology of Time*, 154.

6. Nelson Goodman, *The Structure of Appearance* (Boston: Reidel, 1977), 274.

7. The experience I am suggesting is different from Proust's notion of involuntary memory in which something that draws an earlier moment to the edge of awareness is said to be mirrored at the same time in the past and the present moment so that the event is irreducible to the past or the present. Marcel Proust, *Time Regained, Remembrance of Things Past*, vol. 3 , trans. S. K. Scott Moncrieff (New York: Vintage, 1981).

8. Henri Bergson, *Duration and Simultaneity* (Indianapolis: Bobbs-Merrill, 1965), 52.

9. Gilles Deleuze, *Bergsonism*, trans. Hugh Tominsom and Barbara Habbersim (New York: Zone Books, 1991), 80.

10. Desjarlais, *Sensory Biographies*.

11. Desjarlais, *Sensory Biographies*, 203.

12. I do not deny that sometimes the analogy of time with space is useful—for instance, the similarities between space indicators, personal indictors, and temporal indicators have been pointed out by Goodman *(The Structure of Appearance)*. However, I am struck by the far more frequent references to time as agent rather than space as agent. This is a topic that I cannot hope to explore in any detail here, but let me indicate one difference. People often spoke of both their immediate space and the present time in which they were as *mahaul* or environment. Thus one could say *yahan ka mahaul bahut kharab hai*—the environment of this place is very bad—or *aajkal ka mahaul bahur kharab hai*—the environment these days is very bad. The spatial indicator *yahan* is "here" locating the speaker in space. The temporal indicator *aajkal* (today-tomorrow) refers to the present as a spectral present. However, while one could leave the space one was in, one could not leave the time one was in—one could only arrange one's life keeping into account the bad times or hope that these would pass. This sense of time is also what accounts for the idea that hope lies in a second chance, as we shall see.

13. Deleuze, *Bergsonism*, 62.

14. For an exposition of the relation between the potential, the actual, and the virtual that is a model of clarity, see Paola Marrati, *Gilles Deleuze: Cinéma et philosophie* (Paris: Presses Universitaires de France, 2003).

15. Deleuze, *Bergsonism,* 62, emphasis in original.

16. While ordinary language would speak of the past being brought forward, showing how spatial categories provide the language to think of time, my emphasis is on the way affect is determined by the qualities of the virtual, which, though not actual, still has the quality of the real.

17. In this connection see the important paper by Sylvain Perdigon on what he calls pessoptimism among the Palestinian refugees in Beirut. Here he describes in exquisite detail the quality of the virtual, the actual, and the potential as embodied in everyday life. Sylvain Perdigon, "Yet Another Reflection on Pessoptimism," paper presented at the Institute of Global Studies in Culture, Power, and History, Johns Hopkins University, March 2003.

18. See Arthur Kleinman and Joan Kleinman, "The Appeal of Experience: The Dismay of Images," in Arthur Kleinman et al., *Social Suffering.*

19. Cathy Caruth, *Unclaimed Experience: Trauma, Narrative and History* (Baltimore: Johns Hopkins University Press, 1996).

20. Caruth, *Unclaimed Experience,* 4.

21. Felman, *The Juridical Unconscious.*

22. Caruth, *Unclaimed Experience,* 4.

23. See Veena Das and Arthur Kleinman, "Introduction," in *Remaking a World,* 1–31.

24. Caruth, *Unclaimed Experience,* 63.

25. See Agamben on the category of the Muselmann as embodying the living dead in concentration camps; Agamben, *Remnants of Auschwitz,* 41. For Agamben the category of the Muselmann implies that the inmates sensed that the living dead were not going to die as Jews—yet he does not comment on the fact that the bare life is imagined as another form of life—that of the Muslim— and that it comes to be equated with animal life.

26. See Lawrence Langer, *Holocaust Testimonies: The Ruins of Memory* (New Haven: Yale University Press, 1991) on this point. I am not concerned with the question of the uniqueness of the Holocaust as a theological point but with its historical specificity.

27. Cavell, *The Claim of Reason: Wittgenstein, Skepticism, Morality, and Tragedy* (London: Oxford University Press), 365.

28. See Alf Hiltebeitel, "Draupadi's Garments," *Indo Iranian Journal* 22 (1980): 97–112, and "Draupadi's Hair."

29. I struggle here with the impoverished kinship terminology of English, for to translate *bhabhi* as sister-in-law would be to completely miss the rhetorical force of the word.

30. Cavell, *The Claim of Reason,* 481.

31. For a detailed discussion, see Veena Das, "Kama as Purushartha," in *King, Householder, Renouncer: Essays in Honour of Louis Dumont,* ed. T. N. Madan (Delhi: Sage Publications, 1982).

7. IN THE REGION OF RUMOR

1. One of the most delicate ethnographic renderings of the anthropology of an event and of unfinished stories is Steven Caton's *Yemen Chronicles* (New York: Hill and Wang, 2005). As his work shows, an event that seems to come from nowhere betrays (rather than, say, reveals) the contingency of relationships: it shows how memory is implicated in the creation of the future and how it becomes embedded in poetry and narrative.

2. Bergson, *Duration and Simultaneity.*

3. The idea of the two guards as martyrs was to crystallize much later in the militant literature of the Sikhs. This rendered the assassins as incarnations of two heroic figures, Sukha Singh and Mehtab Singh, who had avenged the dishonor done to Harmandar Sahib in Amritsar in 1752 at the hands of a minor Muslim chieftain, Massaranga, by killing him. To my knowledge this story was not evoked at this point in time, but their action and the risk to their own lives was compared to the suicide squads of different militant groups in the Middle East. I have analyzed the circulation of this story in the militant literature elsewhere; see Das, *Critical Events.* In his extraordinary study of the Dhadi singers in the Punjab during the period of militancy, Michael Nijhawan gives one instance in which police interrogated a singer who was supposed to have eulogized the two Sikh bodyguards, who laughed in turn and replied that he was simply singing what his patron had asked him to sing. For his alleged arrogance, the singer was imprisoned for three years. Nijhawan concludes that one could not think of the commemorative voice of the Dhadi singer as somehow neutral any more than any keepers of history can be regarded as neutral. See Michael Nijhawan, "Dhadi Darbar: Religion, Violence, Agency and Their Historicity in a Panjabi Performative Genre," unpublished Ph.D. dissertation, University of Heidelberg, 2002. Forthcoming as *Dhadi Darbar: Religion, Violence and the Performance of Sikh History* (Delhi: Oxford University Press, 2006).

4. There is an extensive literature on what is variously called the militant movement, the Sikh insurgency, or the terrorist threat in the Punjab in the 1980s—each term embodying a particular political perspective. I found the following texts to be particularly useful: J. S. Grewal and Indu Banga, *Punjab in Prosperity and Violence: Administration, Politics and Social Change 1947–1997* (New Delhi: K. K. Publishers, Institute of Punjab Studies, Chandigarh, 1998); Surinder Singh Jodhka, "Looking Back at the Khalistan Movement: Some Recent Researches on Its Rise and Decline," *Economic and Political Weekly* (April 2001): 1311–18; Rajiv A. Kapur, *Sikh Separatism: The Politics of Faith* (Delhi: Vikas

Publishing House, 1987); Harjot S. Oberoi, *The Construction of Religious Boundaries: Culture, Identity and Diversity in the Sikh Tradition* (Delhi: Oxford University Press, 1997); Shinder Purewal, *Sikh Ethnonationalism and the Political Economy of Punjab* (Delhi: Oxford University Press, 2000). The appalling history of human right violations by the state in India in its counterinsurgency operations are documented in Human Rights Watch, *Punjab in Crisis: Human Rights in India* (New York: Human Rights Watch, 1991), and *Dead Silence: The Legacy of Human Rights Abuses in Punjab* (New York: Human Rights Watch, 1994). It is hard to think of this period in terms of ethnonationalism, since the term renders the phenomenon as a conflict between two ethnicities. However, the militant leadership was not simply representing the subjective will of all Sikhs any more than the state in India was clearly identifiable as a Hindu state. A remarkable study of the complexity of the phenomena under consideration that shows how militancy was understood in the rural areas in which it flourished is Harish K. Puri, Paramjit Singh Judge, and Jagrup Singh Sekhon, *Terrorism in Punjab: Understanding Grassroots Reality* (New Delhi: Har Anand Publications, 1999). Michael Nijhawan's sensitive study of the musical genre of Dhadi is unique in showing how present experiences of torture at the hands of the state were assimilated and given shape in the musical renderings by reference to the earlier stories of martyrdom in the Sikh tradition. He also shows the way that criticism was articulated of both the state and the modern Sikh politicians within this genre. The diasporic dimension has been explored in Brian Keith Axel, *The Nation's Tortured Body: Violence, Representation and the Formation of a Sikh 'Diaspora'* (Durham: Duke University Press, 2001) and Cynthia Keppley Mahmood, *Fighting for Faith and Nation: Dialogues with Sikh Militants* (Philadelphia: University of Pennsylvania Press, 1996).

5. On the theme of how Hindu nationalist discourse regarded the emasculated Hindu, see Thomas Blom Hansen, *Wages of Violence: Naming and Identity in Postcolonial Bombay* (Princeton: Princeton University Press, 2002), especially 93; Sudhir Kakar, "The Construction of a New Hindu Identity," in *Unravelling the Nation: Sectarian Conflict and India's Secular Identity,* ed. Kaushik Basu and Sanjay Subrahmanyam (New Delhi: Penguin Books, 1996); Nandy, *The Illegitimacy of Nationalism;* and various essays in Gyanendra Pandey, ed., *Hindus and Others: The Question of Identity in India Today* (New Delhi: Viking, 1993).

6. On the salience of the symbol of the martyr in Sikh political imaginary, see Michael Nijhawan, "Dhadi Darbar," and J. P. S. Uberoi, *Religion, Civil Society and the State: A Study of Sikhism* (Delhi: Oxford University Press, 1996).

7. This nicely mirrored the anxiety of the Hindus that they were deprived of masculinity in relation to the Muslims that we detected in the early-twentieth-century vernacular tracts and that came to the fore in the post-Partition debates on abduction and recovery of women. Thus, the inauguration of the state in India as founded by men in their capacity as fathers and husbands did not lay to rest the anxieties about masculinity.

8. Recorded cassette in author's collection. This and the quotations below are from recorded speeches circulating on cassette. They do not identify place and time because this was a period of intense confrontation between the state and the militants.

9. Cavell's discussion on how skepticism might be inflected by gender is central to this issue. In his reading of *The Winter's Tale*, Cavell formulated the question as follows: "What interests me here is to get at the intersection of the epistemologist's question of existence, say of the existence of the external world, or what analytical philosophy calls other minds, with Leontes' perplexity of knowing whether his son is his. . . . Leontes' first question to his son is: 'Art thou my boy?' . . . What Leontes is suffering has a cure, namely, to acknowledge his child as his, to own it, something every normal parent will do or seem to do" (*Disowning Knowledge*, 203). It is later, in his study of the Hollywood melodrama of the unknown woman, that Cavell comes to terms with the fact that this is a question that haunts a *father* and not a *parent*. In this later work, he states the question of skepticism as inflected by gender. Here he talks of *The Winter's Tale* as having raised unforgettably "and I might say traumatically the possibility that skepticism is inflected by gender whether one sets oneself aside as masculine or feminine." The gender asymmetry, he observes, is not simply resolvable in terms of presence or absence of doubt but rather calls for an analysis that might be directed not onto the uncertainty about whether one's child is one's own (a male question) but toward the father of one's child (a female question). The anxiety around the uncertainty of genealogy I detected in the speeches of Bhindranwale suggests that there might be important cultural differences around the way that questions of skepticism are posed not only in terms of gender but also in terms of different ways of conceptualizing genealogy and parenthood. See Cavell, *Disowning Knowledge in Seven Plays of Shakespeare*, ch. 6, and *Contesting Tears*, see especially 100–102.

10. To add a further layer to the complicated question of the gender of the nation, I simply note that almost every conceivable imagery, ranging from seeing the nation as a consuming mother to a courtesan, a goddess, a beloved, or a sodomizing father, has made an appearance in the social imagery of different groups at different times. See, for instance, Sudhir Chandra, *The Oppressive Present: Literature and Social Consciousness in Colonial India* (Delhi: Oxford University Press, 1992); Partha Chatterjee, *The Nation and Its Fragments: Colonial and Postcolonial Histories* (Princeton: Princeton University Press, 1993); Lawrence Cohen, "Holi in Banaras and the Mahaland of Modernity," in *Gay and Lesbian Quarterly* 2, no. 1 (1995): 399–424; Sudipta Kaviraj, *The Unhappy Consciousness: Bankimchandra Chattopadhyay and the Formation of Nationalist Discourse in India* (Delhi: Oxford University Press, 1995). Recall the interplay between nation as beloved and nation as mother in chapter 3.

11. The term *Guru* literally means teacher, whereas the term *Sikh* is a derivative of *shishya*, meaning student.

12. It is, of course, ironic that the imagery of Sikhs as a martial race owed its salience to the colonial practices of identifying martial races in India. See Harjot Oberoi, *The Construction of Religious Boundaries: Culture, Identity, and Diversity in the Sikh Tradition* (Chicago: University of Chicago Press, 1994).

13. See *They Massacre Sikhs: A White Paper* by the Sikh Religious Parliament (Amritsar: Shiromani Gurdwara Prabandhak Committee, n.d.). The view of the government on the issue can be seen in *White Paper on Punjab Agitation* (New Delhi: Government of India, July 10, 1984).

14. This point is important to bear in mind since the sword is claimed as an important symbol of masculinity and valor in the Hindu Rajput tradition too, but the flowing beard singles out the Sikh male. Compare Connerton's observation of the past being sedimented in the body: Paul Connerton, *How Societies Remember* (Cambridge: Cambridge University Press, 1989).

15. The Akali Dal is a political party having its base primarily in the Punjab among the Sikhs. It is not, however, the case that all Sikhs owe allegiance to the Akali Dal, since the Congress Party has been its main rival in the state. The latter also has had a long history of Sikh leadership and Sikh support. The interface between religious organizations and political parties in the Punjab is a complicated question; it should be borne in mind, though, that political allegiances for both Sikhs and Hindus cut across political parties. For an early account of the Akali politics, see Mohinder Singh, *The Akali Movement* (Delhi: Macmillan, 1978).

16. The relation between memory and forgetting in constituting the community has been noted in many contexts in recent years. In a very interesting paper, Jan T. Gross shows the importance of memory in the resistance to totalitarianism, and of simultaneous forgetting for the construction of community as purged of its past evil in the case of Polish-Jewish relations during the Second World War. He comments powerfully on the Polish conviction that "a half way victory over totalitarianism's attempts to destroy social solidarity would still be won if the community's history were rescued from the regime's ambition to determine not only the country's future but also its past." Yet the same Polish people developed elaborate myths to conceal from themselves the nature of Polish-Jewish relations and the anti-Semitism in Polish society that led to both covert and overt support being given to the fascist ideology of scapegoating the Jew. Jan T. Gross, "Polish-Jewish Relations during the War: An Interpretation," *Archives européennes de sociologie* 28: 199–214.

17. *They Massacre Sikhs*, 29–30. The history of conflict over publications such as *Rangila Rasool* deserves an analysis of its own, entangled as it was in colonial imagination of censorship and public order, on the one hand, and the creation of new reading publics, on the other. I am grateful to Deepak Mehta for his insights into this issue and look forward to his present study on the social life of such texts.

18. Louis Dumont characterized the relation between priesthood and kinship represented by Brahmins and kingship represented by Kshatriya castes as a

double-headed hierarchy, but the Pandits, despite their ritual purity, always occupied a lower position in the caste hierarchy in the Punjab. On the relation between priesthood and political power, see Louis Dumont, *Homo Hierarchicus: The Caste System and Its Implications,* trans. Mark Sainsbury et al. (Chicago: University of Chicago Press, 1980). Dumont's conception of kingship and of power has been extensively critiqued, but this literature does not concern me here.

19. One can find similar images refracted in the discourse of militant Hinduism, for instance, in speeches made by Sadhvi Rithambra and Uma Bharati (politicians embodying all the symbols of renunciation) where a repudiation of the supposed passivity and emasculation of Hindus provides the subject matter for passionate utterances. Interestingly, the theme of betrayal by the state is as much a part of the repertoire of militant Hindu discourse as of the militant Sikh discourse, although in the case of Hindus the oppositions are played out with reference to the Muslims.

20. Although panic seems to be an accompanying affect of rumors in times of trouble, I am not claiming that all rumors are accompanied by panic. It is useful to distinguish between rumor and gossip. Early theories of gossip emphasized its function of maintaining group unity by providing informal standards of evaluation and control. See Max Gluckman, "Gossip and Scandal," *Current Anthropology* 4, no. 3 (1963): 307–15. Other anthropologists were more interested in seeing how gossip provided a means for individuals to manipulate social rules and assess the limits to which cultural norms may be negotiated. See Robert Paine, "What Is Gossip About? An Alternative Hypothesis," *Man* 2, no. 2 (1967): 272–85. For a discussion on the role of gossip in Punjabi life, see Das, "Masks and Faces."

21. In his essay on the interpretation of rumor, Peter Lienhardt concluded: "I suggest, then, that rumours of the more fantastic sort can represent, and may generally represent, complexities of public feeling that cannot readily be made articulate at a more thoughtful level. In doing so, they join people's sympathies in a consensus of an unthinking, or at least uncritical, kind. And perhaps this explains why the word rumor has a bad connotation that goes beyond mere foolishness. It suggests a surrender to the irrational. Rumors which produce integration without thought are the voice of the mob before the mob itself has gathered" (131). The conclusion reflects the discomfort of the enlightened scholar with the unthinking attitude of the "mob," but in fact the analysis in the body of the text deals with rumors that had nothing to do with the "mob" and much more to do with suspicions of the colonial masters in the colonies. See Peter A. Lienhardt, "The Interpretation of Rumor," in *Studies in Social Anthropology: Essays in Memory of E. E. Evans-Pritchard by His Former Colleagues,* ed. J. H. M. Beattie and R. G. Lienhardt (Oxford: Oxford University Press, 1975), 105–32.

22. George Rudé, *The Crowd in the French Revolution* (Oxford: Clarendon Press, 1959), and *The Crowd in History, 1730–1848* (New York: Wiley, 1964).

23. See Ranajit Guha, *Elementary Aspects of Peasant Insurgency in Colonial India* (Delhi: Oxford University Press, 1983).

24. Guha, *Elementary Aspects*, 256, 226, 251, 264–65. For a very nice application of the role of rumor in understanding the popularity of Gandhi among rural populations, see Shahid Amin, *Event, Metaphor, Memory: Chauri Chaura 1922–1992* (Berkeley: University of California Press, 1995).

25. Homi K. Bhabha, "By Bread Alone: Signs of Violence in the Mid-nineteenth Century," in *Location of Culture* (London: Routledge, 1994), 198–212, quotation from 201.

26. S. Moscovici, *The Age of the Crowd: A Historical Treatise of Mass Psychology* (Cambridge: Cambridge University Press, 1985).

27. See Veena Das, "Introduction: Communities, Riots and Survivors," in *Mirrors of Violence: Communities, Riots and Survivors in South Asia* (Delhi: Oxford University Press, 1990), 1–37.

28. In Austin's classic formulation illocutionary force is distinguished from perlocutionary force in that in the former case one does something *in* saying something, while in the latter case one does something *by* saying something. The presence of the first-person indicative marks out utterances that have illocutionary force. In the case of perlocutionary force the situation is much more complicated, but at least in the case of rumor we can say that its force would be lost if it were tethered to the words of the speaking agent, or for that matter if one were to frame a rumor by saying, "I am spreading the rumor that . . ." Again, when rumor operates within everyday life, we might find that some people get the reputation of being gossipy, others we would trust more. Yet the similarity between the tempo of rumor and the tempo of skepticism, the loss of trust in ordinary functioning words, is apparent in both. See J. L. Austin, *How to Do Things with Words,* ed. J. O. Urmson and Marina Sbisa (Cambridge, MA: Harvard University Press, 1975), and for the relation between skepticism and rumor, Cavell's marvelous discussion of the figure of Iago in *Disowning Knowledge,* ch. 3.

29. In army usage the followers of Bhindranwale were "terrorists," in their own self-understanding they were "martyrs," and in popular usage in the media or in conversations there was a frequent slippage between different kinds of terms. As Kosseleck has repeatedly pointed out, most social scientific concepts are marked by a political plenitude. In this case what is clear is that ordinary people in the Punjab and elsewhere had to bear the burden of much violence due to both the insurgency operations of the militants and the anti-insurgency operations of the police and the army. Thus it would be a mistake to assume that the distribution of terms was neatly distributed among a populace fighting for freedom or justice, on the one hand, and a repressive state apparatus, on the other. See Reinhart Koselleck, *Futures Past: On the Semantics of Historical Time* (Cambridge, MA: MIT Press, 1985). It is apparent that many Sikhs felt extreme

anger at both the actions of the militants in using the Darbar Sahib as a sanctuary and at the government of Indira Gandhi for first having nourished the leadership as a counter against the Akalis in competitive politics and then having acted in this particular manner—which is not to say that somehow the actions were symmetrical.

30. *Paan* shops, small roadside shops where betel leaves and betel nuts are sold, are typical gathering places for exchange of news, gossip, and information. These are strongly gendered spaces: women would not be found standing and gossiping around these shops.

31. Some of the early reports and analysis can be found in the following: Uma Chakravarti and Nandita Haksar, *The Delhi Riots: Three Days in the Life of a Nation* (New Delhi: Lancer International, 1987); Das, "The Anthropology of Violence and the Speech of Victims" and "Our Work to Cry: Your Work to Listen," in *Mirrors of Violence*, 345–99; *Voices from a Scarred City: The Delhi Carnage in Perspective*, Smitu Kothari and Harsh Sethi, eds. (Delhi: Lokayan, 1985); PUDR/PUCL, *Who Are the Guilty? Report of a Joint Inquiry into the Causes and Impact of the Riots in Delhi from 31 October to 10 November* (Delhi, 1984). I believe that among the first academic reporting of the event was a newspaper article by Veena Das, Ranendra K. Das, Ashis Nandy, and D. L. Sheth published in *The Indian Express* on November 7, 1984.

32. This is a common saying that refers to dependents who betray one's trust and do harm to their benefactors.

33. I am tempted to say that the "objective" conditions did not warrant this fear of a plot against the whole of society being hatched by Sikhs. But the problem in this essay is precisely to see a crisis by placing oneself within it and to explain how evil powers come to be attributed to those who are the most vulnerable.

34. I have shown in my earlier work that in the streets where the violence occurred people simply did not use the category of martyrdom, nor did any other ready-made categories come very easily to them. See Das, "Our Work to Cry." Nijhawan has given important examples of the irony with which the Dhadi singers deployed the category of martyrdom when claimed by Sikh politicians whom they did not trust. The point I am trying to make is that although the martyr image is an extremely powerful one, those who have experienced violence do not put their experience into a given category as if reality provided some ready-made categories in which to put experience in. On the difficulties of drawing boundaries between the categories of martyrdom and of feud-related violence, see Das and Bajwa, "Community and Violence in Contemporary Punjab."

35. The first phrase may be translated as "Whoever proclaims this will find fulfillment," and the second phrase as "Eternal is our timeless Lord." In Sikh congregations, the leader of the prayers usually recites the first phrase, and the congregation responds with the second. In everyday encounters, Sikhs greet one

another using the second phrase. This story was much in circulation after Operation Blue Star and was cited in a letter by a senior police official in the Punjab in his resignation letter to the then president of India, Sardar Zail Singh.

36. There was always a "forgetting" at such points in a discussion that statistically more Sikhs had died in terrorist attacks then Hindus.

37. Hindu mythology is replete with such examples, and the expression *devata chaddha hai* (a god has possessed one) and *bhut chaddha hai* (a ghost has possessed one) can both be used in seeking to exorcise a troubling spirit.

38. See Bruce Kapferer, *A Celebration of Demons: Exorcism and Aesthetics of Healing in Sri Lanka* (Washington, DC: Smithsonian Institution Press, 1991), in conjunction with his *Legends of People, Myths of State: Violence, Intolerance, and Political Culture in Sri Lanka and Australia* (Washington, DC: Smithsonian Institution Press, 1998) for some analogies with the situation in Sri Lanka, in which the themes of possession and exorcism made an appearance in political cartoons in relation to the Tamil militants. For an astute critique of Kapferer's use of the category of experience in the text, see David Scott, *Formations of Ritual: Colonial and Anthropological Discourses on the Sinhala Yaktovil* (Minneapolis: University of Minnesota Press, 1994).

39. Valli Kanapathipillai, "July 1983: The Survivor's Experience," in Das, *Mirrors of Violence*, 321–45.

40. Jacques Lacan, "The Other and Psychosis," in *The Psychosis: The Seminars of Jacques Lacan, Book III, 1955–1956*, ed. Jacques-Alain Miller, trans. Russell Grigg (New York: W. W. Norton, 1993).

8. THE FORCE OF THE LOCAL

1. Deleuze, *The Logic of Sense*, 152. A little further in this quotation Deleuze goes on to say that there is much ignominy in saying that everyone has his or her own war or wound, for this is not true of those who are creatures of bitterness or resentment. There is an important picture of freedom in relation to the event that I cannot pursue here.

2. See Strathern, *Partial Relations*, ch. 1.

3. In its simplest meaning localization may be defined as construction of references that allows us to situate the various narrative programs of a discourse spatially. I use the idea here both to give a specific map of the riots as well as to situate the utterances of the crowd.

4. Deepak Mehta has argued that the language of epidemics provided the imaginary for conceiving of the riot as a natural phenomena in British colonial discourse. He shows how this language can be tracked in current discussions of forms of collective violence conceived as "riots" in India. This might be one way in which the fourth person "it" operates.

5. The following account is based upon the newspaper reports of four national dailies—*The Times of India, Indian Express, Hindustan Times,* and *The Statesman.*

6. Recall the rumors described in chapter 7 about trainloads of dead bodies arriving from the Punjab, later found to be false, but these instigated attacks on Sikhs in trains.

7. *Report of the Citizen's Commission: Delhi,* October 31 to November 4, 1985. Five official commissions of inquiry have analyzed the events to affix responsibility, but no closure has been achieved as each inquiry commission leads to protests and offers of new inquiry commissions from the government. Some of these outcomes are directly related to the power and influence of some politicians who were actively engaged in the riots, but other factors are the disappearance of evidence due to the passage of time. The official commissions of inquiry were *Report of the Justice Ranganath Misra Commission of Inquiry,* vols. 1 and 2 (Delhi: Government of India Publications, 1986); *Report of the Ahuja Commmission of Inquiry* (Delhi: Government of India Publications, 1987); *Report of the Kusum Lata Mittal Commission of Inquiry* (Delhi: Government of India Publications, 1990); *Report of the Jain Aggarwal Commission of Inquiry* (Delhi: Government of India Publications, 1993), and as the book goes to press there is the Nanavaty Report submitted in 2005, which I have not been able to study.

8. The nature of public language bears the signature of that time, for as I briefly show in chapter 11, media reports now work with a very different understanding of the "riot." In that sense the work of social scientists and human rights groups that insisted on investigating the violence rather than simply assuming that the popular pictures of crowds were correct has had a lasting effect on the media.

9. Amiya Rao et al., eds., *Report to the Nation: Truth about Delhi Violence* (New Delhi: Citizens for Democracy, 1985), x.

10. See especially People's Union for Civil Liberties and People's Union for Democratic Rights, *Who Are the Guilty?;* Chakravarti and Haksar, *The Delhi Riots;* and the special issue on the 1984 riots of *Illustrated Weekly of India,* December 23, 1984.

11. This committee was set up by the Indian Express Group of newspapers and was steered by the visionary leadership of its then editor, Mr. George Verghese, and a number of retired bureaucrats.

12. In the next chapter, I describe a more nuanced understanding of the state, but I was in no position to appreciate this while the work in the field was in progress.

13. Other voluntary groups organized relief in other affected blocks (including C3 and C4).

14. This was both because we urgently needed information on Sikh households and because there was both hostility to and fear of voluntary groups collecting data on the carnage. Our movements were restricted to certain parts of the neighborhood to minimize danger to the students who formed a major part of the survey teams.

15. The implications of the fact that most Sikhs who resided here were from artisan castes from Rajasthan and not from the Punjab will become clear later. Here I simply note that they did not know Punjabi and had played no part in the movement for Khalistan. Many were members of the Radhaswami sect that worshipped both in *gurudwaras* and in temples.

16. The only work I know that theorizes the work of relief and rehabilitation as simultaneous to communal violence is Mehta and Chatterji, "Boundaries, Names, Alterities," 201–49. In their words, "In their separate but related ways, both violence and relief work establish their genealogies, hence it is an error to see the latter as a direct and unmediated response to violence. As far as genealogy of violence is concerned, the narration of the riots forges a link with prior instances of collective violence. . . . Rehabilitation too operates in similar ways, arrogating an agency for itself" (206–7). What Mehta and Chatterji ask for is a nuanced ethnography of the genealogies of these processes, and their own work is an exemplary discussion of these. Similarly, Arjun Appadurai has examined the implications of the emergence of housing NGOs in Dharavi for understanding the working of democracy in a globalized world. See Arjun Appadurai, "Deep Democracy: Urban Governmentality and the Horizon of Politics," *Public Culture* 14, no. 1 (2002): 21–47.

17. The tola is a traditional measure in wide use for measuring gold. Although the exact weight varied by locality in earlier centuries, the measure was standardized during British rule. A 10 tola bar is the most commonly traded, each weighing 0.375 troy ounces. The value of 10 tolas in markets in 1984 was approximately $1,200.

18. *Jhatka* refers to slaughter of animals according to the Sikh ritual formula and is distinguished from the *halal* shops in which animals are slaughtered for meat according to Islamic rituals.

19. PUCL-PUDR, *Who Are the Guilty? Jhopdi* is a composite term referring to shanties. It is used as an administrative category for houses not built with concrete and usually falls under the slum development programs of the Delhi Development Authority.

20. Allen Feldman's work on political violence in Ireland is relevant here for his theory of political agency and subjectivity. Allen Feldman, *Formations of Violence: The Narrative of the Body and Political Terror in Northern Ireland* (Chicago: University of Chicago Press, 1991).

21. For an excellent description of the housing policies during the Emergency, see Emma Tarlo, *Unsettling Memories* (Berkeley: California University Press, 2002). The national Emergency was declared by Indira Gandhi on June 26,

1975, on the grounds that the security of India was threatened by internal disturbances. It is widely acknowledged that this was purely to keep her own government in power after the election was declared void after a judgment by the Allahabad High Court on June 12, 1975. Mrs. Gandhi's son Sanjay played a major role in the beautification drive as well as the sterilization drive. I discuss this issue in the next chapter.

22. The Siglikars as an artisan caste did not occupy a much higher caste status, but competition among lower castes has been intense in modern politics. For selected references on this aspect of caste politics, see Veena Das, "Caste," in *Encyclopedia of Social and Behavioral Sciences,* ed. Neil J. Smelser and Paul B. Baltes (Amsterdam: Elsevier, 2001), vol. 3, 1529–32.

23. This description is based primarily on the accounts given by the survivors in A4 Block, but many others in the adjoining blocks who were at a distance from the events gave similar accounts. There were others, such as the supporters of the Pradhan from A2 or simply those who feared they might be named as the culprits, who denied these accounts completely.

24. There was also one reported case of a Sikh police constable from the area who was burned to death, but we could not trace the family.

25. This case is discussed in greater detail in chapter 10.

26. In retrospect I realize that my fears were greatly exaggerated, but in my defense I have to say that the henchman of X had threatened me in a menacing manner, and this might have colored my perception of this request.

27. See Stanley J. Tambiah, *Leveling Crowds: Ethnonationalist Conflicts and Collective Violence in South Asia* (Delhi: Vistaar Publications, 1997), 266.

28. Appdurai, *Modernity at Large.*

29. Although, strictly speaking, register refers to variations in natural language in relation to social morphology such as social class or occupation, I use it here to indicate that it is not vocabulary but chains of words that show the social imaginary of groups to which speakers are laying claims. Thus *caste, nation,* or *global world* here are not indexical terms.

30. Benedict Anderson, *Imagined Communities: Reflections on the Origin and Spread of Nationalism* (London: Verso, 1983).

31. The use of the male pronoun is deliberate and appropriate here.

32. This is the famous problem of many hands in which individual agency becomes difficult to fix—hence the lowest officials in an organization are scapegoated to take the blame for organizational failures, but the context here is of judicial culpability and not failure in relation to risk culture in organizations that preoccupied Luhmann. See Niklas Luhmann, *Risk: A Sociological Theory,* trans. Rhodes Barrett (New York: A. de Gruyter, 1993).

33. I do not say this as a criticism, for I believe that there are many contexts in which it is not very useful to look for agency, or in which society presents itself as already made. However, the issue remains as an open one.

34. For instance, speaking of practices, Bourdieu says, "They can therefore only be accounted for by relating the social conditions in which the *habitus* that generated them was constituted, to the social conditions in which it is imple-, mented, that is through the scientific work of performing the interrelationship of these two states of the social world that the *habitus* performs, while concealing it in and through practice." Bourdieu, *The Logic of Practice,* 56.

9. THE SIGNATURE OF THE STATE

1. Walter Benjamin, "Critique of Violence," in *Reflections: Essays, Aphorisms, Autobiographical Writings,* ed. P. Demetz, trans. E. Jephcott (New York: Harcourt Brace Jovanovitch, 1986), 277–301.

2. Fernando Coronil, *The Magical State: Nature, Money and Modernity in Venezuela* (Chicago: University of Chicago Press, 1997).

3. I am perfectly aware of the idea that some fictions belong to life, but I use the idea of magic because it resonates, in some ways, with the representations I have encountered in the process of fieldwork among low-income neighborhoods in Delhi.

4. Michael Taussig, *The Magic of the State* (New York: Routledge, 1997).

5. Derrida, "Signature, Event, Context."

6. I use the idea of writing to suggest modalities, different from that of textual domination in the state's performance of authority, as, for instance, in Brinkley Messick, *The Calligraphic State: Textual Domination and History in an Islamic Society* (Berkeley: University of California Press, 1993).

7. Taussig, *The Magic of the State.*

8. The word literally means "the assembly of five" and refers to the legislative and adjudicatory powers invested in the village or caste elders.

9. For the normal practices in the filing of FIRs in police stations, see Das and Bajwa, "Community and Violence in Contemporary Punjab."

10. The form used in registering the First Information Report I record here was deployed in many cases in the documents that many people showed me, though I cannot vouch that this form was used in all cases. Vrinda Grover has argued that the idea of a "mob" is produced through the suspension of ordinary investigative procedures of policing prescribed in the Criminal Procedure Code. See Vrinda Grover, "Quest for Justice: 1984 Massacre of Sikh Citizens in Delhi," unpublished report, 2002. Pratiksha Baxi offers a close analysis of appellate court decisions to show how the notion of crowd is produced in court judgments and leads to a jurisprudence in which individual agency is suspended by producing the idea of a collective subject. Pratiksha Baxi, "Adjudicating the Riot: Communal Violence, Crowds and Public Tranquility in India," *Domains* (forthcoming).

11. Among the various reports produced by civil rights organizations, see especially PUDR/PUCL and Report of Citizens' Commission *(Who Are the Guilty?)* for evidence of the complicity of various politicians and the police in the riots.

12. I thank Peter Geschiere for this point.

13. Since I assisted the People's Commission and the Police Commission in gathering evidence and helped in getting the compensation to the victims by doing their paperwork along with the NGOs working in this area, the police officer could easily identify me. Besides, in the atmosphere of fear and suspicion, any attempt to even talk to the local police officers could have caused fear among the survivors.

14. The names of policemen are fictitious. Though there is no way for me to directly acknowledge their help in this study, I want to express my profound gratitude to the policemen and lawyers who extended their help to me.

15. Pandit is a Brahmin subcaste, but unlike in many other regions in India, the Brahmins do not enjoy a high status in the Punjab. They are considered dependents of powerful landowning castes. Though their purity is not in question, they are more figures of fun than of awe. In this case the Pandit was a small-time astrologer and palmist. *Pandta* is a form of address.

This is my translation of Tej Singh's description.

16. Forms of civility and legal requirements in India do not permit the use of such terms as "untouchable" in regard to Chamars, because of their stigmatizing connotations. Although in most contexts I would have used a term that is officially accepted such as *scheduled caste,* or one that is coined by these castes—Dalits—here I am using the terms Tej Singh himself used with exquisite irony, because much of the force of his affect would be lost if I substituted these terms with others.

17. I am withholding the name of this park.

18. Notice the similarity in the forms of insult levied by the Siglikar Pradhan and the one internalized by Tej Singh. Insults, whether uttered in the course of rumors, shouted during a riot or public dispute, or internalized as in Tej Singh's account, constitute a rupture at the level of language—words take on weight that distinguishes them from a purely referential usage. See Jacques Lacan, "I've Just Been to the Butcher's," in *The Psychosis: The Seminars of Jacques Lacan,* 42–56.

19. Tarlo, *Unsettling Memories.*

20. See John Dayal and Ajoy Bose, *For Reasons of State: Delhi under Emergency* (Delhi: Ess Ess Publications, 1977), and Shah Commission, *Shah Commission of Inquiry: Third and Final Report* (Delhi: Government of India Publications, 1978).

21. Vinod Mehta, *The Sanjay Story: From Anand Bhavan to Amethi* (Bombay: Jaico Publications, 1978).

22. *Shah Commission of Inquiry.*

23. See Anna Tsing, *In the Realm of the Diamond Queen: Marginality in an Out-of-the-Way Place* (Princeton: Princeton University Press, 1993).

24. Benjamin, "Critique of Violence."

25. John Austin, "A Plea for Excuses," in *Philosophical Papers,* ed. J.M. Urmsom and G.J. Warnock, 3rd ed. (Oxford: Oxford University Press, 1979), 175–205. The notion of "excuse" has been developed in the legal literature in both the battered woman defense and the cultural defense strategy. See Mark Kelman, "Reasonable Evidence of Reasonableness," in *Questions of Evidence: Proof, Practice, and Persuasion across Disciplines,* ed. J. Chandler, A. Davidson, and H.D. Harootunian (Chicago: University of Chicago Press, 1994), and Leti Volpp, "(Mis)Identifying Culture: Asian Women and the 'Cultural Defense,'" *Harvard Women's Law Journal* 17 (1994): 57–101. The way that I deploy Austin's notion of excuses is to argue that the realm of the civil is expanded in admitting such enunciations.

26. See Cavell, *A Pitch of Philosophy.*

27. Deborah Poole, Pradeep Jeganathan, and Mariane Ferme have shown the precariousness of these encounters. See Deborah Poole, "Between Threat and Guarantee," 35–67; Pradeep Jeganathan, "Checkpoint: Anthropology, Identity and the State," 67–81; Mariane C. Ferme, "Deterritorialized Citizenship and the Resonances of the Sierra Leonean State," 81–117, all in Das and Poole, *Anthropology at the Margins of the State.*

28. See Veena Das and Abhijit Dasgupta, "Scientific and Political Representations: Cholera Vaccine in India," *Economic and Political Weekly* 35, nos. 8–9 (2000): 633–45.

29. Hansen, *Wages of Violence.*

30. Claude Lefort, *Democracy and Political Theory* (Cambridge: Polity Press, 1988).

31. Ernest Kantorowicz, *The King's Two Bodies* (Princeton: Princeton University Press, 1957).

32. Hansen, *Wages of Violence,* 129.

33. I am not claiming that theories of Mughal kingship or Hindu kingship would necessarily provide better insights into contemporary political processes in India, but I nevertheless find it puzzling that even if ideas of medieval kingship in Europe were inherited by the political elite in India, they are not subjected to greater scrutiny by Hansen in trying to render them applicable to contemporary India. This is not to propose that no Western notions are applicable and that we can somehow isolate a pristine Indian tradition, but to suggest that we look more closely into the processes of language, life, and labor in their contemporary forms.

34. Hansen, *Wages of Violence,* 130.

35. This felicitous phrase is from Deborah Poole and is deployed by her to indicate not only the instability of the state that makes peasants in Peru vulnerable

to the exercise of arbitrary power but also to the fact that it provides the space for initiatives toward "reinheriting the state." See Poole, "Between Threat and Guarantee."

36. This is part of the contingency of fieldwork, for it is not always possible to attempt such a mapping during the riots, but as Mehta and Chatterji show, walking through such areas with those who were present even long after the event provides an important map. See Deepak Mehta and Roma Chatterji, "Boundaries, Names, Alterities: A Case Study of a 'Communal Riot' in Dharavi, Bombay," in Das et al., *Remaking a World*, 201–50. Yasmeen Arif is presently engaged in an important effort to see if people can render memories as a map in Sultanpuri within a larger project on urban violence directed by Deepak Mehta under the auspices of ISERDD in Delhi.

37. Hansen's chapter on the *mohalla* in this book gives us some history specific to Muslim *mohallas,* but the weight of the chapter is at a level of generality derived from public statements and sporadic interviews that constantly moves the center of gravity to the city, the urban imaginary, and circulation of talk around well-known figures. Paying attention to networks of talk is, of course, crucial for the anthropologist, but as Mehta and Chattterji show, there is a difference between general observations that people might make in relation to questions on, say, Muslim identity and the particular enunciations that rupture the language, especially in the context of violence. What we learn about Muslim identity when a small mentally challenged child says of the riots "We were playing India/Pakistan" or when sitting ethnographies and walking ethnographies construct the neighborhood in completely different ways is of a different order than observations offered in the course of the general and somehow unanchored conversations that Hansen reports. I believe that questions about violence especially open up the issues of language and speech that require closer attention to such ruptures. Mehta and Chatterji, "Boundaries, Names, Alterities."

38. Hansen, *Wages of Violence,* 122, 123.

39. If we see only the intentions of the state in these commissions of inquiry, we fail to appreciate the enormous effort citizens have put into public recognition of wrongs done to victims and survivors. For instance, the lawyer H.S. Phoolka has devoted the last twenty-one years in pursuing cases against perpetrators who were named in the 1984 riots and in organizing civil action to demand the truth. Even as I complete this book, the Nanavati Commission Report was tabled in the Indian Parliament in August 2005. It did not satisfy many civil right groups, but it did evoke an unqualified apology from the prime minister on behalf of the government. The irony was that the present prime minister, himself a Sikh, was not implicated in any way in the organization of the riots. While justice might not have been achieved to the satisfaction of many, it led to the resignation of one of the Congress politicians from his position as minister. On questions of culpability see the forthright paper by

Nandini Sundar, "Toward an Anthropology of Culpability," *American Ethnologist* 31, no. 2 (2004): 145–64.

40. See Gene Ray, "Reading the Lisbon Earthquake: Adorno, Lyotard, and the Contemporary Sublime," *Yale Journal of Criticism* 17, no. 1 (2004): 1–18.

41. Jean-François Lyotard, *The Inhuman: Reflections on Time,* trans. Geoffrey G. Benington and Rachel Bowlby (Stanford: Stanford University Press, 1991).

42. Edmund Burke, *A Philosophical Enquiry into the Origin of Our Ideas of the Sublime and the Beautiful,* ed. Adam Philips (London: Oxford University Press, 1990).

43. Appadurai, "Deep Democracy"; Roma Chatterji, "Plans, Habitation and Slums: The Production of Community in Dharavi, Mumbai," *Occasional Research Paper Series,* September 2003 (Delhi: Iserdd), forthcoming in *Contributions to Indian Sociology (n.s.).*

10. THREE PORTRAITS OF GRIEF AND MOURNING

1. *Ji* is an honorific term used for elders and those senior to show respect.

2. Mita Bose, a teacher of English literature in the University of Delhi, did remarkable rehabilitation work among the survivors and became a close confidant of Shanti. We worked together to set up a summer camp for the children in 1985. I am very grateful for Mita's generosity and her affection.

3. One of the most memorable renderings of this sentence for me was in a dance performance in a mixed Indian classical (Bharat Natyam) and modern dance genre performed by the dancer Navtej Singh, directed by Ein Lal, which was based on an earlier version of this paper. Shanti's words and Navtej's rendering of the man crawling toward the door wanting to open it but unable to do so have become so overlapped in my memory that I cannot think of one without the other.

4. I refer here to the Hindu and Sikh belief that it is the ancestral oblations offered by sons that release a dead man from a particular kind of hell. What is at stake though is the firmness of the belief for Shanti, for Hindu and Sikh texts and practices offer any number of ways of dealing with exceptions.

5. Fire is a polyvalent symbol and appears here in both its malevolent and benevolent aspects. In its malevolent aspect it was used by mobs to burn people alive, but its benevolent aspects of purification and release, as represented by the sacrificial fires of the cremation ground, were denied to the dead. See G. Bachelard, *La psychoanalyse du feu* (Paris: Gallimard, 1949). On fire in death rituals as a sacrificial fire see Das, *Structure and Cognition,* and Jonathan Parry, *Death in Banaras* (Cambridge: Cambridge University Press, 1994). The most complex rendering of this is to be found in the classic study of Charles Malamoud, *Cooking the World: Ritual and Thought in Ancient India,* trans. David White (Delhi: Oxford University Press, 1996).

6. I should make it clear that the park was more a place overgrown with weeds and was used primarily for defecation. Many houses lacked toilets, and though there were public toilets built for use in the locality, these were considered to be dangerous places by the women. When houses were rebuilt after the riots, provision was made for toilets in the house, though in the absence of proper sewage, flush toilets could not be installed.

7. In his classic statement on free association, Freud compared the patient in psychoanalysis with a passenger on a train. The patient's job is to look at the passing scene and describe all its features to his companion, who cannot see outside the window. Despite the powerful imagery that such a model of "remembering" conjures in the mind, it is not very appropriate for remembering recent and traumatic events. Sigmund Freud, "Recommendations to Physicians Practising Psychoanalysis," in *The Complete Psychological Works,* Standard Edition, vol. 12, ed. and trans. James Strachey (New York: W. W. Norton, 1976; first published 1912).

8. Yasmin Arif has now conducted fieldwork in Tilak-Vihar where many widows in two affected neighborhoods were provided housing as compensation partly in response to their own demands. The unintended consequences of this have been explored in a thought-provoking paper in which Arif describes how the area came to be stigmatized as a "widow's colony," and how the intergenerational transmission of the narrative of loss and trauma led to a freezing of the women within the events of 1984. The after-life of the violence is lived by the widows, whose responsibility is now to carry the memory of the violence as symbols of loss for the whole community. Yasmin Arif, "The Delhi Carnage of 1984: The Afterlife of Violence and Loss," *Domains* (forthcoming).

9. This is how at least the survivors interpreted the presence of these "social workers." On the concept of "big men" see Maurice Godelier and Marilyn Strathern, eds., *Big Men and Great Men: Personifications of Power in Melanesia* (Cambridge: Cambridge University Press, 1991).

10. On leviratic marriage in North India see P. Kolenda, "Widowhood among 'Untouchable' Churas," in *Concepts of Person: Kinship, Caste and Marriage in India,* ed. Akos Ostor, Lina Fruzzetti, and Steve Barnet (Delhi: Oxford University Press, 1982). The famous novel by B.S. Bedi, *Ek Chadar Maili Si* (Delhi: Rajkamal Publications, 1969), gives a poignant rendering of the shadows of incest that fall over this form of marriage.

11. See Dipesh Chakrabarty, "Domestic Cruelty and the Birth of the Subject," in *Provincializing Europe: Postcolonial Thought and Historical Difference* (Princeton: Princeton University Press, 2000), 117–49.

12. The implications of naming the widow as the appropriate recipient of compensation by the state meant that even when women established conjugal relations with other men, they continued to represent themselves as widows. The fact that middle-class sensibilities inform bureaucratic sensibilities was obvious to the women.

13. The normal assumption that divorce occurs between spouses is not valid in this case, for upon marriage a woman is seen as the "property" of the conjugal family. Therefore, the conjugal family has to terminate its claims over the woman by the granting of divorce. Similarly, the court papers on which agreements were signed may not have had any legal validity, but these were nonetheless symbols of a formal contract in the community, as I discussed in the last chapter.

14. She was speaking figuratively, for in such cases the marriage is finalized by a simple ceremony of a new *chaddar* or piece of cloth being placed on the woman by the new husband—there is no wedding procession as such. The symmetry, however, between the funeral procession and the marriage procession served as a powerful rhetorical device and is often made in mourning laments.

15. In this context the tireless work done by lawyers, especially H. S. Phoolka, over the last twenty years has been crucial for sustaining some of the cases in court and representing the cases of the victims before the various commissions of inquiry.

16. I kept a diary recording some events and often wrote in Hindi. I was not systematic—between being in the colony, taking my classes in the university, attending meetings at various sites to raise money, or attending to an immediate emergency, I simply could not write regularly. Steven Caton has given the best description of fieldwork in which our sense of what happened is equally made up of memories that went unrecorded, the visceral feel of a place, and how we read gestures, facial expressions, and not only what is spoken. See Caton, *Yemen Chronicles*. Wittgenstein's idea of language as bodying forth is of the utmost relevance here.

17. I must confess that it would be more honest to say that I was unceremoniously turned out, but when I first started writing about these issues, I was apprehensive of saying things about the bureaucracy too bluntly. I have retained those early descriptions.

18. I knew from experience how difficult it was to have a group discussion in which participants did not break into bitter accusations against one another.

19. Like most other languages, Hindi also uses circumlocutions for such bodily functions as defecation and urination. The women wanted to know what these circumlocutions were. One of the points to which they wished to draw attention in their petition was the dangers they faced when they went to perform these functions, either in the fields or in public toilets, where many of the men had been murdered. The polite term for "widow" in Hindi is *vidhava*, and in Punjabi *beva*, but in the community the word most frequently used was *randi*, which can refer to both a widow and a prostitute. This term is never used in polite forms of speech among upper castes. The speech of lower castes, such as the Siglikars, is often marked by the use of such taboo words. Clearly, I appeared to them as someone who could mediate between their world and the outside, defined by class, gender, and culture.

20. They were provided with apartments in multistory complexes in another colony but not with the kind of housing they had requested. This is the colony that came to be known as the "widow's colony" later. The social life of this event in these new spaces is a whole new research subject. Yasmin Arif and Asha Singh are now working in these areas to see how the memory of the riots is lived here.

21. Stanley Cavell, *The Claim of Reason: Wittgenstein, Skepticism, Morality and Tragedy* (New York: Oxford University Press, 1979), 177.

22. Cavell, *The Claim of Reason*, 177–78.

23. In Cavell's words, "What we learn is not just what we have studied; and what we have been taught is not just what we were intended to learn. What we have in our memories is not just what we have memorized." *The Claim of Reason*, 177.

24. See especially Cavell, *The Claim of Reason*, 179, 189.

II. REVISITING TRAUMA, TESTIMONY, AND POLITICAL COMMUNITY

1. Deepak Mehta, "Documents and Testimony: Violence, Witnessing, and Subjectivity in the Bombay Riots—1992–1993," unpublished manuscript.

2. Paul Brass, "Introduction: Discourses of Ethnicity, Communalism, and Violence," in *Riots and Pogroms,* ed. Paul Brass (London: Macmillan,1996), 1–56.

3. "All-Party Panel on Gujarat Riots," *The Statesman,* March 17, 2002.

4. PUDR and PUCL, *Who Are the Guilty?*

5. Nancy Scheper-Hughes, "The Primacy of the Ethical: Toward a Militant Anthropology," *Current Anthropology* 36, no. 3 (1995): 409–20. I do not say that the idea of a militant anthropology is not important, but simply that it did not mark my mode of work. Scheper-Hughes's own work shows the ways that such a vision can be productive.

6. I take this opportunity to record, once again, my gratitude to the lamented C. R. Rajgopalan, whose life and work were testimony to the courage and resilience that many public servants showed at that time.

7. Despite the picture of innocent victims in which people have a stake, those working with the actual processes of rehabilitation after any kind of collective disaster, especially related to violence, are fully aware of the way that local networks develop to siphon off resources in one direction or another. Even distribution of rations could lead to major quarrels among the survivors over who are worthy recipients of relief. On the other side, the kinds of commodities that end up in relief camps after a disaster reflect a whole trajectory of how "charity" is perceived in a globalized world. A recent example was a representative of a global consulting firm who distributed toys of well-known American figures of fiction holding guns to children in relief camps who had just witnessed their parents or other close relatives burned or bludgeoned to death in the

Gujarat riots. For a finely nuanced analysis of how the trajectory of relief inter-acts with the trajectory of violence, see Mehta and Chatterji, "Boundaries, Names, Alterities."

8. Among anthropologists, it is Arthur Kleinman who has struggled con-ceptually and ethically throughout his work with this set of issues, most partic-ularly in his Tanner lectures. See Arthur Kleinman, "Where Our World Is Taking Us: Remaking Moral Experience in the New Era," Tanner Lectures, Stanford University, 2000.

9. For instance, Barkha Dutt has described how after interviewing the chief minister of Gujarat in his residence where he confidently asserted that the situ-ation in Gujarat was now normal, their crew was attacked by a mob barely a mile away from the chief minister's residence. Barkha Dutt, "The Invisible Women," in *Lest We Forget,* ed. Amrita Kumar and Prashun Bhaumik (Delhi: Rupa & Co., 2002), 57–61.

10. Bhrigupati Singh, "My Work in Amman Chowk," *Seminar, Special Issue on Securing South Asia,* 517 (2002): 67–72.

11. Reinhart Koselleck, *Kritik und Krise* (Frankfurt: Suhrkamp, 1973).

12. Achille Mbembe, "African Modes of Self-writing," *Public Culture: Spe-cial Issue on New Imaginaries* 14, no. 2 (2002): 239–75.

13. Mbembe, "African Modes of Self-writing," 259.

14. Mbembe, "African Modes of Self-writing," 245; see especially 259–60.

15. For example, Foucault's examination of "self-writing" looks at the detailed ways in which the act of writing was implicated in the technologies of the self. He locates three different modalities through which writing was used in the philosophical cultivation of the self just before the arrival of Christianity and then in early Christian forms of monastic notation. See Michel Foucault, "Self-writing," in *Ethics, Subjectivity and Truth,* ed. Paul Rabinow (New York: New Press, 1994), 207–23. It seems interesting to me that Mbembe not only transposes the idea of "writing" without locating its place in the historical and cultural traditions he is studying, but is also impatient with any detailed ren-dering of differences within Africa on the relation between the oral and the written, despite his own insistence that differences have been eclipsed in discus-sions that deploy notions of similarity on the basis of race. To be sure, he con-cludes by gesturing toward the mobile and unstable forms that practices of the self generate, but this does not prevent him from speaking of "African thought" or "African subjectivity" frequently in the course of his analysis.

16. It is not my argument that detailed historical work on the conditions under which slavery operated as part of the strategy of selling in the African context is not relevant, but rather that to trace the genealogy of the modern wars in Africa to the ghostly apparitions produced by unresolved guilt but unmediated by the contemporary forces of life and labor seems neither a sketch to be filled out later nor a fragment that points to an impossible totality.

There is the powerful seduction of his language that is more conducive to prophetic pronouncements, but is this good enough ground to accept the diagnosis of the crisis?

17. In his collection of essays on the postcolony, Mbembe talks of hallucinated writing but uses hallucination as a characteristic of power in the postcolony. Writing is understood in terms of the act of rendering this experience in analytical terms while the subject appears as the hallucinated subject "incapable of responsibility for what he says and does." Achille Mbembe, *On the Postcolony* (Berkeley: University of California Press, 2001), 169. As far as I can make out, the concept of writing the self is not deployed in this book.

18. Das and Kleinman, "Introduction," in *Remaking a World.*

19. Max Weber, "Science as Vocation," in *From Max Weber,* ed. H. Gerth and C. Wright Mills (New York: Oxford University Press, 1946).

20. Charles Hale, "CA Forum on Anthropology in Public: Consciousness, Violence and Politics of Memory in Guatemala," *Current Anthropology* 38, no. 5 (1997): 817–38.

21. Mahmood Mamdani, *When Victims Become Killers* (Princeton: Princeton University Press, 2002).

22. Diane Nelson, *Finger in the Wound: Body Politics in Quincentennial Guatemala* (Berkeley: University of California Press, 1999).

23. Michael Hardt and Antonio Negri, *Empire* (Cambridge, MA: Harvard University Press, 2000), 155–56.

24. Fiona Ross, *Speech and Silence: Women's Testimony in the Truth and Reconciliation Commission* (London: Pluto Press, 2003).

ACKNOWLEDGMENTS

My debts to various friends, colleagues, and students for their generosity in sharing ideas, offering criticisms, and helping to reframe issues are many, and I gladly carry these debts with me wherever I go. In Delhi, the intense conversations with Rita Brara, Roma Chatterji, and Deepak Mehta have been inspirational for me for more than two decades. Yasmin Arif, Pratiksha Baxi, Asha Singh, and Mani Shekhar Singh shared their work and their thoughts; Pratiksha was especially diligent in urging me to read important books and papers that I might have otherwise missed. I am very grateful to them.

My colleagues at Johns Hopkins University provided a rich and intellectually engaging environment. I especially thank Naveeda Khan, Deborah Poole, and Pamela Reynolds for reading parts of the manuscript and giving incisive comments. William Connolly, Hent de Vries, Jonathan Goldberg, Ali Khan, Lori Leonard, Paola Marrati, and Michael Moon have offered me an education in literatures that I might otherwise have found beyond my capabilities. I thank them for their generosity. My graduate students have been a source of great joy in my academic life. I learnt so much from discussions in and out of the classroom. Bhrigupati Singh, Sylvain Perdigon, and Aaron Goodfellow set very high standards for my book—I hope I have not disappointed them in this book.

My friends in Colombo, especially Pradeep Jeganathan and Radhika Coomaraswamy, have produced stunning work on violence. It is a pleasure to say how much I have learned from them. As always, I miss Neelan Thiruchelvam and the strength I derived from his imagination, courage, and faith in my work.

I have been blessed in my friendship with Talal Asad, Arthur Kleinman, and Joan Kleinman. They are not only fellow collaborators but also exemplars in their moral orientation to life and work. Though my interactions with Arjun Appadurai, João Biehl, Janet Carsten, Steven Caton, Lawrence Cohen, Claude Imbert, and Stefania Pandolfo have been confined to conferences and meetings in recent years, each conversation was a treasure. Audrey Cantlie, Christopher Davis, Murray Last, and Jonathan Spencer have sustained conversations across continents, shared ideas even when they were fragile, and offered me the kind of trust without which intellectual life withers away. I am extremely grateful to them for all they have offered.

I want to thank Arjun Appadurai, Talal Asad, Steven Caton, Lawrence Cohen, Val Daniel, Michael Herzfeld, Arthur Kleinman, Paul Rabinow, Rayna Rapp, and Bjorn Wittrock for providing me with strength and stability during a very troubling time. I will be indebted to them for many lives.

I was fortunate in receiving a short-term fellowship at SCASS in Uppsala that provided an idyllic time in which to think and write. The two anonymous reviewers for the University of California Press gave very useful suggestions, and David Anderson, Chalon Emmons, Randy Heyman, Caroline Knapp, and my editor, Stan Holwitz, were models of patience and persistence. Becky Daniels helped in the preparation of the manuscript with good cheer. Sahar Jalal and Todd Meyers helped me think of images for the book jacket. I am grateful for all this support.

My love for the everyday comes from my family—to Ranen, Saumya, Christiana, Jishnu, Carolina, Sanmay, Jennifer, Nayan, and Lucas, and to the memory of Iota as also to Dev Bhaiya, I owe my existence, my obsession with kinship, and my particular take on excuses.

In Stanley Cavell's writing, I found a philosophical friendship that has sustained my thought over terrains that were hard for me. I offer my gratitude to him. And for her blessings, I gratefully thank ma.

I am grateful to the following publishers for permission to reproduce chapters that appeared in an earlier form in the following publications. Chapter 2 appeared as "National Honor and Practical Kinship: Unwanted Women and Children," in *Conceiving the New World Order,* ed. Faye Ginsburg and Rayna Rapp (Berkeley: University of California Press, 1995), © 1995 The Regents of the University of California. Chapter 3 appeared as "Language and Body: Transactions in the Construction of Pain" in *Social Suffering,* ed. Arthur Kleinman, Veena Das, and Margaret Lock (Berkeley: University of California Press, 1997), © 1997 The Regents of the University of California. Chapter 4 appeared as "The Act of Witnessing: Violence, Poisonous Knowledge and Subjectivity" in *Violence and Subjectivity,* ed. Veena Das, Arthur Kleinman, Mamphela Ramphele, and Pamela Reynolds (Berkeley: University of California Press, 2000), © 2000 The Regents of the University of California. Chapter 5 appeared as "Violence and the Work of Time" in *Signifying Identities: Anthropological Perspectives on Boundaries and Contested Values*, ed. Anthony P. Cohen (London: Routledge, 2000). Chapter 7 appeared as "Crisis and Representation: Rumor and the Circulation of Hate," in *Disturbing Remains: Memory, History, and Crisis in the Twentieth Century*, ed. Michael Roth and Charles G. Salas (Los Angeles: Getty Research Institute, 2001). Chapter 8 appeared as "Spatialization of Violence: A 'Communal Riot' in Delhi," in *Unravelling the Nation: Sectarian Conflict and India's Secular Identity*, ed. Kaushik Basu and Sanjay Subrahmanyam (New Delhi: Penguin Books, 1996). Chapter 9 appeared as "The Signature of the State: The Paradox of Illegibility," in *Anthropology in the Margins of the State*, ed. Veena Das and Deborah Poole (Santa Fe, NM: SAR Press, 2004), copyright © 2004 by the School of American Research, Santa Fe, New Mexico. Chapter 10 appeared as "Our Work to Cry: Your Work to Listen" in *Mirrors of Violence: Communities, Riots and Survivors in South Asia*, ed. Veena Das (Delhi: Oxford University Press, 1990). Chapter 11 appeared as "Trauma and Testimony: Implications for Political Community," *Anthropological Theory* 3, no. 3 (2003): 293–307.

Veena Das
October 2005

INDEX

179, 185–87, 193, 196, 204; bad, 40,
48, 50–51; biological, 215; blame for,
69; fear of, 35; good, 40, 48, 50–51;
rituals, 50–51, 60, 191; time and, 99;
untimely, 68, 235n15; without heroism,
190–91; zones of, 56, 60–61. *See also*
mourning
Deleuze, Giles, 91–92, 98–100, 135–36
Derrida, Jacques, 8–9, 163
Descartes, René, xii, xiii, xiv, 41
desire, 27, 61, 64, 71, 219
Desjarlais, Robert, 65–66, 75, 98–99
destruction. *See* devastation, space of
devastation, space of, 5–6, 62, 74, 101,
214, 217
Dickens, Charles, 91
disappointment, 2, 40, 68
documents, 164–65, 168, 174, 178
doubt, 7, 77, 90, 112. *See also* skepticism
Draupadi, 104, 216
duration, 95, 98, 100, 200
Durkheim, Emile, 180

emergency, 110, 122, 134, 150, 161,
172–74
Emerson, Ralph Waldo, 39, 226n20
ethnography, 50, 86, 100, 103, 174, 215–17,
226n21; practice of, 2, 13, 93, 98,
143, 159, 161, 181, 259n37; state of,
207, 219
events, 5, 7, 37, 54, 56, 62, 98, 101, 117,
120, 123, 127, 134–36, 195, 205, 213,
217–18; as collective and individual,
135; constructions and counter-
constructions of, 109; critical, 2, 7,
134; and the everyday, 1, 7, 136, 149,
218, 223n1; as foundational, 21, 32;
genealogy of, 109; interpretation
of, 167; language and, 109, 223n1;
national, 11; public, 96–97; simultaneity of, 97; and time, 96–97; traumatic,
103, 111; unfinished, 129; unfolding of,
72, 120; witnessing of, 209
eventual, 2, 103, 120
everyday, x, xiii, 7, 17, 57, 90–91, 111,
135–36, 159, 163, 167, 172, 188, 216–218;
descent into, 62, 216; engagement

with, 80, 102; as eventful, 2; as recovered, 62, 218; register of, 215; return
to, 134; voice in, 2–3
everyday life, xiii–xiv, 1, 2, 9, 11, 13, 15, 37,
45, 50–52, 54–55, 73, 90–91, 101–3,
105, 117–18, 134, 159, 164, 175, 178,
180–81, 200, 205, 207, 218–19;
dangers of, 16; descent into, 15, 62,
74, 221; *habitus* and, 159; heterogeneity of, 136; language of, 225n10;
little deaths of, xiii; as recovered,
101; tactics of, 104; violence of, 136,
149; witnessing of, 102; women
and, xiii
evil, 113, 116, 129, 186
excuses, 164, 178–79, 258n25
exile, 67, 77
experience, 4, 6, 7, 8, 39, 54, 59, 63, 102,
216–17; of abduction, 89; absence
from, 104; collective, 217; edges of,
87; heterogeneity of, 73; subject and,
224n6; traumatic, 102; unclaimed,
103–4, 214; unassimilated, 101–2, 205;
of violence, 111
eyes, 4, 62, 74; evidence of, 122. *See also*
vision

family, 2, 9, 10, 11, 12, 14, 24–25, 28–29,
33, 34, 36, 47, 53–54, 61, 63–65, 68–71,
74, 76, 81–82, 86, 88, 144, 147, 152,
164–66, 183, 188, 192, 195, 200, 208,
218; narratives, 86; planning programs,
173; sovereignty and, 59–60; state
and, 64
fathers, 8, 56–57; and daughters, 34, 46–48,
57, 76; and sons, 32, 70, 86, 112–13.
See also relations
fear, 9, 12, 46, 126, 142, 171, 181, 194; and
anticipation, 225n15
Felman, Shoshana, 19, 102
fieldwork. *See* ethnography
Filmer, Sir Robert, 34
forms of life, xi, 4, 15, 16, 88–90, 200–201;
and agreement, 88; experimentation
with, 86; and forms of death, 118, 132;
horizontal and vertical differences in,
89–90; human, 88

martyrdom, 56, 114, 116, 127

martyrs, 45, 110, 112–13, 127, 130, 203, 251n34

Marx, Karl, xii

masculinity, 81, 87, 89, 110–13, 119, 193, 246n7; femininity and, 110, 113–15, 117. *See also* men; nation

Mbembe, Achille, 211–14, 217, 219

McTaggart, John E. M, 96

Mehta, Deepak, 14, 205

memories, 10–11, 54, 71, 72–73, 76, 90, 98, 109, 185. *See also* memory; past

memory, 8, 38, 55, 67–68, 76, 99, 149, 167, 195–96, 200, 213–14; collective, 95; social, 117, 120, 127. *See also* memories; past

men: as citizens, 56; as heads of households, 25–27, 29, 32, 33, 38; as husbands and fathers, 28, 110, 161, 179, 205, 246n7; as monsters, 56, 205; world of, 187

Menon, Ritu, 54

militancy: causes of, 131; discourse of, 111–14, 117, 120, 124; among Hindu groups, 11; in the Punjab, 108–9; reflections on, 171–72; and sanctuary, 120; among Sikhs, 111, 131, 168, 170

mobs, 14, 73, 126–28, 138–39, 209; in law, 256n10. *See also* crowds

modernity, 45–46, 196

money, 188–89, 196–97

motherhood, 8, 99, 186–87, 189

mothers, 63, 187; and failure, 186, 193; Indira Gandhi as mother, 153–54, 159. *See also* motherhood; relations

mourning, 5, 39, 48–49, 51, 54, 57, 62, 77, 101, 184, 194–95, 214, 216–17; gendered division in, xiii, 38, 48, 57, 62, 193; work of, xiii, 38, 48, 57, 59, 193. *See also* grief

Muslims, 13, 18, 20, 32, 36, 41, 147, 208; atrocities against, 209; mobs of, 73, 87; violence against, 3, 14, 19, 206

myth, xii, 20, 60, 62, 103–4, 115, 130–31, 161, 181; in philosophy, xii

naming, struggle over, 205–6. *See also* language

narrative, 47, 53, 57, 64, 72, 75, 80–81, 87, 217, 220; continuity of, 29; of Lahore, 64; localizing of, 142; management of, 81; official, 116, 216; oral, 71; pluralization of, 149; shifts in, 187; staging of, 80; tropes of, 53. *See also* stories; story

nation, 16, 23, 26, 42–46, 53, 55–56, 112–13, 116, 159, 205; and honor, 24, 26, 56, 58; as icon, 42–44, 74, 88; inauguration of, 19, 21; magnified image of, 45, 52; as masculine, 13, 18, 19, 25, 59, 112–13, 247n10; as motherland, 113; politics of, 160; and sexuality, 52–53, 56; and violence, 2; and women, 52, 90

nation-state, 2, 34, 38, 59

nationalism, 38, 41, 53, 110; and communalism, 46; discourse of, 20, 154; ideology of, 45; revolutionary, 42

Negri, Antonio, 230

neighborhoods, 126, 174–75, 204

neighbors, 155–57, 168, 184, 186, 189–91

Nehru, Jawaharlal, 23, 56

Nelson, Diane, 219

nonviolence: militant Sikhs on, 113–14; Gandhian politics and, 203

norms, 63, 69, 73, 78, 87, 166, 189, 207, 211–12

Nussbaum, Martha, 76

Obeyesekere, Gananath, 70

Operation Blue Star, 109, 117, 119–20, 122–24, 129, 169; Hindu and Sikh versions of, 130–31

ordinary, 1, 3, 6, 7, 11, 15, 42, 134, 218, 221; descent into, 7, 77; as eventful, 7; flight from, 160; and ordinary language, x; and ordinary people, 18; suspicion of, 6; turn towards, 92, 101. *See also* everyday; everyday life

other, xiv, 6, 16, 17, 39, 40, 57, 132, 134, 211; being with, 76; denial of, xiii; fear of, 134; knowledge of, 41, 107; living

with, 4; as made of stone, 107;
minds of, xii; philosophical problem
of, xiii; psychic annihilation of, xiii;
recognition of, 80; singularity of, 105;
words of, 39
otherness, 105

pain, xi–xii, 6, 18, 38, 39, 40, 47, 55–56,
90, 113, 128, 133, 211, 221; and the body,
39–41; and language, 38, 39, 55, 57;
ownership of, 41; play of, 61; standing
words for, xii
Pandey, Gyanendra, 18, 19, 21
panic, 117, 127, 134, 179; phenomenology of,
97, 111
Partition, 2, 7, 9, 10, 11, 14, 16, 18–20,
26, 33, 36, 46, 52, 54, 58, 64–65, 69,
75–78, 81–82, 91, 93, 97, 102, 108, 115,
134, 161, 220; disorder of, 54; horror
of, 18, 95; memorialization of, 19;
memories of, 73, 76; neglect of, 18;
signature of, 13; stories of, 132; as
total event, xii; violence of, 52, 54,
62, 72, 75, 79–80, 87, 90, 215. See also
nation; riots
past, 11, 29, 73, 82, 88, 97–100, 109, 122,
132, 184, 192, 210, 215–16, 219;
actualization of, 108; construction
of, 114; direct possession of, 76; as
frozen, 99; reenactment of, 102; regions
of, 99–100, 102, 108; simultaneity
of, 97; as unfinished, 134. See also
Bergson, Henri; memories;
memory
pastness, feeling of, 97
Patel, Kamlabehn, 24
peace, 68, 85, 91, 184; for the dead, 187–88,
190–91; refusal of, xiii
perpetrators, 77, 90, 98, 110–11, 149, 164,
166, 208–9, 219–20
Plato, x, xii
pogroms, 205–6
police, 24–25, 121, 124, 139–42, 147, 153,
156–57, 159–60, 164–65, 167, 169–71,
176, 191, 204, 208–9
politics, 119, 131, 174, 193, 196–97, 203, 217,
219–20. See also nation
pollution, 104, 195, 216

power, 78, 82, 151, 161–62, 178, 187, 189
present, 29, 80, 97, 106, 134, 192, 205, 210,
215; appeal to, 100; blindness to, 98,
111, 124; solipsism of, 98. See also
Bergson, Henri; future; past
public sphere, 101, 211
purity, 18–19, 25, 32, 47

Rangila Rasul, 115. See also Hindu-Muslim
relations
rape, 13–14, 25, 27–28, 34, 47, 53–54, 59,
82, 90–91, 119, 127, 133, 226n23;
mass, 19
real: claims over, 120–21, 123; stabilization
of, 130; and the symbolic, 134
recognition, 106–7, 218. See also
acknowledgment
relations, 3–4, 6, 8, 69, 72, 73, 135,
212; between brothers, 67; between
brothers and sisters, 57, 60–61, 63,
65–68, 77; distrust of, 77; between
fathers and sons, 77, 112–14, 231n21;
between husbands and wives, 72;
among men, 112; between mothers
and daughters, 188–90; between
parents and daughters, 47, 65–66;
repairing of, 77–78, 80, 193; uncertainty of, 81; among women, 188–89,
193. See also fathers; mothers;
relationships; Strathern,
Marilyn
relationships, 8, 11, 48, 62, 64, 70–71,
100; caring, 63, 75; death of, 60;
effacement of, 66; formulation of,
72; history of, 105; suspension of,
73; temporal depth of, 71–72, 75;
work on, 78, 87, 99. See also fathers;
mothers; relations; Strathern,
Marilyn
relief: in camps, 24, 127, 140, 164, 185,
208, 210; distribution of, 198; and
rehabilitation, 12–13, 123, 127–28,
142, 144–45, 198, 207–10;
theorizing, 254n16; work, 144,
194
repetition, 90, 102–3, 205
revenge, 110, 86, 105–6, 110–11, 126, 120, 136,
156, 159, 186, 203

violence (*continued*)

ordinary, 7, 78; actualization of, 134, 149; authorization of, 110; as inert, 81, 86; collective, 14, 132, 205–6; communal, 14, 20, 116, 206; and everyday life, xiii, 45, 205; experimentation with, 86; extraordinary and everyday, 91, 149; founding and maintaining, 161–62, 179–80; gendered acts of, 59; local, 142–43; memories of, 90; models of, 208; narratives of, 57, 80; of Partition, 11, 16; and the other, xiii; sectarian, 102; sexual and reproductive, 23; showing of, 10; sociality and, 153; spatialization of, 110; stories of, 8; subjectivity and, 59, 213; theoretical stance toward, 101; trauma and, 134, 150; unfolding of, 136; wakefulness to, 80; in the weave of life, 80, 87–88, 211; witnessing of, 60

virtual, 99–100, 134

vision: suspicion of, 61; and voice, 62. *See also* eyes

voice, 2, 8, 9, 16, 57, 59–60, 62, 69, 102, 104, 117, 187, 196, 201–2, 213, 215; abrogation of, 197; emergence of, 61; in the everyday, 2; experimentation with, 87; parable of, 102; patriarchal, 189; repression of, 6, 19, 36, 64; simulacrum of, 92; speech and, 8, 225n13; subject and, 62; vision and, 62; world annihilating, 8

voluntary groups and organizations, 141, 144, 160

Weber, Max, 218

weddings. *See* marriage

widowhood, 68, 75; patriarchal norms of, 69, 110, 116, 155

widows, 33, 50–51, 62, 68, 76, 92, 93, 105, 144, 198; remarriage, 73, 166, 195–96

Wittgenstein, Ludwig, ix, xii, xiv, 2, 4, 5, 15–17, 62, 65, 68, 93–94, 97, 104, 119, 224nn5,6,7, 225n10; anthropological register in, ix–x, 7–9;

the child in, 199–200; on culture, x–xi; on the everyday, xiv; on forms of life, xi, 88–90; on language, ix, x; the modern subject in, x, xiii; on pain, xi, 39–41, 48, 57; on philosophical grammar, 66–67; and skepticism, xi, xii, 9, 11, 23, 26

witness, xiv, 5, 48, 57, 59–60, 72, 74, 77, 209; bearing, 50–52, 62, 102–3; passive, 54

witnessing, 12, 52, 54, 57, 59, 76, 80, 102, 221, 237n2

woman: as citizen, 34; destiny of, 68–69; figure of abducted, 19–21, 26, 28, 32, 33, 37, 49, 53; life of, 74, 82; in Rousseau, 34; as seductress, 35; sex and, 82; as witness, 74

women, 9, 12, 29, 34, 38, 42, 53, 186, 195, 199; abduction of, xii, 13, 19, 20, 21, 22–26, 28, 36, 58, 59, 88, 91, 133; bodies of, 46, 52; and care, 63; as citizens, 26, 49, 62; and consent, 53, 60; and death, 48–51, 53, 92, 238n; and everyday life, xiii, xiv; exchange of, 21, 24, 34, 56; and healing, 73; Hindu, 33; in Manto, 56; and mourning, xiii; Muslim, 27, 56, 88, 179; and pain, 89; and patriarchy, 71; and pollution, 154; recovery of, 21–26, 88, 91, 110–11, 179; and reproduction, 49, 54–55, 60; rights of, 28; in Rousseau, 61; and seduction, 62; as sexual and reproductive beings, 26, 32, 33; and sexuality, 18–19, 49, 58, 60; in Sikh militant discourse, 113–114; and silence, xii; sitting in stillness, 104, 194, 216; and speech, 57, 83; subjectivity of, 59; suffering of, 20, 37; violation of, 19, 37, 57, 221; violence against, 13, 23, 25, 38, 52, 88; and voice, 37, 96

words, 8, 10, 39, 46, 57, 62, 65, 94, 105, 200, 202–4; battle over, 82; bodying forth of, 40; everyday, 89; frozen quality of, 11, 90; and gesture, 194; and home, 221, 225n14; lethal, 105; without life, 8; numbness of, 8, 221;

perlocutionary force of, 119; poverty of, 91; relation to, xii; spectral quality of, 8; standing, xii; threats embodied in, 98; trust in, 117

world, 2, 4, 8, 39, 58, 64, 101, 203–4; boundaries of, 5; building of, 58; devotion to, 221; inhabiting, 5, 59, 76–77, 209; limit of, 224n5; loss of, 54; obliteration of, 134; remaking of, 5, 20, 38; as shadow, 132, 134. *See also* subject

wounds, 12, 101–2, 104, 135, 213, 229n5

writing, 2, 17, 169, 207, 216, 221; body of, 41; fantasy of, 89; as hallucinatory, 212, 215; protocols of, 206; the self, 212, 214–15

Text:	11.25/13.5 Adobe Garamond
Display:	Adobe Garamond; Perpetua
Compositor:	International Typesetting and Composition
Cartographer:	Bill Nelson
Printer and binder:	Maple-Vail Manufacturing Group